0
1/4
1/2
1
MILES
NORTHERN
CONSTITUTIONALIST
SECTOR
Duarte
Bridge
AVE. DE LAS AMERICAS
San Isidro Air Base — 9 MILES
Ozama River
AVE. MELLA
National
Palace
Ozama
Fortress
CUIDAD NUEVA
AVE. GEORGE WASHINGTON
RIKI
Caribbean Sea
Santo Domingo

Intervention and Negotiation

THE UNITED STATES AND THE DOMINICAN REVOLUTION

Intervention and Negotiation

THE UNITED STATES AND THE DOMINICAN REVOLUTION

by Jerome Slater

Foreword by Professor Hans J. Morgenthau

HARPER & ROW, PUBLISHERS
NEW YORK, EVANSTON, AND LONDON

Grateful acknowledgment is made for permission to include material that previously appeared, in somewhat different form, in the following publications:

The OAS and United States Foreign Policy, by Jerome Slater, The Ohio State University Press, © 1967 by The Ohio State University Press.

"The Limits of Legitimization in International Organizations: The OAS and the Dominican Crisis," by Jerome Slater, *International Organization*, Vol. XXIII, No. 1, © 1969 by The World Peace Foundation.

"The Decline of the OAS," by Jerome Slater, *International Journal*, Vol. XXIV, No. 3, © 1969 by the *International Journal*.

FIRST EDITION

LIBRARY OF CONGRESS CATALOG CARD NUMBER: 70-95985

To my Dominican friends,
and to the Dominican people—may their future
redeem the tragic past

Contents

Foreword

HANS J. MORGENTHAU

THE INTERVENTION in the Dominican Republic of 1965 has faded into our historic recollection as an isolated event, justified or unjustified, which hardly needs concern us anymore. The reasons for this lack of concern are twofold. On the one hand, the intervention in the Dominican Republic, on the face of it, appears to be justified by the risk of a Communist take-over, and more importantly, again on the face of it, it appears to have been successful. On the other hand, our intervention in Vietnam continues to raise such a host of intractable political, military, and moral issues that by comparison the intervention in the Dominican Republic presents itself as a historic incident without consequences, which can teach us nothing.

However, this is a highly distorted historic perspective. The causes and results of the intervention in the Dominican Republic deserve to be well understood both for intellectual and political reasons. Professor Slater has set himself the task to provide that understanding. It is the first comprehensive attempt to do so, and the results are indeed highly illuminating. They illuminate not only the factors which led us into this intervention and determined our policies during and after it, but, more importantly, they shed an illuminating light upon the assumptions and expectations which have determined the foreign policies of the United States outside Europe.

It becomes obvious from Professor Slater's painstaking and objective analysis—the author leans over backwards in trying to see the situation from the vantage point of our government—that the main motivating force propelling us into intervention was the fear of Communism. President Johnson articulated that force when he said that we cannot have another Communist government in the Western hemisphere. By doing this, he also implicitly pointed to the historic precedent which obsessed our policy-makers: the communization of Cuba. What had happened in Cuba could not be permitted to happen in the Dominican Republic. This obsession determined not only our policy but also our perception of reality from which our policy derived. Our diplomatic representatives on the spot reported not what was actually happening, but their fantasies as to what ought to have happened in view of their assumptions about the omnipresence of Communist conspirators and the identity of leftist and Communist revolution. Thus even if one assumes for the sake of argument that it would have been in the interest of the United States to oppose a Communist revolution in the Dominican Republic, the lacking evidence of such a risk vitiates our intervention.

The other motivating force of our policy leading to intervention was the fear of public opinion. Our policy-makers were obsessed by the fear that American public opinion would refuse to support a policy which would not prevent another Communist take-over in the Western hemisphere. Professor Slater has no difficulty in showing the fallacy of this conception of public opinion as a kind of given limiting factor, impervious to presidential direction.

Not only did the intervention in the Dominican Republic not serve the interests of the United States, but the way it was executed actually violated those interests. Let us take a look at the sequence of events: Juan Bosch, elected in a free election whose democratic enthusiasm I witnessed on the spot, was overthrown by a military *coup d'état,* and the revolution against which the United States intervened was staged by the "constitutionalists" on behalf of the legitimate regime of Bosch, a declared friend of the United States. When we intervened, this revolution was on the verge of success, having decimated the military forces. Our intervention restored the crucial political power of the military, which has been the bane of the Dominican Republic. It has been the main source of instability, backwardness, misery, and government by assassination. In other words, insofar as there exists today a Communist danger in the Dominican Republic, it is the outgrowth of the very evil which our intervention restored to power. As Professor Slater puts it,

> In the long run, perhaps the most serious criticism that can be made of U.S. policy after the intervention itself is that, having intervened, it refused to use the opportunity to effect really sweeping military reform, thereby creating the essential prerequisite for major political and social change in the Dominican Republic. . . . its policy is conditioned on the very explicit premise that, whatever its faults, the Dominican military is an essential force for "order" and "stability" and that, therefore, nothing must be done that would seriously weaken it.

The aim of American policy was not "fundamental change" but "essential preservation" of a status quo which, even if it were viable, is not worth preserving.

Professor Slater adds: "This is a long-standing policy, not only applicable to the Dominican Republic but to all Latin America. . . ." He could have added: "and throughout the world with the exception of Europe." For what his study shows with great clarity and in convincing detail is a perception of the world and a frame of mind in our policy-makers, which permeates our foreign policy outside Europe. The result was relatively benign in the Dominican Republic, at least in the short run, while it has been catastrophic in Vietnam. As long as that perception and outlook persist, compelling policy-makers to react to a sudden emergency in terms consonant with them, there will be other Vietnams, and other counter-productive interventions, similar to that in the Dominican Republic. It is, then, not enough to criticize our interventionist moves in the Dominican Republic and Vietnam. The lesson we must draw from these experiences is that the cause of the evil is not in these particular actions but in a state of mind that has caused them. This book indeed provides that lesson.

Preface

ALONG WITH THE WAR in Vietnam, the U.S. intervention in the Dominican revolution of 1965 has come to represent in the United States and all over the world the bankruptcy of recent American foreign policy. In the field of scholarship, one of its major effects has been to lend impetus to a new school of historical "revisionism" that has reexamined the entire range of U.S. cold war policies and, in some versions, has emphasized the role of U.S. "imperialism" since World War II. Yet, despite its drama and significance, the Dominican crisis itself has received remarkably little detailed attention and careful analysis. While the literature on the Vietnam situation would take many years to absorb, *there is not a single book or article in any language* that analyzes the full range of U.S. policy in the Dominican revolution from the military intervention of April, 1965, to the withdrawal of U.S. troops in September, 1966. It is difficult to account for this; perhaps the best explanation is that the nature of U.S. policy in the Dominican Republic seemed so self-evident that it was thought there was little to be said about it. In addition, the escalating crisis in Vietnam served to deflect attention from the relative—or apparent—quiet that prevailed in the Dominican Republic within a few months of the intervention.

The major works to date are books by John Bartlow Martin,

Tad Szulc, and Dan Kurzman, and a series of articles by Theodore Draper.[1]* All of them suffer from serious drawbacks. The Szulc and Kurzman books, though excellent in terms of what they set out to do, are journalists' accounts that focus almost exclusively on the intervention and the immediate period thereafter, touching hardly at all on the evolution of U.S. policy in the next year and a half. Moreover, written as they were at the height of the crisis and before events had fully worked themselves out, they inevitably suffer from incompleteness and lack of perspective. Martin's book, similarly, deals only with the first weeks of the crisis and in any event is an apologia for his personal role and for U.S. policy in general. The most important writings are those of Theodore Draper, whose interpretations of U.S. policy have come to be almost unquestioningly accepted by most serious students of American foreign policy. Seldom has the work of one man so thoroughly dominated discourse on such an important event. Yet, it is my belief that despite its brilliance, the Draper analysis is seriously flawed in a number of very important ways, as I hope to be able to demonstrate throughout this book.†

In addition to describing U.S. policy in the Dominican Republic from 1965 until today, this book will seek to answer the following questions: Why did the Dominican revolution of 1965 occur, who were its main participants, and what did it represent? What was the extent of Communist participation in the revolution

* Superior numbers refer to Notes, page 223.

† For a similar analysis of the writings on the Dominican crisis, see Howard J. Wiarda, "The Dominican Revolution in Perspective," *Polity* (Vol. I, No. 1), fall, 1968. Professor Wiarda concludes that while there is a good deal of polemical and one-sided material, there has been a dearth of serious and scholarly studies and none at all "which fully covers the diverse themes and events or places them in perspective" (p. 119). Draper's writing, he argues, "smacks of a kind of 'devil theory' of events, glosses over facts that are incompatible with his analysis, and at times allows ideological and value considerations to get in the way of impartial analysis" (p. 121).

and what was the danger of a Communist takeover if the United States had not intervened? At what point did the United States begin to oppose the revolution and what factors lay behind its decision to intervene militarily? What were the short- and long-term objectives of the United States once its troops had landed and by what methods did it seek to realize those objectives? Did the United States seek to impose reactionary and dictatorial rule in the Dominican Republic? How did U.S. policy evolve over the year and a half its troops occupied the country? How was a political settlement reached and on what was it based? What roles did the UN and the OAS play in the crisis? To what extent were the elections of 1965 genuinely honest and free? What would U.S. policy have been if Juan Bosch had won the elections? What is U.S. policy in the Dominican Republic now?

I have also sought to make judgments about Washington's Dominican policies and to place them in the context of general U.S. foreign policy during the Johnson Administration. Would a second Communist revolution in the Caribbean have posed any threat to the United States? Even if it would, was the intervention in the Dominican Republic necessary? What could the United States have done before the intervention to preclude military action? How might the intervention itself have been differently handled? What criticisms should be made of U.S. policy in the post-intervention period? How did it all turn out—was the intervention in retrospect a "success"? If so, what were its costs? Did the Dominican intervention reflect a larger pathology of U.S. foreign policy under Lyndon Johnson? Did U.S. policy reflect a wider hostility to the democratic left in Latin America, or, alternatively, a general counterrevolutionary policy?

Finally, I have attempted to derive some lessons from the Dominican crisis and apply them to future U.S. policy. What weaknesses in the foreign-policy machinery were revealed by the crisis? What kinds of criticisms can be made about the underlying premises and general attitudes of key U.S. policy-makers? What are the prospects for future Carribbean uprisings similar to the Dominican revolution of 1965? Given the prevailing circumstances in the Caribbean and the general outlook in Washington, what is the likelihood of further U.S. military interventions? What can or should be done to avert them?

The research for this book was mostly undertaken in 1967, when I was on leave of absence from my teaching position, under a grant from the Social Science Research Council. This grant, along with a 1968 summer fellowship from the State University of New York, was the sole source of financial support for this study. Research for the book was based on the following sources: all or almost all U.S. and Dominican books and articles on the crisis, including those in major Dominican newspapers and news magazines; the entire set of UN and OAS records, most of which have not been used in previous studies, including hundreds of telegrams and reports by UN and OAS missions in the Dominican Republic; and about eighty interviews on a not-for-attribution basis with key Dominican, U.S., and OAS officials, most of whom were not only willing but anxious to talk freely.

In addition, in the course of my research I was given access to a great number of papers, memoirs, and documents which are not now in the public domain. I accepted access to all such materials only on the clear and explicit condition that I would be free to use them in whatever way I chose, submitting the manuscript for clearance or approval to no one. The sole condition I accepted—or, for that matter, I was asked to accept—was that no direct citation be made of materials stemming from nonpublic sources. Because of this restriction, the evidence for a number of statements in the book cannot be disclosed. However, no important assertions based on access to nonpublic material will be made unless in my judgment the source is unquestionably accurate and reliable.

It is evident that there are important problems inherent in this procedure. Much of the analysis cannot be verified by other scholars who will have not seen certain materials, although it should be added that the use of unattributed material from private interviews is a commonly-accepted practice that raises the same issue. There is also the danger that I may have become somehow biased, corrupted, or at least (in the current cliché) "co-opted," thus making my judgments, particularly when they challenge some of the accepted wisdom about U.S. policy, suspect. Nonetheless, it remains my strong belief that the value of more-complete knowledge about a highly significant event in recent American history outweighs all such problems. I can only hope that I have fully recognized the dangers and successfully guarded against them: the sole criterion I have been guided by is that of strict adherence to the truth; no relevant data, no matter on whom it reflected favorably or unfavorably, has been omitted; and the analysis and conclusions of the book are mine and mine alone.

As another safeguard, I have asked a number of respected colleagues and experts on Dominican affairs to read the manuscript and comment specifically on whether any of my analysis seemed unsupported by the evidence I adduce or that is otherwise available, although naturally I have not accepted all their criticisms and none of them bear the slightest responsibility for any errors of fact or interpretation that remain. In this connection, I would like to express my deep appreciation to Mr. Robert D. Crassweller of the Council on Foreign Relations, Dr. Abraham F. Lowenthal of the Ford Foundation, and Professors

Joseph S. Nye of Harvard University, Howard J. Wiarda of the University of Massachusetts, José Moreno of the University of Pittsburgh, and Charles R. Planck and Terry W. Nardin of the State University of New York at Buffalo.

Above all, I am indebted to my wife, Judith, who has served as research assistant, editor, and intellectual critic. Without her constant and demanding scrutiny at every stage, this book would be far less than it is.

JEROME SLATER

Intervention and Negotiation

THE UNITED STATES AND
THE DOMINICAN REVOLUTION

1

Background to Revolution

SEVERAL MILES OUTSIDE Santo Domingo, at a point where a quiet two-lane highway winds very close to the sea, stands a stolid, unadorned, rectangular block of cement, about the size of an ancient Egyptian coffin. It is an empty scene—on one side of the road, a narrow stretch of desolate black coral, abruptly ending at a cliff overlooking the sea; on the other side, miles of flat, piny scrubland. There are few signs of life except, perhaps, off in the distance, a small naked boy tending a few scrawny goats.

As one carefully picks his way across the sharp coral to get a closer look at the Dominican national monument to the assassination of Rafael Trujillo (the Dominicans call it the *ajusticiamiento*—the execution), who was shot to death on this spot on the night of May 30, 1961, as he sped toward a visit with his mistress, it becomes evident that the block is not completely uninscribed. Across its face, in a rough hand, are scrawled the words "*Asi les pasara a los Comunistas*"—thus to the Communists. During the Dominican revolution of April, 1965, someone ripped off and threw into the sea a plaque commemorating "the Martyrs of the 30th of May"—most of whom were caught, tortured, and murdered in the terrible weeks following the *ajusticiamiento*—and substituted his own inspirational message. Four years later, no one had yet bothered to remove the paint and restore the plaque.

In this scene is revealed the depths of the bitter tragedy of the Dominican Republic. No soldier guards the monument to those who liberated their country from thirty years of one of the worst tyrannies of the twentieth century; no one does anything about, or even protests the desecration of, their memory. And no wonder. Not only may retribution from the still-powerful Trujillista elements in the country be feared, but even more to the point, most of the "Martyrs of the 30th of May" were of dubious material for legendary status and came very late to herohood. The majority were simply old cronies of Trujillo who, for one sordid reason or another, had fallen out with "the Chief" and had therefore decided to do him in. Thus, appropriately, in gangland style ended the reign of the gangsters.

The Era of Trujillo was the logical culmination of a century of endemic instability, all-pervasive violence, and the complete absence of democratic, effective, and responsible political institutions in the Dominican Republic. Ever since the small Caribbean country—the Dominican Republic is about the size of New Hampshire and Vermont combined, with a population of about four million—had gained independence from Haiti in 1844, its history had been, as a Trujillo biographer puts it, "a tale of struggle, sorrow, and disaster so prolonged that it has no parallel in the annals of the hemisphere."[1] For more than a century, anarchy, slaughter, and civil war alternated with long periods of feudal dictatorship, with only brief intervals of decent government.[2] Out of this tradition came Trujillo, the most murderously effective of the long line of Dominican *caudillos*. For thirty years Trujillo dominated his country to a degree unprecedented in Latin American history, eventually gaining nearly complete control over the nation's Army, politics, businesses, plantations, labor movements, and even to an astonishing degree its social life and its women.[3]

A good part of the responsibility for this time of corruption and carnage must be borne by the United States. Ever since the Monroe Doctrine had been enunciated in 1823, the United States had sought to exclude European political and economic involvement in the Western hemisphere. In the early part of the twentieth century, this general policy took the form of active American opposition to Caribbean political instability or economic indebtedness to European creditors, which could end in foreign intervention. As a result, the United States *itself* intervened in a number of Caribbean countries to "restore order."

One such intervention took place in 1916 in the Dominican Republic, when the Marines were landed to put an end to a budding civil war. For the next eight years Marine officers imposed tight authoritarian rule over the Dominican Republic. As evidence of their high-handed and often brutal methods became available in the United States, public opposition grew, until in 1922 the well-known American diplomat Sumner Welles was given the task of preparing for the withdrawal of the occupying forces.[4]

In 1924 the Marines finally departed, but not before they had created in their own image a Dominican National Guard to continue the maintenance of law and order. The Dominican armed forces had traditionally been the major source of political power in the country, as Sumner Welles had pointed out in his classic history of the Dominican Republic: "Generally underpaid and almost invariably undisciplined, the military . . . was inevitably the means through which . . . revolutions were engineered."[5] Prior to the American occupation, however, there was no national army worthy of the name, for the local barracks and police forces tended to be under the control of the regional *caudillos* that ruled the Dominican Republic until Trujillo broke their power.

Perhaps understanding that the creation of a truly centralized armed force had opened up new possibilities for national political power, in 1919, at the age of twenty-eight, Trujillo joined the Guard. Not much is known of his earlier life. Born into a middle-class family in the small town of San Cristóbal, Trujillo drifted through an adolescence and early manhood marked by petty thievery, violence, and general dissipation. Nonetheless, as a Guard officer he made a considerable impression upon a series of his Marine superiors, and rose rapidly through the ranks. By 1928 Trujillo was Chief of the Guard, and had converted it into his private army. In 1930, dispensing with the remaining formalities, "the bastard son of the occupation forces"[6] openly took over the government by terrorist tactics. Within a few years all opponents or potential opponents were out of the country, silent or silenced; the Dominican economy had passed into the hands of the Trujillo family (it is estimated that by 1960 the family owned over half the arable land, controlled almost all the sugar industry—the main Dominican crop—and employed over two-thirds of the entire Dominican labor force); and the thirty-year reign of terror had descended.

United States policy toward the Dominican Republic during the Trujillo era reflected in microcosm its general Latin American policy.[7] Throughout the twentieth century, the crucial objective of U.S. policy in the hemisphere had been to prevent the coming to power of any Latin American government or political movement that could threaten the security of the United States or its predominant position in the hemisphere. In practice, the safest way to do this was to support the existing, generally conservative governments in Latin America and to throw the weight of U.S. influence against populist movements that threatened to disrupt the political status quo. The nature of the governments of the Latin American states was irrelevant, so long as they kept peace and quiet at home and went along with fundamental U.S. policies abroad.

The American relationship with Trujillo typified the marriage of convenience with Latin American dictatorships. Trujillo, the U.S. Ambassador in Santo Domingo once reported, had only one foreign policy: "maintaining friendly relations with the United States."[8] To do so he not only religiously followed U.S. foreign policy—the Dominican Republic was the first Latin American state to "declare war" on the Axis powers immediately following Pearl Harbor and yielded to no one in strident anti-Communism after the war—but he also spent vast sums of money in the United States on public relations, on donations to the campaign chests of both parties, and perhaps even on outright bribery.* And to a very good end, indeed; until 1956, voices questioning U.S. support of Trujillo were few and had no effect on Washington's policy.† Occasional congressional resolutions condemning U.S. policy, for example, typically were defeated by 401-3 margins. Catholic leaders were pleased by Trujillo's public piety and anti-Communism; Jewish groups were grateful for his World War II publicity gesture of inviting

* According to Trujillo's former police chief Arturo Espaillat, the Dominican dictator spent at least $5,000,000 on bribes to key Congressmen and State Department officials.[9] However, he does not name names and a *New York Times* investigation of Dominican archives after the fall of Trujillo failed to turn up corroborating evidence.[10]

† With one brief exception: immediately after World War II the new U.S. Assistant Secretary of State for Latin American Affairs, Spruille Braden, pressed for an active policy of opposition to Latin American dictators, taking as his main targets Trujillo and Juan Perón of Argentina. Soon after the collapse of the U.S. effort to dissuade the Argentine public from voting for Perón in the 1946 Argentine elections, however, Braden left the State Department and the United States reverted to its traditional policies.

some five hundred refugees of Nazism to settle in the Dominican Republic; powerful Southern Democrats (like Ellender of Louisiana, Eastland of Mississippi, and Smathers of Florida) were impressed by the general way in which Trujillo maintained law and order; and government officials were happy with Trujillo's unswerving devotion to the latest U.S. policy line. Even those who viewed his regime with faint distaste did not find it difficult to subordinate their feelings to the larger necessities of state; no one put it more succinctly than Franklin Delano Roosevelt himself: "He may be an S.O.B., but at least he's *our* S.O.B."[11]

Public outrage in 1956 at the kidnapping from the streets of New York and subsequent murder in the Dominican Republic of Professor Jesús de Galíndez of Columbia University, an outspoken opponent of Trujillo, marked the beginning of the end of the tacit alliance. A complete break, however, did not occur until the general shift in Washington's Latin American policy following the stoning of Vice-President Richard Nixon in several Latin American capitals in 1958 and, more importantly, the 1959 Castro victory in Cuba. The anti-Nixon riots symbolized the extent of anti-Americanism in Latin America, arising in good part because of U.S. support for Latin American dictatorships. The Castro revolution focused attention on a far more fundamental problem, Latin American political and social unrest.

Although the extent of rising mass dissatisfaction with the status quo in Latin America had been well known to serious hemispheric observers for years, its implications were ignored or not understood by U.S. policy makers. But the revolt against Fulgencio Batista sharply dramatized this discontent, making it painfully obvious that rightist dictatorships, through their repression of all political opposition and their reactionary social and economic policies, were creating an environment ripe for Communist exploitation. As a result, the United States sharply reversed its Latin American policy and began emphasizing the need for democracy and modernization of Latin American economic and social institutions. The new policy gradually coalesced into the Alliance for Progress in 1961, but it was foreshadowed by a new attitude toward Trujillo beginning in early 1960.

This shift was also a response to internal Dominican developments. Toward the end of 1959, for the first time since he had come to power, Trujillo's grip on the country began to slip. A number of clandestine opposition groups formed and the situation suddenly became more fluid. The general Dominican environment, in fact, was thought to be uncomfortably similar to that during the last days of Batista in Cuba, and serious concern developed in the Eisenhower Administration that a sudden collapse of Trujillo's rule could lead to chaos and the emergence of a second Castro. "Batista is to Castro as Trujillo is to ——," was the implicit assumption, and Washington wanted to insure it could help fill in the blank. As a result, then, the United States began to cast about for a means to get rid of Trujillo but at the same time to insure a "responsible" successor.

During the next two years in the Dominican Republic the United States engaged in its most massive intervention in the internal affairs of a Latin American state since the inauguration of the Good Neighbor Policy. A wide variety of the instruments of power and influence available to Washington—including multilateral diplomacy and political pressures, unilateral economic rewards and sanctions, and even the threat of military intervention—were brought to bear to induce a liberalization of the Dominican political structure.

From the beginning the United States was able to maneuver

under a cover provided by the Organization of American States (OAS). In early 1960 Trujillo had committed the serious indiscretion of trying to kill his arch-enemy, President Rómulo Betancourt of Venezuela, who symbolized the (brief) rise of the democratic left in Latin America in the late fifties and who had become the leading anti-Trujillo spokesman of the hemisphere. Faced with Trujillo's rather flagrant violation of the inter-American principle of nonintervention, the OAS imposed sanctions on Trujillo, including a collective break in diplomatic relations and an embargo on petroleum and armaments.

Even more important, the United States took advantage of this opportunity to cut back drastically its purchases of Dominican sugar, the country's major export, citing the OAS actions as its authority. (This action cost the Dominican Republic over $22,000,000 at a time when its economy was in a bad decline; moreover, it struck directly at Trujillo's personal financial base.) Congressional hearings on the sugar embargo clearly demonstrated the major shift in U.S. policy. In a surprisingly blunt statement, heretofore unremarked, Under Secretary of State C. Douglas Dillon referred to Trujillo as "a tyrant, a torturer and a murderer," and all but admitted that the real objective of U.S. policy was to bring down the Trujillo regime.[12]

Formally, the OAS measures had been imposed solely because of Trujillo's "aggression" against Venezuela and were therefore to be discontinued when the Dominican Republic ceased to "constitute a danger to the peace and security of the hemisphere."[13] Actually, the United States was able to persuade the OAS to use the sanctions as leverage over internal Dominican politics after the assassination of Trujillo. Immediately after the assassination, the OAS, under United States leadership, established a presence in the Dominican Republic in the form of a four-nation committee (including, of course, the United States), and for the next eighteen months the United States was able to use this opening as well as the prospect of the resumption of normal diplomatic and economic relations to exert great influence on internal Dominican events.

The framework for U.S. policy in this period was summed up in President Kennedy's famous post-*ajusticiamiento* remark: "There are three possibilities . . . in descending order of preference: a decent democratic regime, a continuation of the Trujillo regime, or a Castro regime. We ought to aim at the first but we really can't renounce the second until we are sure that we can avoid the third."[14]

The strategy, then, was to use the OAS-U.S. sanctions to press for the very gradual liberalization of the Trujillo structure, with free elections as the ultimate goal. The trick was to move quickly enough to meet growing Dominican pressures for real democracy and reform, as well as to prevent a potential Castroite movement from capitalizing on the discontent, but yet not so quickly that the United States and the Dominican "moderates" would lose control over the situation. The vehicle for this hedge was Joaquín Balaguer, widely considered to be the most moderate and uncorrupted of the Trujillo retinue, who in the spring of 1961 was serving as Trujillo's puppet President. "Balaguer is our only tool," said Kennedy. "The anti-Communist liberals aren't strong enough. We must use our influence to take Balaguer along the road to democracy."[15]

The main obstacle, however, proved to be not the Dominican Castroites but the remaining members of the Trujillo family, with their continuing control over major elements of the military. The crisis came in November, 1961, when two of the Trujillo brothers, alarmed at the small steps that had been taken toward democracy, began apparent preparations for a coup. In response, a U.S. Navy task force was sent to the scene to patrol just outside Dominican waters in plain sight of Santo Domingo, while in Washington Dean Rusk was warning that the United States would not "remain idle" if the Trujillos tried to "reassert dictatorial domination."[16] It was not a bluff, for the administration let it be known that it intended to land Marines in the event of an attempt against the Balaguer regime. In the face of this show of force, the plot collapsed and a few days later the Trujillo family fled the country.

With the left remaining quiescent and the Trujillos out, the State Department felt freer to step up pressures for further democratization. While the Navy lingered on near the coast, U.S. pressures forced Balaguer to step aside in favor of a seven-man Council of State, dominated by the generally conservative but anti-Trujillo Unión Cívica Nacional (UCN). The council was to be a transitional body, ruling only until elections, which were scheduled for December, 1962.

In those elections, prepared for, presided over, and guaranteed by the OAS and the U.S. Embassy, the surprise winner was Juan Bosch, who defeated Viriato Fiallo of the UCN. Bosch, born in 1909, was a writer and an intellectual who had gone into exile in 1937. Living mostly in Puerto Rico and Costa Rica (where he taught political science for a while), he became an active leader of the anti-Trujillo opposition and a close friend of many Latin American leaders of the democratic left, particularly Betancourt, Luis Muñoz-Marín of Puerto Rico, and José Figueres of Costa Rica. In 1961 he returned to the Dominican Republic as the head of the social democratic Partido Revolucionario Dominicano (PRD). His promises of social reform, his magnetic personality, and his brilliant oratory enabled him easily to defeat the colorless, paternalistic Fiallo.

Bosch took office on February 27, 1963, amidst high hopes

and great fanfare in the Dominican Republic, the United States, and the rest of the hemisphere. After thirty years, the Dominican Republic had returned to the democratic fold, and now it was to be a showcase for the newly launched Alliance for Progress. There was no doubt over the depth of the U.S. commitment to Bosch. Shortly before the elections the U.S. Ambassador, John Bartlow Martin, brought together Fiallo and Bosch and told them: "We, the United States . . . support free elections. . . . We intend to exert our influence to see that such elections are held. We intend to see that the winner is able to take office. We intend to use our influence to see that his government is not dominated by the military or by police."[17] * And just before taking office Bosch was invited to Washington and given the grand treatment, ending with a long and cordial private discussion with President Kennedy.[19]

Somehow, though, the glow was to fade quickly, to a great degree because of the reporting of Martin. A prominent free-lance journalist associated with progressive causes, Martin had been a speech writer for Adlai Stevenson and John F. Kennedy. In 1937 he had visited the Dominican Republic for several months and had later written a magazine article attacking the Trujillo dictatorship, one of the first American writers to have done so. Despite his liberal background, though, Martin was not very taken with Bosch or his party: he considered the PRD "too doctrinaire, too ideological . . . its lower ranks filled with some of the worst elements in Dominican political life,"[20] while he thought Bosch was, among other things, "emotionally unstable," "arrogant, vain, erratic,"[21] an opinion, to be sure, that

* In a remarkable historical parallel, just prior to the 1916 civil war (ending with a U.S. intervention) Secretary of State Bryant had told Dominican political leaders that the United States "will use all means in its power to aid in the holding of free and fair elections and will support the constitutionally elected president."[18]

was shared by many others. Even before the elections, Martin had concluded: "We could not trust Juan Bosch. For President he would not do . . . he was a reckless political plunger, willing to risk everything, including the democratic system itself, to gain a personal political objective."[22]

After the elections, Martin's opinion of Bosch sank even lower. In part because Bosch refused to modify sections of a new constitution (primarily those providing for sweeping welfare benefits, prohibiting very large landownings, and downgrading the influence of the Catholic Church) that displeased the Army, the Church and the "tutumpotes,"* Martin concluded that Bosch was "a divider, a splitter, a schemer, a destroyer."[23] Moreover, his alleged administrative incompetence and chaotic governing style elicited Martin's contempt. One story Martin tells is particularly revealing. After relating, exasperatedly, how Bosch's motorcade got lost one day after attending a Mass in Santiago, he concluded: "Any government that can't find its way home from Mass deserves to fall."[24]

What was really ominous, though, was Bosch's nationalism. Martin seemed to judge Dominicans in good part by whether or not they were anti-American, sometimes even implying his suspicion that anti-American Dominicans might really be pro-Communist. Thus, while Martin stresses that he didn't believe Bosch was a Communist, at several points he betrays his fear that Bosch's nationalism and commitment to (not very radical) social reform might, after all, be only a front, underneath which the possibility could not be ignored that he was a "deep-cover Communist."[25]

As a result, even though at times Martin thought that Bosch

* "Tutumpotes," a play on the Latin words for all-powerful, was Bosch's term for the oligarchy.

*over*estimated the Communists and "feared them unreasonably,"[26] and even though by his own analysis there was no real Communist danger in the Dominican Republic,* Martin continually plagued Bosch for demonstrations of his anti-Communist orthodoxy.

Thus, in the course of Bosch's brief administration, Martin, the lifelong liberal and devoted admirer of Adlai Stevenson, pressed the following measures on the Dominican President: the elimination of agrarian reform measures involving land confiscation; a major effort to control "subversion" through the training of an antisubversive force; the closing of leftist schools; the illegal harassment or detention of Dominicans traveling to Cuba; and finally, as rightist pressures mounted, the "wholesale roundup," imprisonment, or deportation of both the extreme right and left![28] Bosch himself has provided the best comment on all this: "To prove that I was a democrat, I would have had to follow Trujillo's old pattern: imprison, deport or kill anyone accused of being a Communist. I would, furthermore, have had to abide by the judgment of any old general or colonel whom God had given the special right of knowing who was and who was not a Communist."[29]

Thanks to Martin's reporting and the increasingly vituperative Dominican rightist and business attacks on Bosch, the State Department quickly soured on the first democratically elected Dominican President in over thirty years. Martin himself complains, apparently seeing no connection to his own attitude and reporting, that U.S. loans to the Bosch government were far below those given to the conservative and unelected Council of State

* A CIA investigation instigated by Martin found a "surprisingly small" number of Communists in Dominican public life and Martin himself estimated that "communism could count on not more than one hundred well-trained, fully committed, and fully disciplined Dominicans."[27]

and that a number of AID projects requested by the embassy were turned down.*

At the same time, evidence of U.S. disenchantment with Bosch encouraged Dominican plots to overthrow him. Finally, on September 25, a group of dissident military men led by Colonel Elías Wessin y Wessin, commander of the key Armed Forces Training Center (CEFA) near Santo Domingo, deposed Bosch and sent him into exile. The excuse, as always, was that Bosch was delivering the country to the Communists. Although Martin did not really agree with this assessment, despite his own dark forebodings, and went to great lengths to prevent the coup, his insistent playing on the Communist theme undoubtedly had helped legitimize the Dominican military's proclaimed fears and undercut U.S. efforts to persuade them to stay out of politics.†

The standard cliché about the fall of Bosch is that "he wasn't overthrown, he overthrew himself." Or, as the State Department put it, "The forces arrayed against him were largely of his own creation."[33] It is true that Bosch had important weaknesses as a political leader and it is possible that a less erratic and shrewder politician, such as, say, Rómulo Betancourt, might have prolonged his tenure by manipulation, evasion, and subtle balancing.

* According to Martin, as of May, 1963, the State Department had given "not a cent" to Bosch, as compared with over $50 million committed to the Council of State (and $24 million later given to the Reid government).[30] However, according to official AID figures, $24,250,000 was eventually authorized to the Bosch government.[31]

† I have no evidence either to confirm or to deny the widely-reported stories that U.S. military attachés in Santo Domingo secretly "told" their counterparts in the Dominican military to overthrow Bosch or that they at least knew about and acquiesced in the plans for the coup. However, there is no doubt that the views of the U.S. military mission in the Dominican Republic carry a great deal of weight with the Dominican military; Martin related that at one point when rumors of a coup were rife the attachés were told by their Dominican counterparts: "If you tell us to go [overthrow Bosch], we'll go"[32]—and there is equally little doubt that the attachés had a very low opinion of Bosch.

But, nonetheless, the crucial reason for Bosch's downfall was that he meant what he said about ruling by democratic methods, respecting the civil liberties of leftist opponents, and effecting major political, economic, and social changes. Given the diehard resistance to this course by Dominican military men, business interests, rightist or opportunistic politicians, and elements of the Church hierarchy, it is far from clear that anyone could have survived, at least without making such far-reaching concessions to the forces of reaction as to make survival almost pointless. As José Figueres has put it, "God Himself would have done a bad job in the Dominican Republic."[34]

The coup was greeted in Washington with distaste but, because of the disillusion with Bosch, not with action effective enough to reverse it. When in the last frantic hours before the coup Martin had asked for an aircraft carrier to be sent to Dominican waters in a show of force, the State Department had sharply refused and warned Martin not to tie his moves to save Bosch to any U.S. commitment. "The Department . . . [can] do little more to save Bosch in view of his past performance," Martin was told. "Now he must save himself."[35] Thus, not only would military force not be used or even threatened, but there would be no repeat of the heavy economic pressures that had been so effective in the post-Trujillo period. To be sure, diplomatic relations were suspended and economic and military aid was temporarily cut off, but the *golpistas* all over Latin America know that if Washington limits its reaction to those measures they have little to be concerned about. They merely need to sit tight for a few months, discover a few guerrillas in the hills, and make vague promises about returning to constitutionality in the future, and in very short order relations with Washington will slide back to normal.

And that was precisely the pattern in the Dominican Republic. At first, the mild U.S. pressures focused on ways to return to constitutional rule, although not, let it be noted, to Bosch. "I take it we don't want Bosch back," said Kennedy on reading Martin's position paper on U.S. objectives. "No, Mr. President." "Why not?" "Because he isn't a President."[36]

When the pressures failed to work, the State Department went from one "fall-back position" to another. At first, the department had hoped to exact significant concessions from the post-Bosch junta in exchange for recognition and the resumption of economic assistance: free political activity for non-Communist parties, the appointment of a PRD leader to head the junta and the broadening of the cabinet to include other PRD followers, the removal of the military leaders of the coup, and social and economic reforms.[37] But, when the junta remained adamant, Washington began to fear that its pressures might encourage a leftist guerrilla uprising or, alternatively, that the junta would turn to full-scale repression of all its Dominican opponents. As the weeks went by, the State Department progressively softened its position: "Little by little we retreated. . . . One by one we gave up our objectives, until we were left with almost nothing."[38] Finally, in mid-December, 1963, with a handful of the inevitable "guerrillas" in the hills and a piece of paper from the junta promising "free elections" in a year and a half, the United States capitulated.

Perhaps it should be noted at this point that Martin's detailed account of this period makes it very clear that the main lines of U.S. strategy vis-à-vis the coup were formulated in the Kennedy Administration and that the decision to recognize the junta, which flowed inevitably from that strategy, was initiated by Martin and other Kennedy appointees in the State Department, not by either President Johnson or his new Assistant Secretary of State, Thomas Mann. Thus, the usual interpretation of this period, seeing great significance in the fact that Johnson recognized the Dominican junta only three weeks after the assassination of Kennedy and stressing the sharp contrast between the Kennedy and Johnson policies toward the coup, is quite wrong.[39]

In the next eighteen months, although the embassy withdrew from the sort of day-to-day participation in internal Dominican politics that had characterized the Martin period, the United States resumed economic assistance to, and established cordial relations with, the junta, which was soon dominated by Donald Reid Cabral.* Reid, a cool, wealthy, conservative owner of an automobile agency, was a member of one of the most prominent Dominican families and had served as one of the Vice-Presidents in the earlier Council of State. The new U.S. Ambassador, W. Tapley Bennett, was a courtly southern gentleman, a career foreign service officer of the old school. He had no trouble getting along with "Donny" Reid, whom he considered a force for stability. In the Dominican Republic Reid was widely known as "El Americano";† some even considered him to be—who knows?—an agent of the CIA.

* According to Draper, the United States "poured money" into the Reid government to the tune of $100 million, more than had been made available to any prior regime.[40] According to official U.S. Government figures, though, about $24 million in AID funds was authorized to the Reid government, of which only about $10.4 million was actually spent. Assistance from other sources (Export-Import Bank, surplus food commodities, etc.) amounted to $21 million authorized, $8 million spent.[41]

† In a more elegant version, Bosch referred to Reid as "the latest-model American Latin American, auto-sales-manager version."[42]

2

The Revolution

BY EARLY 1965, the Reid government was in deep trouble. Whatever chance it might have had to gain popular support had been lost as a result of Reid's lack of personal charisma and mildly authoritarian ruling methods, as well as the government's stiff austerity program that, imposed on an already marginal economy (the annual per capita income in the Dominican Republic is less than $250), had resulted in very high unemployment and widespread discontent. While immediately after the September, 1963, *golpe* the public reaction had seemed apathetic (perhaps in part accounting for the failure of the United States to react more vigorously), a year later sentiment for a return to constitutional government in general and to Juan Bosch in particular had substantially spread, especially among students, intellectuals, and professionals. In late January of 1965 the PRD and its main rival on the moderate left, the PRSC (Social Christians), met with Bosch at his exile home in Puerto Rico and signed the "Pact of Río Piedras," committing both groups to cooperate in efforts to reestablish the constitutional government.* The next month, when the pact was published in the still uncensored Dominican press, two thousand leading professionals and intellectuals signed a public procla-

* Draper has effectively refuted charges that Dominican Communist leaders were a secret party to the pact and thereafter worked closely with Bosch in planning the revolution.[1]

mation supporting it, a noteworthy act in a country with little tradition of civic participation, let alone of open pressures on the government. Meanwhile, the armed forces, the government's last bastion of power, were becoming disgruntled by Reid's efforts to stamp out a military smuggling racket and to get rid of some of the most venal of the old Trujillista hangovers.

The final straw was Reid's increasingly obvious intention to cancel the elections scheduled for the fall of 1965 or to rig them to maintain himself in power. By early spring nearly everyone in the country knew that a major blowup was imminent, including Ambassador Bennett, who a few weeks before the revolution informed the State Department that "Little foxes, some of them red, are chewing at the grapes."[2] *

The revolution of April, 1965, began not so much as a revolution in the true sense of the word, but as a military coup designed to topple the Reid government. In the early morning of Saturday, April 24, two Army barracks under the leadership of a small group of young colonels acting in concert with PRD leaders seized and imprisoned the Army Chief of Staff and declared themselves in revolt against the government. Within a few hours a number of other officers had joined the uprising and taken their units with them, swelling the ranks of the "constitutionalists" to about one thousand to fifteen hundred men.†

The original participants in the coup were a rather mixed bag, not all of them being simply pro-Boschists or democratic idealists. Many, among them the initiators of the April 24th action, had indeed opposed the 1963 *golpe*, were ashamed of the military's antidemocratic history, and had established close con-

* Also, Haynes Johnson, in *Fulbright the Dissenter* (Doubleday, 1968), asserts that the U.S. Government had tipped off Reid that a coup was imminent, although the CIA thought it would not occur before June 1 (p. 208).

† The quotation marks are not meant to convey irony. From here on, the titles will generally be those that the participants chose for themselves.

tacts with Bosch. Others, however, had rather doubtful qualifications as revolutionary heroes. Some were pro-Balaguer Trujillistas who had been plotting on their own and who had joined the movement because they assumed its aim was not the direct return of Bosch to the Presidency but the holding of new elections. In such elections, they believed, Balaguer would stand a good chance of winning.* Still others, men like Francisco Caamaño, Rafael Fernández Domínguez, Manuel Ramón Montes Arache and André Rivière, soon to emerge as the leading military figures in the constitutionalist camp, were career men with disreputable, or at least questionable, pasts. Caamaño's father, a Trujillo general, was known as "Butcher" Caamaño for his enthusiastic services to "the Chief," and Francisco himself had served as the head of the hated police riot squad that was anti-Bosch and had specialized in breaking up leftist demonstrations in the Council of State days;† moreover, Caamaño had been involved in the infamous Palma Sola massacre of 1962, in which members of a religious sect had been brutally murdered by a police unit. Fernández was also the son of a Trujillo general and was a former associate of Wessin. Montes Arache, who brought his tough frogman unit with him into the constitutionalist camp, had organized the group under Trujillo to serve as the elite shock troops of the Navy. Later he had been put in charge of a unit of highly "anti-Communist" commandos, and was rumored to have been in charge of the Betancourt assassination attempt. One of Montes Arache's

* In 1968, Colonel Miguel Hernando Ramírez, a leading constitutionalist commander in the first few days of the revolution and heretofore thought to be a Bosch man, declared that one of the main aims of the uprising had been to make it possible for Balaguer to return to the country.[3]

† The riot squad was widely known as the "Cascos Blancos" (White Hats); not only their headgear but their training and tactics were inspired by the late W. H. Parker's Los Angeles police force, which, at John Bartlow Martin's insistence, had been invited by the Council of State to set up an "anti-subversive" force.

lieutenants, Ilio Capozi, was a former Italian SS officer, and Rivière was a professional French mercenary with a long pro-fascist record including, most recently, service with the OAS (Organisation Armée Secrète) in Algeria. Perhaps, as Bennett suggested, such men were seeking atonement for their past,[4] or perhaps they were simply opportunists and adventurers.[5]

Whatever the motives and in many cases the dubious democratic credentials of the initial participants, the uprising soon gained considerable popular support, drawing its sustenance from the widespread discontent with the status quo.[6] The Dominican Republic is a highly underdeveloped country, with most of the population living in "abysmal and grinding poverty."[7] For a while under Trujillo there had been considerable economic growth, but in the mid-fifties a serious slump had set in. Throughout the early 1960's, as a result of political instability as well as worsening terms of trade for Dominican exports, the decline continued. Moreover, the limited fruits of this impoverished economy were inequitably distributed, with huge gaps between the tiny, closed upper class and the rest of the population, consisting mainly of landless, illiterate peasants barely subsisting on the edge of society. At the same time, an urban proletariat was rapidly developing. As was typical of so many other underdeveloped countries, the 1950's saw a major migration of the peasants into the towns and cities, where, however, industrial growth was too slow to absorb them. As a result, tens of thousands of unemployed, bitter men were thrown together in abominable slums on the outside of the cities. Most of them were in Santo Domingo.

Nor was discontent solely economic by any means, for (especially among the still-small but growing middle groups) hatred of a corrupt and brutal military establishment and contempt for a politics of cynicism, demagoguery, opportunism, and repression was rife. Finally, in the five years following Trujillo's assassination, mass attitudes had dramatically reflected the classic pattern of rapidly rising expectations curdling into bitter frustration as substantial change failed to develop. As early as 1962, a carefully structured attitude study had concluded that "an extremely serious situation of popular discontent and frustration, fraught with a dangerous potential for upheaval, exists in the Dominican Republic. Never have we seen the danger signals so unmistakably clear."[8]

The catalyst for the transformation of the April uprising from a coup to at least a partial populist uprising was provided by two events. First, PRD leaders, working closely with the constitutionalist military, seized Radio Santo Domingo and urged the populace to take to the streets in support of the movement. Second, and even more important, late Saturday night and early Sunday morning constitutionalist officers passed out arms to thousands of civilians (estimates range from 2,500 to 10,000) in order to broaden the base of the movement and counter any possible reaction from the bulk of the armed forces. Until that point, the civilians working with the constitutionalists were mostly middle-class, college-educated students, lawyers, engineers, technicians, and young businessmen, frustrated by a system in which they had no purpose and no meaningful future. With the passing out of the arms large sectors of the urban lower class joined the ranks, giving the movement something of a mass base as well as providing most of the actual *combatientes*.[9]

On Sunday morning Reid resigned and went into hiding, the military having ignored his orders to crush the uprising. Because of Reid's widespread unpopularity and the still unclear nature and ultimate purpose of the movement, the regular military leadership had been unwilling to take decisive action. On Sunday afternoon the constitutionalists named José Molina

Ureña as provisional President.* Molina was a leading Bosch supporter, and as the last president of the Chamber of Deputies, dissolved after the 1963 coup, he was constitutionally in the line of sucession to the Presidency.

It seems well established that several important military commanders, particularly former Chief of Police Belisario Peguero and Navy Chief of Staff Francisco Rivera Caminero, initially offered their allegiance to the Molina government. Moreover, the constitutionalists claim that other commanders and key political figures, including Antonio Imbert, also rushed to offer support, although these reports cannot be verified.† As Sunday wore on, however, the situation began to change, largely because the pro-Bosch nature of the movement was becoming increasingly obvious. For one thing, Molina Ureña announced that he would remain in office only until Bosch's return to the country. For another, all day Sunday jubilant crowds were surging through the streets of Santo Domingo, as hundreds of autos rhythmically honked for Bosch's return: ta-ta-ta, ta-ta; *re-gre-sa, Juan Bo'*.

Thus, there no longer could be much doubt that a victory of the revolution would result in the direct return of Bosch to the Presidency, rather than in new elections as had originally been planned.‡ This was another matter, for the regular military de-

* Not much is known about Bosch's role during this stage of the revolution, although apparently he was in continuing telephone contact with the constitutionalists. According to Moreno, the choice of Molina Ureña was Bosch's.

† Abraham Lowenthal writes that several of the most discredited Trujillo generals who had been cashiered from the military after 1961 joined the constitutionalists in the early days, probably in hopes of gaining reinstatement if the constitutionalists succeeded in establishing a new government.[10]

‡ In 1968, Antonio Martínez Francisco, the Secretary General of the PRD during the revolution, said that the original agreement between Bosch and sympathetic military men called for a military junta to rule the country temporarily after the overthrow of the Reid government, pending the holding of new elections within ninety days. Once Reid had fallen, Martínez charges, Bosch ignored the agreement and called for a return to "constitutionality," that is, the immediate restoration of his Presidency.[11]

tested and feared Bosch, judging, undoubtedly correctly, that a triumphant Bosch backed by the defecting constitutionalist military and what amounted to a well-armed civilian militia would probably seek to destroy their power and position in the Dominican Republic. As a result, by late Sunday afternoon the bulk of the military, particularly the key San Isidro Air Force Base dominated by Wessin y Wessin, had decided to actively resist the revolution.

Another apparently important factor in the military's decision to fight was the action of the U.S. Embassy.* Working mainly through its military attachés, the embassy began urgently pressing the military chiefs to unite and forcibly resist the rebellion: "Our attachés have stressed to the three military leaders . . . our strong feeling that everything possible should be done to prevent a Communist takeover."[12]† Undoubtedly, this U.S. intervention proved decisive with those commanders who were still wavering. In Santiago, for example, the importunings of the U.S. Consul barely averted the defection of an important

* Draper strongly implies that U.S. pressures alone account for the shift in the military's position from neutrality to active opposition to the revolution. This is a serious oversimplification, for Wessin and many other Dominican generals needed little external encouragement to resist a Boschist movement.

† The constitutionalists claim to have a tape recording of one of the attachés "ordering" the military to fight, presumably accounting for Bosch's assertion that "during the first days of the revolution . . . the bombing was specially and specifically ordered by the American military mission."[13] According to one highly reliable Dominican who claims to have heard the recording, however, the U.S. officer merely urged the military to resist and told them they had U.S. "support" if they did. This seems much more plausible, and it would be entirely consistent with U.S. policy at that moment, which was "reluctantly" to support forcible resistance to Bosch.[14] Thus, there is no reason to think the attachés exceeded their instructions or operated on the basis of "Pentagon policy," as most Dominicans believe and as Draper seems to accept: "In the incalculable mass of words written about the Dominican crisis, very few have been devoted to the military attachés and the CIA agents. Yet their activity may get us closer to the real U.S. policy than all the diplomatic messages between Washington and Santo Domingo. While the diplomats may have been trying to make up their minds, the military attachés apparently acted."[15]

Army base and the passing out of arms to thousands of pro-Bosch civilians. Back in the capital, Rivera Caminero, who had shifted back and forth a couple of times, finally ascertained to his satisfaction which way the wind was blowing and rejoined the Wessin forces. At about 4:30 Sunday afternoon planes from San Isidro bombed the National Palace and constitutionalist military encampments (even at this point, according to Wessin, Air Force Chief of Staff Juan de los Santos had to be forced at gunpoint to order his planes to attack[16]), and the civil war had begun.

The American determination to oppose the revolution and to use its great influence to rally the military against it, then, was made no later than Sunday morning (the beginning of the second day) and perhaps even sooner.* There seems to be little doubt that in part this decision stemmed from the general hostility to Bosch throughout the U.S. Government. As Draper has pointed out, the embassy's actions in the early days of the revolution can be seen not as a hasty and panicky reaction to a rapidly unfolding crisis but as an implementation of Washington's existing policy of frowning on the return of Juan Bosch to the Presidency.[18] It was probably no accident, for example, that the State Department had assigned the two top embassy positions to conservatives who instinctively distrusted not only Bosch but the PRD in general, and who had almost no ties with even the moderate left. "Tap didn't seem to know anyone to the left of the Rotary Club," one embassy official is quoted as remarking, while William Connett, the Deputy Chief of Mission, "seemed to be ill at ease with people who were not correctly dressed."[19]

Nonetheless, whatever the feelings about Bosch, by far the

* Cf. Geyelin: "The full weight of the U.S. Government on the scene had been committed to blocking the rebellion before it was twenty-four hours old."[17]

more important factor in the decision to intervene was the embassy's specific assessment, reached almost at the outset, that there was a significant degree of Communist participation in the revolution.* As a result, on Sunday morning the State Department,† which had earlier decided not to take even diplomatic action to attempt to prop up or restore Reid, instructed Connett (Bennett was in the United States at the outset of the revolution and didn't return until April 27) that in view of signs that Dominican Communists were playing prominent roles in the uprising as well as the appearance of extreme leftist elements in the street demonstrations, the embassy should contact the leaders of the Dominican armed forces and urge them to form a provisional government that could restore order, prevent a Communist takeover, and prepare the country for free elections. It was at this point that the embassy's military attachés contacted the Dominican chiefs of staff, told them of Washington's reactions and, at a minimum, acquiesced in Wessin's decision to bomb the constitutionalists.

* See pages 35-44 below for a discussion of the Communist role in the revolution. Geyelin and Szulc, making use of their access to the initial exchanges between the embassy and the State Department, have pointed out that, in Geyelin's words, "the firm conclusion [was] reached at a remarkably early stage [by the embassy] . . . that a rebel victory would carry with it an unacceptable risk of a Communist regime."[20]

† It is my strong impression that the key officials in Washington in the early weeks of the crisis were Kennedy M. Crockett, Chief of the State Department's Bureau of Caribbean affairs, Under Secretary of State Thomas Mann, Under Secretary of State George Ball, and McGeorge Bundy in the White House. It does not appear as though Secretary of Defense McNamara or "the Pentagon" in general played a major role in the development of U.S. policy. Nor, for that matter, does it appear that Dean Rusk was at the center of affairs, not very surprising in light of increasing evidence that, except for Vietnam, the Secretary of State was often on the sidelines of major foreign-policy decisions throughout the Kennedy and Johnson administrations. However, I cannot be confident of the accuracy of this assessment, as I did not focus my research on the internal policy-making process during the Dominican crisis. Hereinafter, I will use the terms "the United States," "Washington," and "the State Department" more or less interchangeably to represent overall U.S. policy, normally without further specification on how that policy was arrived at.

As of the next day, Monday the 26th, however, the revolution was still alive and the embassy was worrying about the effect of Bosch's possible return. Because of the extremist participation in the coup, the embassy reported, as well as Communist advocacy of Bosch's return as favorable to their interests, Bosch's reinstatement would not be in the interests of the United States. Nonetheless, Connett concluded with apparent reluctance, since no effective case could yet be made that the movement was under Communist *control,* the United States should not physically prevent Bosch's return. Such action, he warned, would cast the United States in the role of intervening against a popular democratic revolution.

As it turned out, of course, Bosch did not attempt to return. The precise circumstances surrounding this dramatic aspect of the revolution are shrouded by conflicting testimony, but it is nearly certain that, as Connett advised, the United States took no direct action to prevent him from doing so.[21] In fact, to the annoyance of Bennett, no move was made even to cut Bosch's communications with the constitutionalists, which would not have been much of a problem in view of Bosch's residence on U.S. soil in Puerto Rico. On the other hand, it also seems clear that the United States was not willing to facilitate Bosch's return, except perhaps on terms that were obviously unacceptable to him—that he make a strong statement "recognizing" the Communist danger in Santo Domingo and accepted the presence of U.S. forces in the Dominican Republic until the danger passed.[22]

Bosch himself blames his failure to return on the refusal of the United States to assist him, and Draper defends his inaction as based on a "difficult political decision." Be that as it may, almost all Dominicans I interviewed, including constitutionalist and PRD leaders, consider Bosch's apparent insistence on U.S.

authorization and protection bitterly ironic and argue that Bosch could and should have found ways to get back to his country and assume command at the outset of the revolution. To be sure, the risks to his life would have been considerable, but no greater than those being run by his followers in Santo Domingo. The spectacle of Bosch's fiery exhortations to the constitutionalists from the safety of Puerto Rico was uncomfortably reminiscent of the prizefight manager telling his boy to get in there and fight, they can't hurt us. It was to cost Bosch dearly in the elections of 1966.

By Tuesday, April 27, with the constitutionalists under heavy military attack and the revolution having failed to spread to the countryside or to any major city outside Santo Domingo, the movement appeared doomed. Since Sunday afternoon the constitutionalists had been under continuous attack from Wessin's planes. Tad Szulc described the scene: "In the ancient Dominican capital blood was flowing freely. Rebel army units and civilian bands were firing across the city at the positions of the Wessin forces. Planes streaked overhead, machine gunning the streets and dropping bombs on the rebels and the civilian population. Casualties were mounting and hospitals were filling up with the wounded."[23] (Later estimates were that about two thousand people lost their lives in the fighting prior to the U.S. intervention.) Most of the fighting centered on the Duarte Bridge spanning the Ozama River, where a force of tanks from the San Isidro base was attempting to enter the city.

Late that afternoon, with the tanks apparently about to break through the rebel defenses, a number of leading PRD officials and constitutionalist officers, including Molina Ureña and Caamaño, went to the U.S. Embassy for the second time in three days in order to request U.S. help in ending the conflict. On the first occasion, immediately following the bombing of the National

Palace on Sunday afternoon, Antonio Guzmán of the PRD had asked the second secretary of the embassy—Bennett had not yet returned and Connett made himself unavailable—to get Wessin to stop the air attacks. According to constitutionalist sources, the response was not only negative but the U.S. official added that "if I had Wessin's power, I would use it too." Ambassador Bennett's reaction to the second plea hardly differed. Accusing the PRD officials of allowing "Communists" to take advantage of the movement and of tolerating looting and atrocities, Bennett flatly refused either to use his influence to end the bombing or to mediate settlement talks between the constitutionalists and the military. There was only one course for the constitutionalists, he advised—to surrender.[24]

As Draper and others have pointed out, Bennett's reaction was not an emotional blunder, but was entirely consistent with U.S. policy. Having determined that the revolution must fail, Bennett obviously saw no point in interposing U.S. authority and rescuing the constitutionalists at the moment when they were apparently on the verge of total defeat. Immediately after this conversation Bennett reported to Washington that the revolution had entered the "mop-up" stage, which, he conceded, might be somewhat "rough."[25] A number of constitutionalist leaders, including Molina Ureña, apparently shared the embassy's assessment, for immediately following the highly-charged meeting they fled into the political asylum of Latin American embassies.

But not all of them. A participant at the now famous embassy confrontation vividly recalls that at the moment when Bennett labeled the revolution "Communist" and told the leaders to surrender, a big, barrel-chested man whom he had never seen before jumped to his feet and said, "Son of a bitch! I know what *I'm* going to do." It was Francisco Caamaño, and he was not going to strangle Bennett on the spot as the startled assemblage for a moment feared, but was on his way to the bridge to rally his forces for a last-ditch stand.

Somehow, at that moment the tide turned. Exhorted and directed by Radio Santo Domingo, thousands of people converged on the bridge. Armed only with small arms and Molotov cocktails, they were ready to confront Wessin's armor. As the tanks crossed the bridge they were immediately bottled up in the narrow streets of the old city and were either destroyed or forced to surrender. Those that were captured intact were quickly taken over by the constitutionalist military and thrown back into action, this time with the word "People" painted across their sides.[26] On the other side of the river the remainder of the Wessin force refused to cross the bridge, and many began to desert.

The revolutionaries then turned their attention to the police stations inside the city. Post after post fell to the constitutionalists, whose armaments increasingly swelled as they captured new armories, until finally the main fortress at Fortaleza Ozama was overrun. (Amidst the carnage was a note of black humor: the last detachment of surrendering Cascos Blancos, having been told they were facing a Communist rebellion, pleaded for their lives by crying "Viva Fidel! Viva el Comunismo! Viva Cuba!")[27]

The collapse of the police and military, ominously reminiscent of the last days of Batista, was the final straw for the U.S. Embassy. At 5 P.M. April 28, with the city belonging to the revolution, and the "loyalists" in terror that the constitutionalists were about to go on the offensive and attack San Isidro itself, Bennett's famous "critic" telegram, recommending the immediate landing of U.S. troops, arrived in Washington.[28] That night, when the first contingents of the 82nd Airborne Division arrived at San Isidro, they found the "strong man" of the Dominican armed forces, the dreaded Wessin y Wessin, in tears: "If you had not come," he cried, "they would have killed us."[29]

There is not the slightest doubt that the primary, indeed the overwhelming factor in the U.S. decision to intervene was the belief in both the embassy and the State Department that the apparently imminent constitutionalist victory would pose an unacceptable risk of a Communist takeover. As has been indicated, from the very outset of the revolt the embassy had been warning, and with increasing urgency, of Communist participation, until, finally, Bennett reported on the afternoon of the 28th that "the issue here is now a fight between Castro-type elements and those who oppose."[30] As both the embassy and the State Department saw it, even if Bosch should be reinstalled in the Presidency he would soon be discarded by the better-organized and more-determined extremists and there would be a Communist takeover within six months.

If there were any doubts in Washington as to whether the evidence justified the momentous decision to intervene, they were buried by an overwhelming predisposition throughout the U.S. Government to err on the "safe" side—that is, to move hard and fast to ensure that the Cuban scenario would not again be repeated in the hemisphere. Castro had somehow slipped by, the feeling was, concealing his true colors until he had consolidated his revolution and established close ties with the Soviet Union, thus making the risks of direct U.S. intervention prohibitive. The missile crisis of 1962 had actually solidified Castro's position, for it had apparently been resolved on the basis of an at least tacit U.S. commitment not to invade Cuba. But it had also firmly implanted the determination that come what may there would be No Second Cuba.*

No doubt the escalating war in Vietnam also contributed to the disposition to intervene without awaiting further events. As is well known, Johnson and Rusk tended to see revolutions and general political instability involving a Communist element as part of a larger pattern—"what we've got they want" was the way the President once put it. Given this grim siege mentality that seemingly pervaded the Johnson Administration in the spring of 1965, then, it was almost inevitable that the two crises would be seen to be intimately related. "What can we do in Vietnam if we can't clean up the Dominican Republic?" Johnson was reported as saying.[33]†

To this day, some high officials insist, even privately, that fear for the safety of American lives was not a pretext but a very real factor in the initial decision to intervene, although they concede that the Communist issue soon became the dominant consideration. There is some evidence that in a very limited sense this contention is true. There was no doubt that all existing "authority" in Santo Domingo had collapsed and that with armed crowds surging unchecked through the streets the *potential* for truly frightening chaos was real. One incident seems to have been particularly instrumental in shaping Washington's

* Note Adam Yarmolinsky's comment: "Fevered images of Soviet nuclear weapons emplaced on the green hills of Hispaniola may have been a factor contributing to the decision to intervene in the Dominican Republic."[31] Senator Fulbright has pointed to another aspect of what Geyelin has called "the Cuban syndrome," not as exalted as *raison d'état* but perhaps as powerful: "The specter of a second Communist state in the hemisphere—and its probable repercussions within the United States and possible effects on the careers of those who might be held responsible—seems to have been the most important single factor in distorting the judgment of otherwise sensible and competent men."[32]

† Cf. also Seyom Brown's suggestion that the Dominican intervention "possibly reflected an intention to demonstrate to the world, particularly to the larger Communist powers who might be contemplating increased assistance to Ho Chi Minh, that . . . our patience could wear thin, and we *might* even overreact."[34]

image of what was happening. On the morning of April 27 about a thousand American citizens—businessmen, tourists, embassy dependents—were gathered in the lobby of Santo Domingo's main hotel, being readied for helicopter evacuation to U.S. ships lying offshore. Suddenly a band of armed constitutionalists burst into the hotel, lined the Americans against the wall, and fired a number of machine-gun bursts over their heads. No one was hurt, and it later turned out that the rebels had not been seeking deliberately to terrorize the Americans but were looking for an extreme right-wing propagandist who had taken shelter in the hotel. A short time later, according to Martin, the constitutionalists agreed to cooperate fully in the evacuation of Americans.[35] Just the same, the embassy's report on the hotel incident apparently deeply concerned the State Department.

Moreover, some of the newspaper correspondents who were very critical of subsequent U.S. policy agreed that a "complete breakdown of order" had occurred and that the landing of U.S. troops to protect lives was justified.[36] As it turned out, not only was not a single American attacked but there were remarkably few constitutionalist atrocities of any sort. What few attacks did occur were highly selective, aimed almost exclusively at a few extreme rightists, and then mainly at their property. Indeed, many more innocent citizens died as a result of the Air Force bombing and strafing than at the hands of the constitutionalists.[37] Nonetheless, the embassy, perhaps because of its ideological predisposition, apparently believed the rumors of wild pillaging and the execution of hundreds and it might well have convinced Washington that a bloodbath was an imminent possibility.

Perhaps it should also be pointed out that in the first day or so after the armed intervention Washington's instructions to the embassy stressed that at least "for the time being" the mission of the troops was only to protect U.S. lives and that no decision had yet been made to use them in such a way as to influence the outcome of the civil war. However, the crucial points are: (1) the strong possibility of using military force to prevent a constitutionalist victory was explicitly envisaged as early as Sunday afternoon, the second day of the revolution[38] ("We don't want to intervene unless the outcome is in doubt," was the way the department put it);[39] (2) at least part of the reason for even the initial troop landings was to have them available for direct intervention if that proved necessary; (3) in fact, within forty-eight hours paratroopers *were* deployed in a manner designed to forestall a constitutionalist victory, taking over the Duarte Bridge and the eastern banks of the Ozama River in order to prevent an attack on San Isidro; and, finally, (4) U.S. troops remained in the Dominican Republic in a political-military occupation for nearly seventeen months after the initial intervention.

Thus, the continuing debate over whether the publicly announced reasons were genuine or not is pointless.[40] Perhaps Art Buchwald had the last word in a column widely read and enjoyed in the Dominican Republic. One Sydney, the last U.S. citizen waiting in line to be evacuated, is refused permission to leave. Instead he is taken to a hotel and surrounded by massive amounts of soldiers, heavy artillery, and tanks. After a few days, tired of being so protected, Sydney calls the White House and demands to talk with President Johnson. The President points out that if he insists on leaving all the troops would have to leave too, since the United States is in the Dominican Republic only to protect American lives. Sydney is still unhappy. "Sydney, have you ever heard of the Monroe Doctrine?" the President then asks. "You form part of it. Your name will go into the history books along with Teddy Roosevelt and Admiral Dewey, and when school teachers ask their students who saved the Dominican Republic from going Communist, the students will answer: Sydney!"[41]

On the other hand, if Buchwald's school teachers base their lectures on most of what has so far been written on the Dominican crisis, they are likely to believe that the Communist danger was all but nonexistent. If that is so, the administration has nothing to blame but its own remarkably inept public performance, so devastatingly demolished by the leading journalists. The only evidence ever presented to justify the decision to intervene was lists of some fifty-three, fifty-eight, or seventy-five "Communists" said to be in the Dominican Republic and active among the constitutionalists. Not only would the presence of such a trivial number of Communists hardly demonstrate a Red Peril but, in fact, the reporters soon were able to show that not everyone on the list was a Communist, and that many of the genuine Communists were dead, in jail, or outside the country.[42] Small wonder, then, that the resort to such McCarthyite tactics convinced many that the various lists were, in Draper's words, "ex post facto jobs, hastily put together to justify an already adopted policy."[43]

This assumption that the whole affair was a hoax or cover-up is, however, incorrect. Almost all serious Dominican and foreign observers who were in the Dominican Republic during the revolution and to whom I talked, including many who are highly critical of the U.S. intervention, agree on the existence of *some* degree of danger.[44] * Moreover, the Johnson Administration's decision to intervene was based not merely on the presence of a few Communists in the constitutionalist camp but on what appeared to be a widespread pattern of events. Some of the more decisive factors, in Washington's view, were intelligence reports on the activities and plans of the Dominican Communist leader-

* Perhaps it bears reiteration that my interviews were on a not-for-attribution basis.

ship (the United States had apparently penetrated the Communist party structure, for Charles Roberts has revealed that information was being received "from such well-placed sources that to reveal them would have resulted in the sudden death of the informants"[45]); warnings from some PRD leaders that they were losing control over the situation; constitutionalist propaganda and rhetoric that frequently was Castroite in tone and substance;* and, most important, evidence of a major Communist role in the arming, training, and leadership of the guerrilla warfare "commando" units in the constitutionalist zone.[47]

This last is crucial, for the critics have tended to focus on the demonstrable lack of significant Communist influence among the initial leaders and official spokesmen of the revolution—the PRD officials and the constitutionalist military—ignoring the incontrovertible evidence of a very considerable Communist role among the rank-and-file armed civilians, who soon outnumbered the original military participants by almost four to one.[48] The leaders of the three Communist parties, particularly of the Castroite 14th of June, had taken advantage of the passing out of arms to take to the streets and form highly organized and disciplined units under the command of students and Communist leaders trained in guerrilla warfare tactics, some, undoubtedly, in Cuba.† How much of an eventual threat these

* Herbert Dinerstein has noted that most judgments on whether a revolutionary uprising is likely to result in a Communist takeover are made on the basis of models in the minds of the analysts.[46] This seems particularly striking in the Dominican situation—not only was the Cuban revolution in the minds of embassy officials but at least one U.S. diplomat was sure he saw the same "pattern" of events that had led to a Communist-dominated government in Guatemala in 1954.

† José Moreno, who supported and participated in the constitutionalist movement, is very explicit on the central role of MPD (Movimiento Popular Dominicano) and 14th of June activists in the commandos and on the spontaneous emergence in leadership roles of men with "a high degree of radicalism" after the first few days of the revolution.[49] See also the analysis by Bryant Wedge, who found that Communists played an important role in organizing the street fighting.[50]

militant and well-armed "commandos" may have posed is certainly debatable, but in the context of revolution, near-anarchy, shattered and discredited political institutions, and a tradition of political violence, reasonable men could and did take the matter seriously.[51]

There is now evidence, in fact, that the assessment of the Communist leaders themselves was quite similar to that of the embassy. To be sure, the analysis may be self-serving and prove nothing, but it is nonetheless interesting:

> In a few days the military movement of April 24th became transformed into a revolutionary struggle of the armed masses that overthrew the despotic government and broke the reactionary military apparatus controlled by the United States. . . . In the immediate course of the revolution the Commandos arose as the organization through which the people combatted the enemy and exercised the new power that was formed. It was, without a doubt, a true revolution. It is true that the revolution began with the objective of reestablishing the liberal bourgeois government of Bosch and the Constitution of 1963, but the destruction of the old state apparatus and substitution of the people in arms for the national army gave it a much more profound character and presented the possibility, almost the certainty, of transforming the movement in a short period into an anti-imperialistic, socialist revolution. The North American imperialists understood this. . . . They feared, and it was logical . . . that a new Cuba in the Caribbean would be produced.[52]

Similar conclusions were reached by others besides the U.S. Embassy and the Communist leaders. (It is perhaps worth noting that Bennett's belief that U.S. intervention was necessary to prevent a Communist takeover was not his alone but was concurred in by all twelve political and military officers of the embassy; later, Thomas Mann claimed that "all those in our Government who had full access to official information" agreed with the need for intervention.)[53] For example, the five Latin American members of an OAS investigating commission unanimously reported that, had the United States not intervened, the

Dominican revolution "could rapidly have been converted into a Communist insurrection."[54] To be sure, most of the committee members represented conservative governments, but the delegate of the one fairly liberal state, Colombia, went even further, arguing that "we are in a struggle against international communism," in which the hemispheric states could not "sit on the balcony to watch the end of the tragedy . . . as if we were at a bullfight waiting for the crew."[55] Some members of the United Nations mission also privately agreed that the possibility of a Communist seizure of power could not have been discounted.[56] Finally, my interviewing revealed that a number of foreign diplomats stationed in Santo Domingo fully shared the U.S. assessment and welcomed the intervention; there were also repeated U.S. reports, the reliability of which I cannot verify, that the liberal Apostolic Nuncio, who was considered to be very sympathetic to the constitutionalists and later was to play an important go-between role, actually became increasingly disenchanted with the revolution, even concluding at one point that the constitutionalist leadership was under the control of foreign Communist groups.

What does all this add up to? Two things are certain. On the one hand Communist or Castroite groups were an important element in the constitutionalist camp, but, on the other, they never succeeded in getting "control" of the movement, as the Johnson Administration for a brief time asserted. It is probable that for some time *no one* was in complete control of what, after all, was in good part a spontaneous, unstructured uprising, a series of unplanned chain reactions, a letting-go after thirty-five years of silence. But, as will be shown later, if *any* group can be said to have been dominant, it was clearly the moderate leftist PRD leadership and the anti-Communist constitutionalist military under Caamaño.

In any case, though, the U.S. decision to intervene had not been based on an assessment that the Communists were already in control but merely that they posed a serious threat. Once again, Johnsonian overkill succeeded only in destroying the credibility of the administration's entire case, for his May 2nd statement that the revolution had been "taken over and really seized and placed into the hands of a band of Communist conspirators" went considerably beyond what most State Department analysts believed to be the case. To be sure, Johnson's speech seems to have been based on the overwrought reports of John Bartlow Martin, who arrived in the Dominican Republic after the intervention and whose liberal background lent his observations a wholly undeserved credence. The unsupported Johnson-Martin charges were so vigorously challenged that within a few days the administration had dropped them and returned to its original rationale.*

Even more absurd were the half-hearted attempts, particularly by the ever-predictable Mann, to link the revolution to "international Communism," the "Sino-Soviet conspiracy" [!], or, more modestly, to Cuba.[58] While some of the guerrilla leaders probably had received training in Cuba, all but a tiny handful of the constitutionalists were Dominican, and not a shred of evidence exists linking any Communist country to the planning, organization, or direction of the movement, before, during, or after the initial uprising.

In short, the only intellectually respectable question is whether there was a major threat of indigenous Communists or extremists gaining control of a chaotic situation and successfully imposing a Castroite government. The safest answer would have to

* As Draper, Szulc and others have pointed out, Martin's book provides practically no evidence to support his contention. Instead, we are offered some emotional obscurantism: "It is not names of Communists, or numbers, that is important. It is the process itself—the fusion process of the bloodbath."[57]

be that no one can possibly know, for an unfolding revolutionary process had been aborted by outside intervention at its very outset. Nonetheless, the most reliable, sophisticated observers and the best evidence tend to discount the seriousness and immediacy of the danger.

To begin with, on the eve of the revolution the Dominican Communists were very few in number, divided into three quarreling parties, and had hardly any popular support. In 1962 an attitude study found that while 65 percent of Dominicans questioned mentioned the United States as the country which has a political system and a way of life that the Dominican Republic should emulate, less than one-half of one percent mentioned a desire to imitate any Communist country, and there were no mentions of Cuba at all! Eighty-six percent thought that if the Dominican Communists came to power they would work for the interests of the Soviet Union and Communism rather than for those of the Dominican Republic, and 11 percent didn't know. Overall, pro-Communist sentiment was estimated to be about 3 percent.[59] *

Moreover, just two weeks before the revolution the House Committee on Foreign Affairs released the results of its investigation into "Communism in Latin America," clearly based on CIA material. According to the report, Venezuela, Guatemala, and Colombia were the primary targets for Communist subversion; just to be on the safe side, Paraguay, Panama, Honduras, Haiti, and El Salvador were also cited as countries to be watched.[61] No mention of the Dominican Republic, where apparently all was quiet.

Second, as has been mentioned, there is no evidence of any

* To be sure, the liberal Mexican analyst Victor Alba has written that, while the Communists did not have much influence with the masses, their impact was considerably greater on the middle class, the intellectuals, and the students.[60]

Communist participation in the planning of the initial pro-Bosch military coup. On the contrary, Draper's assiduous research has convincingly demonstrated that the Communists considered Bosch a lackey of U.S. imperialism, were excluded from the PRD-PRSC Pact of Río Piedras, and were by their own admission unprepared for the uprising and therefore unable to head it.[62]

Third, U.S. intelligence agencies are not famous for erring on the side of tolerance in their reporting on who is and who is not a Communist, and nowhere were their sources more unreliable than in the Dominican Republic. One key Dominican political leader who was able to observe some of the CIA operations reports that the agency tended to accept information from any source whatever, and points out that since the Trujillo era Dominicans have been notoriously prone to label all their enemies as "Communists." By way of example, he notes that the CIA considered half the members of the García-Godoy cabinet, ranging from moderately liberal to conservative in their political views, to be "risky." Also revealing is the story told by a wealthy oligarch sympathetic to the constitutionalists. On the first day of the revolution he received a telephone call suggesting that he contact all his friends and ask each to tell the American Embassy that the revolutionaries were "Communists." It was an old tactic, used earlier by the rightists in order to discredit Bosch, but who can tell what effect such telephone calls may have had on Connett, who with only six months in the Dominican Republic was still new to the game? (This story may also help explain the few physical attacks on self-styled "anti-Communists" which so concerned the embassy, for they were mainly directed against the semi-fascist extreme rightists who had been prominent in the 1963 coup against Bosch and had been poisoning Dominican political discourse for years.)

Fourth, the Castroite radio and television propaganda and the presence of Communist leaders at the National Palace and other revolutionary command posts may have reflected, as the constitutionalists subsequently explained, only the utter chaos of the first few days of the revolution and the consequent ease with which any one could wander in and out of government installations and issue *pronunciamientos*.

Finally, and perhaps most crucially, the Dominican Communists (unlike, say, the Chinese Communists or the Vietcong) had no mass base or even the rudiments of an organization network in the countryside, nor did they have any charismatic leaders with the great prestige and widespread popular appeal of a Castro or a Ho Chi Minh.

For the sake of argument, however, let us assume that the State Department analysis was correct—that the United States intervention came just in time to prevent a Communist-dominated uprising from defeating the last remaining military forces in and around Santo Domingo. Even in that case, though, the revolution would still not have been completely victorious, for several military units outside the Santo Domingo area were still intact.* To be sure, the apparently imminent collapse of the San Isidro forces would have been a major psychological as well as military blow, but the more manifestly Communist the revolution, the more likely that the regular military would continue to resist. And in the last analysis, even if the entire military structure had completely disintegrated, the Communist revolutionary leadership would still have been a long way short

* However, according to Martin the Dominican armed forces had "virtually disintegrated" by the time the United States intervened. He estimates that of a military structure of nearly 30,000 men, the San Isidro generals could command the loyalty of no more than 1,500 soldiers, 900 air men, part of the Navy, 1,000 policemen, and "several thousand virtually useless soldiers scattered in garrisons around the country."[63]

of consolidating their control over the revolutionary forces themselves, let alone over the entire country. The constitutionalist military and other anti-Communist elements in the revolution had been willing to accept Communist support only on the principle that the enemy of my enemy is my friend, and only so long as they were in a fight for survival. Once victorious, though, the non-Communist elements in the movement would undoubtedly have fought to resist a Communist takeover, turning for support, if necessary, to the still-uncommitted, highly anti-Communist peasantry, comprising almost 70 percent of the Dominican population.[64]

In short, even assuming the United States is in some way justified in intervening to abort an indigenous Latin American Communist revolution (a point I shall take up in the Conclusions), its intervention in the Dominican Republic was at the very least highly premature. To recapitulate: (1) the Communists probably did not pose an immediate threat to dominate the revolution; (2) even if they had posed such a threat, the revolution was far short of nationwide victory; and (3) even if *that* occurred, it was highly likely that the movement would then have become divided and the civil war would have entered a new phase, the outcome of which would have been far from certain.

Note, however, that this interpretation, stressing the uncertainties of the situation, differs markedly from the widely-accepted but much too facile assumption, stemming largely from the writings of Theodore Draper, that the U.S. intervention prevented an imminent *Boschist* victory. Draper, in my view, not only underestimates the diversity of the constitutionalist movement (which contained a powerful and generally conservative pro-Balaguer grouping as well as significant Communist elements), but, more importantly, he overestimates the strength of the movement in its entirety, vis-à-vis its internal opponents. As I have argued, the movement had not won over or defeated important military units outside Santo Domingo, had not spread to the countryside, and insofar as it stood for the return of Bosch without new elections may very well not have had majority support. Even if the constitutionalists had eventually won out, about all that can be said with confidence is that Bosch would have been brought back and installed in the Presidency, but that is not to say he would have been able to stabilize his leadership over the revolutionary activists in the short run, let alone over the entire country over the longer run. Obviously the U.S. political and then military intervention changed the course of a revolutionary process, but how that process would otherwise have unfolded no one is given to know.

3

The Objectives of the Intervention

SOME OF THE STRONGEST criticism of the Johnson Administration has been directed not only at the intervention itself, but at what appeared to be Washington's longer-term objectives in the Dominican Republic once the real or imagined possibility of a Communist takeover had been eliminated. The generally accepted interpretation, stemming primarily from the widely read, forceful analyses of Theodore Draper and Senator William Fulbright, is that the United States deliberately set out to restore the Dominican "status quo." Thus, in their view the United States had compounded the offense of intervention by "turning its back on social revolution" in favor of support for "a corrupt, reactionary military oligarchy."[1] * Later, the theory goes, the policy was partially modified because of the vociferous domestic and foreign reaction as well as pressures from more liberal elements inside the administration.

In retrospect and with far more evidence now available, this interpretation seems almost certainly incorrect. But, before turning to this matter, it is first necessary to deal with an even

* Draper put it this way: "The intervention was an unmitigated political disaster . . . because it demonstrated that the United States did not know the difference between reform and revolution, between what was at most a little social democracy and Communism."[2]

more damning view, which sees the "real" purpose of the intervention as the maintenance of U.S. corporate domination of the Dominican economy and/or, more simply, the protection of the investments of a few corporations, under threat from a nationalist revolution.[3] Proponents of this thesis, especially as represented by Fred Goff and Michael Locker, point out that the La Romana sugar complex, which produces one-third of the Dominican cane output, was a subsidiary of the American-owned South Puerto Rico Sugar Corporation. Moreover, "a considerable number of individuals with financial, legal and social connections to the East Coast sugar complex were well stationed throughout the upper echelons of the United States government."[4] For example, Abe Fortas for twenty years had been a director of the Sucrest Corporation, the third-largest East Coast cane refiner; Adolph Berle was a postwar board chairman of Sucrest; and Ellsworth Bunker was a past chairman, president, and director of the National Sugar Refining Corporation, the second-largest East Coast cane refiner.[5] From this, it is concluded that American policy was a response to the needs of sugar corporations.

The argument does not seem very persuasive. The mere fact that an American corporation had a possible stake in the outcome of the Dominican revolution does not demonstrate that high government officials acted on that interest, regardless of their past connections. In two years of intensive research on the intervention I never once saw or heard mentioned a reference by a United States official to past, existing, or potential threats to American economic interests in the Dominican Republic. Indeed, the Goff-Locker argument does not even pretend to develop concrete evidence demonstrating linkages between corporate interests and high national policies, but instead rests on mere assertion and on a rather flagrant post-hoc, ergo-propter-hoc reasoning style. It is certainly true that U.S. corporations had investments in the Dominican Republic, although in rather inconsequential amounts as compared with those in dozens of other countries around the world. It is also the case that nationalist governments frequently place restrictions on foreign investment. If, however, the existence of these two factors alone were sufficient to produce U.S. military interventions, then the Marines would have been in nearly perpetual motion since the end of the Second World War.

Aside from the absence of confirming evidence, the argument is not inherently plausible. First of all, the "East Coast sugar complex," much less the U.S. economy as a whole, has no real need of Dominican sugar. There is an oversupply of world sugar and should Dominican sources suddenly dry up—highly unlikely, in any event, no matter what the nature of Dominican politics, given the crucial role of sugar experts in the Dominican economy—the United States could easily allocate its quota to dozens of other countries which every year clamor to be let into the lucrative U.S. market. Secondly, even if we should accept the implication that men of the experience and caliber of Berle, Fortas,* and Bunker acted on the basis of their past corporate connections rather than in the national interest as they saw it, the record makes it reasonably clear that none of them played an important role in the decision to intervene. From all the available evidence, Berle was not involved in the crisis at all, Fortas only marginally so, and Bunker only well after the troops had landed.

Finally, the quasi-Marxian interpretation is hardly consistent

* Revelations concerning Mr. Fortas's conflicts of interest while a Supreme Court Justice might seem to undercut this argument, but it should be noted that advocating a U.S. military invasion of another state out of sympathy to past business associates is quite a different matter from the indiscretions that Mr. Fortas apparently committed in the Wolfson case, unfortunate as they may have been.

with common sense, for it asks us to believe that the President of the United States took a momentous action that he fully realized would have enormous and perhaps unpredictable domestic and international repercussions for years to come, simply in order to avert a threat that might or might not have existed to a couple of hundred million dollars' worth of private investment bearing no demonstrable relationship to the security or economic well-being of the United States as a whole.*

The argument that for *political* reasons—*raisons d'état*—the United States in its Dominican policy deliberately set out to restore the status quo, or even to establish a conservative military dictatorship, must be taken far more seriously, however, for the United States's willingness to work with and support safely anti-Communist governments no matter what their domestic political coloration is well known and only too amply demonstrated. Nonetheless, that is *not* the course the United States took in the Dominican Republic, appearances to the contrary notwithstanding. There is no doubt, as I hope to demonstrate throughout this book, that from the very outset of the intervention the Johnson Administration was not only committed to the reestablishment of democratic government through genuinely free elections in the near future, but also intended to use the opportunity to begin gradually to reform and restructure the Dominican military establishment, the main bulwark of the status quo.

* Perhaps it should be emphasized that I have limited myself here to dealing only with the economic-determinist arguments that in fact have been made, not with more sophisticated interpretations that *might* have been offered. For example, an intelligent Marxist presumably would stress the overall impact of the capitalist system on general American foreign policy: policy makers being products of that system, they genuinely believe that radical nationalist movements are a threat to international order and stability. Thus, the argument might run, nationalizations of private enterprises are given far greater significance than the direct impact of such actions would seem to warrant, for they are seen as symbolic augurs of much worse things to come. A discussion of this approach would be beyond the scope of this book.

That point having been made, however, there is an important qualification. If the United States had been interested *only* in the reestablishment of democracy, it obviously could have brought Bosch back to the country and reinstated him in office to serve out the remainder of his constitutional term. When asked why this was not done, the Secretary of State replied that the Bosch government had "lasted seven months. . . . What is important about a constitution in the government is that it have the consent of the people at the time, of the day."[6] As Draper remarks: "According to this principle, whenever a democratically elected government and a democratically enacted constitution was overthrown by force, the slate is wiped clean and the golpistas have the right to demand 'consent' to a new constitution. Every coup, in effect, automatically voids the 'consent' given to the previous constitution, however democratically enacted."[7]

The point, of course, was that although the Johnson Administration was willing to take its chances on a new election, it was not willing to actively help Bosch regain office. Indeed, several high administration officials privately admit that the decision to seek elections was strongly influenced by the U.S. assessment, based primarily on polls taken in the Dominican Republic just before the revolution, that in an election between Balaguer and Bosch, Balaguer would win. Such an admission suggests that, had the assessment been different, it might have been a fair question whether elections would have been sought. One should be wary of making too much of this, however. Many U.S. officials point out that the hopeful expectation of a Bosch defeat was based on the thinnest of evidence, and that no one knew whether Balaguer would even run for the Presidency, let alone how the intervention would alter the Dominican political climate. Moreover, once the decision was adopted, it became firm U.S. policy, even in the face of a later expectation that Bosch, after all, would probably win the elections.

If all this is so, why then did the liberal community so seriously misunderstand U.S. intentions? A good part of the explanation lies in Draper's widely accepted analysis that the United States intervened against a "virtually nonexistent" threat, and, what was worse, he strongly implies, *knew* the threat to be nonexistent.[8] Dismiss the argument that there was a serious Communist threat or, at least, that the administration thought that there was, and you must then look for the "real" reasons behind the official rhetoric. It is this route that leads to the belief that the intervention was based on raw economic imperialism or, more plausibly, opposition to even non-Communist economic, political, and social change.

Much of Draper's argument is built around President Johnson's ill-considered statement of May 2: "What began as a popular democratic revolution was taken over . . . by Communists." As Draper, Szulc, Geyelin, and many others have conclusively shown, though, the United States was opposed to that "popular democratic revolution" from the very beginning. Thus, the inference can be drawn that the later claims of Communist participation were (as quoted earlier) "ex post facto jobs, hastily put together to justify an already adopted policy."[9] And what could that policy be other than an opposition to Bosch's political philosophy, if not to the Latin American democratic left in general?

At first glance this indictment appears persuasive, but ultimately it is unconvincing. First, as I have attempted to show, the Communist threat was not in fact nonexistent, even if probably exaggerated. Second, and even more important, the U.S. Government most certainly did not consider the threat to be nonexistent, and Johnson's rhetoric to the contrary notwithstanding, Communist participation in the revolution was emphasized by the U.S. Embassy from the very beginning. As early as April

25, for example, the State Department told the embassy that it was concerned with the reported participation of extreme leftist elements in the demonstrations leading to the overthrow of the Reid government and instructed it to work for a provisional government capable of restoring order and preventing a Communist takeover. Thus, Draper is simply incorrect—and it is a very important error—when he says that "the United States was given the opportunity to support the 'popular democratic revolution' *before the Communist issue was raised*."[10]

Whatever the objective correctness or incorrectness of U.S. fears, then, the demonstrable fact that the fears existed adequately accounts for U.S. opposition to the revolution. Now, it is perfectly possible and even probable that the emerging pro-Bosch orientation of the revolution contributed to and strengthened the U.S. determination to oppose it.* Nonetheless, it was not Bosch's liberalism per se that worried the administration, but rather that his anti-Americanism as well as his alleged weakness, political incompetence, and generally erratic behavior would make him an easy mark for the Communists; as has already been noted, a number of high State Department officials were gloomily predicting that, even if Bosch should succeed in regaining office, the Communists would shortly outmaneuver him and take over the government.

To be sure, at this point it might be objected that even if it is true that the administration was hostile to Bosch because of his alleged softness-on-Communism rather than his populist democratic philosophy as such, in operational policy the distinction disappears. Is it not the case, the argument might go, that the United States has normally opposed even clearly non-Communist

* For example, "J. B. Bender" admits that the embassy became concerned as it learned of the PRD participation and leadership in the coup, and that the effect of the embassy's policy was anti-PRD, but he too stresses that the more fundamental embassy fear was that chaos and anarchy would benefit the Communists.[11]

revolutionary movements and liberal governments, regardless of the personalities and capabilities of their leaders, because they are seen as inherently soft on, or at least naïve about, Communism? This is apparently Draper's view, for he quotes former U.S. official deLesseps Morrison's fulminations on the vulnerability of the democratic left in Latin America to Communist infiltration, adding that these views are "common currency in U.S. diplomatic and political circles."[12]

No doubt such opinions do exist in the United States Government, but they do not appear to be dominant, for it is demonstrably untrue that the United States has normally opposed the democratic left in Latin America. On the contrary, in the last decade Washington has firmly backed and materially aided reform governments in Honduras, Bolivia, Peru, Venezuela, and Chile. And even in the Dominican Republic the United States initially gave warm support to Bosch in 1963, and as we shall see, the same Johnson Administration that in 1965 opposed his return to the Presidency soon thereafter sought out, installed in the Presidency, and strongly supported Héctor García-Godoy, whose political and social philosophy was not very different from Bosch's.* (Not very different, that is, from Bosch's *former* political and social philosophy. Since the 1966 elections, Bosch has all but abandoned his commitment to democracy.)

Still, it may be pointed out that what I have called the Draper-Fulbright interpretation of U.S. intentions does not rest merely on the initial U.S. decision to intervene but on American actions

* Note Seyom Brown's comment that the political policy followed by the United States after the intervention "turned out to be very similar to the policies of the constitutionalists we refused to support and against whom we intervened."[13] While he attributes this to a shift in U.S. policy forced by intimations of political disaster, it is my contention that this course was the one the Administration intended to follow from the very beginning. Once again, Brown's assessment appears to be based on the premise that the administration initially intervened against the constitutionalist philosophy, such as it was, rather than against the Communist element in the constitutionalist camp.

in the Dominican Republic *after* the intervention, particularly the early support of the Dominican military and Washington's creation of the reactionary military dictatorship of Antonio Imbert.

It is certainly true that the United States was not "neutral" between the constitutionalists and the military in the first weeks of the crisis, as was so absurdly and unnecessarily claimed by the Johnson Administration. Obviously, if the United States had been indifferent about the outcome of the revolution, it wouldn't have intervened in the first place, so it was hardly surprising that its initial actions were not exactly even-handed in either intention or effect. Indeed, the immediate objective of the intervention was to preserve the Dominican military from destruction. To the specific Dominican circumstances was added the weight of a long-held article of faith among U.S. policy makers—that the military in underdeveloped countries, particularly in Latin America, are the major, or in some cases the only organized force for "order and stability." That is the rationale that underlies the military assistance programs and other devices (U.S.-run military schools for Latin American officers, joint sea-air maneuvers, the Inter-American Defense Board, etc.) designed to gain access to, and influence over, Latin America's most powerful political group, as well as to strengthen the capabilities of that group to maintain domestic tranquillity. Nowhere in Latin America was this policy more apparent than in the Dominican Republic, where ever since Trujillo's assassination Washington's nightmare of Another Castro had been reflected in a major Pentagon effort to indoctrinate, train, and equip the Dominican armed forces for "counterinsurgency." Small wonder, then, that Bennett's urgent warning of the imminent collapse of the military touched a highly sensitive nerve.

Once the landing of the Marines had eliminated the possibility of a constitutionalist offensive and restored the morale of the weeping generals of San Isidro, the administration's overriding concern became that of preventing the revolution from spreading to the rest of the country. A new Cuba would be catastrophic enough without adding to it in the same package a new Vietnam.

The coordinated effort included economic, military, and political components. Thus, the large-scale emergency relief and economic-assistance program, begun shortly after the troop landings, stemmed not only from humanitarian impulses but from the desire to eliminate conditions that might intensify the crisis, particularly major food shortages precipitated by the breakdown of the Dominican economy. Although the actual physical damage from the fighting was not very great, internal communications and distribution processes had been disrupted during the revolution. Moreover, the constitutionalist zone in Santo Domingo, now cut off from the rest of the country, was the economic heart of the nation, including within its thirty square blocks or so the Dominican Republic's major port, the bulk of its warehouses, and most of its banks and corporation headquarters.

Once the immediate crisis had been relieved by massive U.S. food distribution (including to the constitutionalist zone), the $60 million OAS-U.S. program focused on quick-impact public-works projects to relieve unemployment as well as on loans to enable public utilities, agricultural enterprises, businesses, and the National Sugar Corporation to resume operation. By mid-summer the economy had been restored to 75-80 percent of its pre-crisis level.[14]

On the military side, massive amounts of heavy equipment and armor as well as over twenty-two thousand troops poured into the country (to the amazement of embassy personnel, who were expecting only a few thousand Marines) in an attempt to avert new trouble through an awesome demonstration of power or, at worst, to prepare for a nationwide occupation.* At the same time, a number of small U.S. teams were stationed throughout the countryside to establish a U.S. presence, survey economic needs, report on local political conditions, and, not least, develop working relations with local police and military units and ensure against any defections to the constitutionalists. Among the more important of such groups were Special Forces units in civilian clothes, ostensibly functioning, in their well-known style, as medical teams.

Even more important, on May 3rd, U.S. troops established an armed corridor through the middle of Santo Domingo, ostensibly to set up an "international security zone" under OAS auspices, but actually to divide the constitutionalist sector in two, cut off the main body of rebel fighters from their access to the countryside, and bottle them up in a small downtown area with their backs to the sea. Once that was done, the United States then stood by in mid-May while Wessin's reconstituted forces attacked and brutally destroyed the weaker of the two constitutionalist zones.

At the time, whether or not U.S. troops played a direct role in this attack was a subject of bitter controversy. It still remains, in my view, one of the unsolved mysteries of the Dominican affair, although the exact degree of U.S. involvement is essentially beside the point. According to many of the newspaper and television reporters in Santo Domingo, U.S. troops not only allowed Wessin's soldiers to pass freely through their own sup-

* John McDermott has suggested that the necessity to apply "overwhelming force . . . early in a somewhat unpredictable way" was one of the lessons derived by the U.S. Government from its failures in Vietnam.[15] In addition to the twenty-two thousand troops in the Dominican Republic, about ten thousand naval and air support troops were stationed aboard a naval task force just off shore, and many more were on an alert status in the United States.

posedly neutral lines but in some cases actually joined in the fighting.[16] (For example, on May 20th the *New York Times* reported that in a variety of ways the Imbert offensive was being "visibly aided by United States troops," who were seen "firing at rebels retreating toward the [United States–held] corridor.") These allegations are vigorously and angrily denied by U.S. officials, even privately and long after the affair. Moreover, during the events in question, the embassy reassured Washington, in response to an urgent State Department request for a report on the matter, that the newspaper stories were palpably false. There were several lower-level unauthorized actions and mistakes, the embassy admitted, but it reiterated that U.S. forces were still under strict orders not to allow the movement of any armed groups through their lines.*

On the other hand, it is also the case that earlier in May U.S. generals were instructed to explain to Dominican military commanders that the projected corridor through the city would help free loyalist forces to take the offensive. Moreover, they were ordered to help their Dominican counterparts draw up plans for attacking the constitutionalists, with the rebel forces north of the corridor specifically suggested as the first target. Furthermore, several days before the fighting began the State Department asked the embassy to prepare a contingency plan for opening up the northern zone for the resumption of normal industrial operations (which, in the circumstances, could only be done by military force), in the event efforts to bring together Imbert and Caamaño failed.

Thus, whether or not U.S. troops participated directly or indirectly in the fighting, the record (including my interviews) leaves little doubt that Washington at a minimum acquiesced

* It *was* possible for Wessin to attack without passing through U.S. lines, by circling around the city and attacking from the North or West.

in the Wessin drive in the hope of eliminating a constitutionalist channel to the countryside, increasing the pressures on the constitutionalists in the negotiating process, and reopening the important industrial area in the northern sectors of the city to desperately needed economic production. However politically costly and morally questionable these tactics were, the fact remains that they *were* only tactics, not (as many took them to be) the first indications of established policy. Once the situation had been stabilized, the presumed danger of a Communist takeover eliminated, and the revolution clearly contained in Santo Domingo, the United States then moved to disassociate itself from the military and to prevent it from attacking the constitutionalists or otherwise disrupting the forthcoming negotiations. Perhaps the first indicator of the changing U.S. tactics was a State Department request that the embassy tell Wessin to stop promoting the idea that the United States was supporting him; it would be particularly helpful, Washington noted, if Wessin could be persuaded to stop playing "The Star-Spangled Banner" over the armed forces radio station. Other, more substantial steps included firm warnings to the military not to take further aggressive action, the placement of U.S. trucks on Dominican airfields to prevent the Air Force from attacking constitutionalist positions, the posting of IAPF (Inter-American Peace Force) units around oil-storage depots to deny fuel to Dominican mechanized units, and the permanent stationing of tanks and artillery across access points to the constitutionalist zone.

The creation of the Imbert junta was another matter, however, coming as it did well after any Communist "danger" had been contained. Shortly after the fall of Reid, the military, under United States prodding, had set up a three-man provisional junta, ostensibly to rule only until new elections could be called.

The leader of the junta, one Colonel Benoit, had assured himself of a revered place in Dominican history by officially requesting the U.S. intervention. Unremarkably, Colonel Benoit was not a very popular man and so, within a few days after the intervention, the United States began to cast about for a new government. With luck, such a government could exercise its authority throughout the country and thus preclude outright occupation rule if the revolution should spread to the interior. Moreover, on the you-can't-fight-something-with-nothing principle, the existence of a more conservative alternative to the Caamaño government* might be useful in the coming negotiations, generating strong (even if somewhat artificial) pressures toward the "middle solution" that Washington had in mind. Thus, the new government was to be only a stopgap, although to play even that role it was necessary that it have a considerable amount of genuine support. As the embassy put it in reporting on the implications of the formation of the constitutionalist government, the first priority was to find a good man who not only could be propped up but would deserve to be propped up when the inevitable adverse winds began to blow.

Not an easy task, and made no easier by assigning it to John Bartlow Martin. However badly it turned out, though, the very presence of Martin in the country was quite revealing of the administration's intentions. Within two days of the intervention, Johnson had called Martin out of private life and asked him to "supplement" the embassy in gathering facts, establishing a new junta, and in developing contacts with the non-Communist left. (In retrospect it is clear that sending Martin was also part of a

* On May 4 the constitutionalists announced their own election of Colonel Caamaño to succeed Molina Ureña (still in asylum) as "provisional President" of the country.

broader decision to remove Bennett from the mainstream of policy information and advice, for Martin was succeeded by a host of other special presidential representatives, including Adam Yarmolinsky, Cyrus Vance, McGeorge Bundy and, finally, Ellsworth Bunker, all of whom had clear authority over the embassy. Three factors appear to have been involved: the continuing liberal criticism of Bennett's performance; the decision to seek a political solution, perforce requiring negotiations with groups that considered Bennett as *persona non grata;* and, possibly, the administration's own concern over the reliability of Bennett's conservative, anti-constitutionalist, and self-justifying reporting.)[17] Given Martin's mission, it is clear that the crucial reason he was chosen was that he was thought to be a lifelong liberal and a sympathetic friend of Juan Bosch.[18]

As the old saw has it, though, with friends like Martin, Bosch didn't need any enemies. Unfortunately for everyone, Martin's account of his tenure as U.S. Ambassador during the Bosch government was not yet in print. It is worthwhile to return again to this remarkably self-revealing book, for it sheds a great deal of light on its author's performance in 1965.

As we have seen, it turned out that contrary to everyone's impression, especially Bosch's,[19] Martin had only contempt for the former Dominican President and not much use for the PRD in general. In that respect, consequently, he was hardly very different from Bennett. Even more important, Martin is disclosed, by his own hand, as a man of quite astonishing judgment.

There is no doubt that Martin was an intelligent man of progressive views, who was deeply committed to helping the shattered Dominican nation recuperate from thirty years of tyranny. However, he was also extremely emotional and moody, given to acting on his impulses and subject to rapid shifts from hope and elation to dark despair. In the end, his emotionalism was to overwhelm his judgment and make a mockery of his manifestly decent instincts.*

Added to his romanticism was a strong streak of paternalism, if not downright imperialism: "We would hold this place for the President, our President," he vowed.[22] And he plunged in, the reincarnated British colonial administrator, White Man in the Tropics model. Not so much that he loved power for its own sake, perhaps, but that the "child-like" Dominicans (a recurring phrase) "didn't seem very capable of ruling."[23] Therefore, he concluded, "it was up to us to save the political system, since no one else seemed able to."[24] In his two years as ambassador, Martin was involved in the intrigue and manipulation of day-to-day politics in the Dominican Republic to an extent unprecedented in a supposedly sovereign, unoccupied country. (Martin relates a 1962 conversation with Bosch. "He said, 'This government is no good. No one wants this government.' [the Council of State]. I said, 'We do.' I said it quietly and coldly."[25] Later, during Bosch's administration Martin was to draft amendments to the Dominican constitution, and at one point he even wrote a speech for Bosch!)

Another Martin characteristic was a certain attraction to what the Latins call *machismo* (worship of the strong, "manly" virtues): "Although I shared everyone's misgivings [about two dangerous Dominican figures], I saw something else in them:

* Throughout Martin's book there is a recurring image of the Dominican leaders "locked inextricably together, stumbling in the dark along the edge of a wind-swept precipice."[20] This sort of romanticized fatalism may serve a psychological function for Martin himself, since it tends to absolve him of responsibility for his own failures. Martin's painful ulcer did not help matters, as he himself recognizes; writing about his difficulties in 1962, he notes: "Though the situation was in truth bad, part of my malaise probably was due to an ulcer attack."[21] Significantly, his ulcer again flared up during his 1965 mission.

Manhood, for one."[26] Or, "While Bosch was safe in exile, Imbert was out on the highway with a .45, killing Trujillo."[27]*

Finally, Martin was a fierce and indiscriminate anti-Communist, having, moreover, a conception of Communism that in an experienced man of public affairs can only be termed as shockingly simple-minded. The Dominican "Castro/Communists" were, in Martin's view, literally controlled by "Moscow," "Havana," or even "Peking."[28] There were no national, indigenous Communists or Castroite radicals, then, not on the evidence but by definition—"under the term Castro/Communist I mean to include people who took money and instructions from Communist parties outside the Republic, submitted to their discipline, and acted as their agents."[29]

It all came devastatingly together—the sentimentalism, the paternalism, the *machismo,* and the simplistic anti-Communism —in Martin's relationship with Imbert and Wessin y Wessin. Take, for example, Martin's advice to Bosch on how to bring the increasingly restive military under control: First, enact a Dominican version of the Smith Act, even though unconstitutional, to facilitate harder action against the "Communists" and "the left," including mass deportations. Second, ease up on the de-Trujillo-ization process and give the military greater autonomy. Third, reorganize the government—for Chief of Police, Imbert; for Minister of Defense, Wessin. *Wessin!* "Bosch looked surprised. . . . I said Wessin was strong, brave, patriotic, and, so far as we knew, honest. He was almost fanatically anti-Communist. [At

* Besides being politically irrelevant, the implication is extremely unfair. Bosch, as it happened, was one of the main organizers of an ill-fated 1947 expedition against Trujillo and over the years had continued as one of the main leaders of the anti-Trujillo exiles, thus making himself a prime target for murder, as other Trujillo opponents were murdered by the dictator's henchmen while "safe in exile." Imbert, on the other hand, had been one of those henchmen until his disaffection at the very end of the Trujillo era.

another point, Martin refers to him as a Dominican (Joseph) McCarthy.] Full responsibility probably would moderate his fanaticism. Appointing him undoubtedly would blunt the politicians' attacks on the Communist issue."[30] Yes, and blunt the whole point of the Bosch government. It was as if a liberal determined to end racism in the United States were elected President and then appointed Strom Thurmond as Chief Justice of the Supreme Court, George Wallace as Attorney General, and Lester Maddox as head of the Civil Rights Commission, in order to "blunt" conservative criticism.

To be sure, Martin's feelings about Imbert and Wessin were somewhat ambivalent, the least one would expect from an Adlai Stevenson liberal. At times he worries about Wessin's fanaticism and other unsavory characteristics; still, he admits to being "greatly impressed" by him, for, whatever his faults, "He was a man."[31] As for Imbert, according to Martin he had been the "Number one problem" in his efforts to ensure the holding of free elections in 1962. A "political primitive" who sought only power, he was fully capable, feared Martin, of setting up a ruthless dictatorship and becoming a new Trujillo.[32]

Yet, somehow, Martin was drawn to Imbert and remained on very good terms with him, frequently giving him friendly lectures on the dangers of abusing power.[33] Whatever Imbert's baser instincts, he could, Martin seemed to assume, be made to respond to the voice of reason, personified by Martin himself of course, much as the naughty but redeemable boy can be controlled by the kind but firm father. (At one point, Martin refers to Imbert as being "almost like a wayward schoolboy."[34]) For Imbert did, according to Martin, have his good points: he was a very "complex and interesting man," a "sentimental, even kind" man, a man who was "fond of children."[35] Besides, unlike the hapless Bosch, he didn't "botch things." Martin's example: "When I wanted to be sure a deportation would work smoothly, I turned to them [Imbert and his colleague Amiama Tió]."[36]

Like the sparrow mesmerized by the snake, Martin was to be undone by his peculiar, somewhat reluctant fascination for Imbert. From all the available evidence, it appears that Martin arrived in Santo Domingo on his special mission of April, 1965, dead set in the conviction that Imbert, and only Imbert, was the man to save the Dominican Republic, not to mention the United States, from catastrophe. It was a notion shared by practically no one else on the scene, except, of course, Imbert.

Martin's instructions appear to have been quite broad, specifying only that a new government composed of respected, noncontroversial Dominicans be created. To be sure, Imbert was mentioned as one among many possibilities, but only if he was politically acceptable to a broad range of Dominican opinion and, in any event, not to be *head* of the government. Moreover, the State Department quite explicitly told Martin that even this new government would be only an interim one and would not be given diplomatic recognition by the United States.

All of these qualifications and restrictions were ignored by Martin. (It was not the first time that he had exceeded his instructions. In September of 1963, as pressures against the Dominican Government mounted, Martin wrote a *fake* cable, in which he had the State Department instructing him to threaten the generals with a diplomatic and economic break if they overthrew Bosch.[37]*) To the subsequent mystification of a number of high embassy and State Department officials (many of whom openly express contempt for Martin's performance), Martin went straight to his old friend Tony Imbert and offered him the

* Martin never actually used these "instructions," in view of a later genuine cable from Washington warning him not to tie his efforts to save Bosch to any commitment by the United States.

Presidency, promising him, moreover, a "blank check" and recognition within twenty-four hours![38] "I do it," said Tony. "For my country. Not for myself."[39]

Only then, after Imbert's selfless acceptance, did Martin turn to other Dominicans to ask them to serve *under* Imbert. But no one of any stature would come near an Imbert government. As the embassy reported to the State Department, those who were willing to serve were not qualified and those who were qualified were not willing. Members of the conservative wing of the PRD, Balaguerists, and nonpolitical professional men—all refused.

A prominent Dominican who was asked to join the Imbert government has related his conversation with Martin:

After a few minutes of Martin hard-sell on the need of patriotic men to come to the aid of their country in its hour of need, the man broke in to ask: "But aren't you aware of the image that this man Imbert has in this country?"

"Yes, but the United States press considers him a hero because of the Trujillo assassination."*

"I'm sorry to have to remind you, Mr. Ambassador, that Imbert will be ruling for the Dominican people, not the North American press."

The Imbert government, then, was a creature of John Bartlow Martin, not of the U.S. Embassy, the State Department, or the Johnson Administration. Moreover, even Martin, of course, did not deliberately set out to establish a military dictatorship, but turned to Imbert because he saw him as a man of action, a doer, yet one who was "pro-American" and could be controlled: "Tony

* Martin himself knew better, pointing out in his book that Imbert had acted out of a personal grudge and that, far from being considered a national hero, he was suspected and feared by most Dominicans as a potential new Trujillo.[40]

will never go against us," said Martin to a Dominican friend.* In short, the establishment of the dictatorial Imbert government, widely taken to be certain evidence of a cold-blooded reactionary policy,† is far better understood not as a manifestation of "policy" at all, but rather of the simple ineptness of one man, who was given wide presidential latitude to operate in a rapidly changing situation precisely because of the expectation that he could produce a liberal solution. Within a few weeks, McGeorge Bundy was in the Dominican Republic attempting to undo the damage.

So far I have sought only to show that apparently antidemocratic United States actions were far more complex and subject to quite different interpretations than initially appeared to be the case. There is also more positive evidence supporting my view that the Johnson Administration never had the intention of supporting, or acquiescing in, a return to dictatorship or the "status quo" in the Dominican Republic.

Draper has made a great deal of the fact that the initial U.S. response to the fall of the Reid Cabral government was not to support "the Boschist revolution" but to press for the establishment of "a military junta."[43] What he neglects to point out, however, is that (1) the junta was to be established by negotia-

* In his book Martin referred to Imbert and Amiama as "reasonable men, realistic men, not hot-headed patriots or melodramatic *poseurs* ready to fling themselves over the cliff." He then elaborates: "They would listen to me, at least up to a point, and they respected the power of the United States."[41]

† Note, for example, the judgment of the Canadian political scientist John McLaren, who argues that "the Johnson Administration had for some time shown a predilection for Latin American governments whose anticommunism outweighed their desire for democracy. Such regimes, it was felt, could be relied upon more readily than their democratic counterparts to support American attempts to contain communism within the hemisphere. . . . This contention is borne out in the Dominican context by unswerving support for the Reid Cabral regime . . . and the preference for a junta led by the right wing General Imbert during the fluid situation immediately succeeding [the revolution]."[42]

tions among military leaders of *both* sides of the conflict; (2) State Department instructions to the embassy repeatedly emphasized that the junta was to be only a provisional stopgap to end the conflict, and that free and fair elections were to be held at the earliest practicable date; and (3) the establishment of a military junta to preside over free elections was precisely the original objective of many, perhaps most, of the constitutionalist leadership, including a number of Boschists.[44]

Another indicator of United States policy was the State Department's strong opposition to any attempt of the Trujillo family to take advantage of the chaotic situation to return to the Dominican Republic and reestablish their rule. All the U.S. embassies in countries harboring the Trujillos were instructed to request the local governments to keep them under surveillance and prevent them from leaving the country. (This in fact was done, and the Trujillos were kept out of the Dominican Republic.)

Still more significantly, there was a general consensus among U.S. policy makers (including Bennett) that the intervention should be used at least to begin the process of restructuring the Dominican military establishment, and on numerous occasions the State Department reminded the embassy to keep this central objective of U.S. policy in mind. Although most action to implement this policy was to await the installation of the García-Godoy government, in mid-May eight old-line Trujillo generals—the last of the pre-*ajusticiamiento* military leaders still in service—were suddenly removed from their commands and sent out of the country. Formally, the action was taken by the Imbert junta, but the idea and impetus for it stemmed from the U.S. Embassy—in fact, the actual arrest and disarmament of the generals took place at a "meeting" called by the embassy—and Imbert's agreement to the action may very well have been a precondition for even temporary support of his "government."

Also significant was the fact that the Johnson Administration established continuing contacts with Bosch immediately after the intervention, in an effort to win his support for a constitutionalism-without-Bosch compromise (later to take shape in the "Guzmán formula"). Negotiations began with a May 1 telephone call from Abe Fortas to the former President, and were continued in the next two days in talks between Martin and Bosch in Puerto Rico. Thus, Draper is wrong in his claim that the administration "refused to recognize his [Bosch's] existence" until a May 15th visit by McGeorge Bundy. He can sustain this assertion only by making some debater's points: Fortas is dismissed as an "unofficial intermediary" and Rusk's assertion that Martin was only a "private citizen" is taken at face value.[45] The difference in dates is important, for it will be recalled that one of Draper's main theses is that the administration shifted to a more liberal policy in the Dominican Republic only as a result of internal conflicts and external pressures.

Even more significant was the administration's effort, though ultimately unsuccessful, to involve three leading Latin American liberals in its Dominican policy making (the so-called "wise man formula").[46] On April 29, one day after the intervention, former presidents Rómulo Betancourt of Venezuela and José Figueres of of Costa Rica, and former governor Luis Muñoz-Marín of Puerto Rico, all of them old colleagues of Juan Bosch, were asked if they would be willing to lead an OAS mission to the Dominican Republic to find a political solution. The key point apparently was that all three were strongly anti-Communist, and thus could be relied upon to use their influence to prevent a political victory for the Dominican extremists; it may also have helped that at least one of them was known to have become disgusted with Bosch's performance both in the Presidency and during the revolution. Nonetheless, as all of them had practically legendary status as crusaders for democracy and social reform in Latin America, Washington hardly would have turned to them if it had intended to establish a conservative, nondemocratic government.

In direct conversations with President Johnson, the "wise men" set out a number of substantial conditions for undertaking a political role in the crisis. The United States would have to agree to: (1) the establishment of an inter-American military force under the complete control of the three Latin American officials and made up of contingents drawn only from the democratic countries of Latin America (the tentative plan was to rely primarily on troops from Venezuela and Colombia, to be headed by a Venezuelan general close to Betancourt); (2) the gradual withdrawal of U.S. troops as this force came into existence; (3) a temporary OAS trusteeship under their own political leadership, pending the reestablishment of the 1963 constitution and the formation of a provisional government composed of anti-Communist but pro-democratic Dominicans that would rule the country until free elections could be held; (4) the reduction and reform of the Dominican armed forces; and (5) large-scale economic assistance from the United States and international institutions.

This was a stiff order indeed, for accession to points (1) and (2) would have amounted to the granting of control of a major U.S. political and military operation to three non-Americans. Yet, the "wise men" have said both publicly and in private conversations that they believe that the administration's talks with them were held in good faith and that their proposals were generally acceptable. In my own conversations with administration officials, including with those usually identified as hard-liners, there was a unanimous insistence that the administration's confidence in the anti-Communist credentials of the three Latin

American leaders made their proposals "in principle" quite acceptable to the U.S. Government, providing that OAS approval could be obtained. Moreover, it is certainly demonstrable that the political solution envisaged in the proposal closely paralleled the course that the United States itself was later to follow.

Still, there are some ambiguities surrounding the eventual demise of the formula. According to both the U.S. Government and the "wise men" themselves,[47] the major stumbling block was the opposition of the conservative and/or dictatorial Latin American states, that is to say a majority of the OAS membership; particularly crucial, it is said, was the strong opposition of Brazil, the only Latin American state that had pledged a significant contribution to the proposed Inter-American Peace Force (IAPF). On the other hand, there is some feeling among OAS delegates that the United States didn't push the proposal against the easily predictable opposition as hard as it might have, and that had it done so it was possible that enough recalcitrants might have reluctantly gone along to produce the necessary two-thirds majority. Some U.S. officials also believe that the State Department did not put all its muscle behind the plan, perhaps reflecting coolness to it by some sectors of the government. In any case, though, the "wise men" soon began to have second thoughts of their own, as a consequence of growing Latin American opposition to U.S. policy. The final straw, it appears, was the decision of the Venezuelan and Colombian governments, under heavy domestic pressure, not to contribute to the IAPF.

Even after the quiet demise of the wise-man formula in mid-May, however, the Johnson Administration continued to make efforts to liberalize subsequent OAS committees involved in the Dominican crisis. For example, Mexico, Chile, and Peru, all of them bitterly critical of the intervention and sympathetic to the constitutionalists, were sounded out on their willingness to participate in efforts to find a political settlement (they all refused). Later, the United States pressed for the inclusion of Gonzalo Facio of Costa Rica on the three-man committee that eventually succeeded in working out a settlement. Facio was probably the most-outspoken liberal, pro-democratic, and anti-military OAS delegate; for precisely that reason he was vetoed by other Central American governments.

In brief, despite some apparent ambiguities and inconsistencies here and there, the evidence, both positive and negative, overwhelmingly points to an early and firm U.S. decision to avoid a return to the pre- and post-Bosch status quo in the Dominican Republic and, on the contrary, to use the opportunity to work for democratic and progressive government. Moreover, while Washington obviously hoped for the emergence in leadership positions of gradualist, pro-American reformers rather than nationalistic radicals, there is every indication (as will be discussed later) that it was prepared to abide by the results of genuinely free elections, at least after it became clear that there was no chance of an openly Castroite government winning such elections.*

* This final qualification is not meant to imply that it is my view that the United States would normally intervene by military means to overturn a Latin American Castroite government that had come to power through the electoral process. On the contrary, I would consider such interventions, as opposed to quite different interventions against Communist *revolutions*, to be extremely unlikely, because of the enormous political costs they would entail. In the Dominican context, however, once the United States had the troops on the ground, it was hardly likely that it would have remained aloof if the Communists had later emerged as a real political threat. As it turned out, of course, they did not, and the issue never arose.

4

The Initial Negotiations

WHATEVER ITS LONG-TERM OBJECTIVES, in the first weeks of the crisis the Johnson Administration very seriously considered a military "solution" to the immediate problem of what to do about the constitutionalists.* Martin tells us how close the United States came to a direct attack or at least to support of a Dominican military move, either of which courses would surely have been a political and moral disaster. The first contingent of about four hundred Marines had landed early Wednesday evening, April 28. Their initial mission had been specifically limited to guarding the Hotel Embajador, the embarkation point for American citizens and other foreigners trying to get out of the country. No decision had yet been made to employ the troops in such a way as to affect the civil war, although that possibility was explicitly envisaged if events so dictated. The first hint of impending military action came the next morning, when Bennett was told to "consider urgently whether he ought to use a few U.S. officers to help San Isidro develop operational plans to take the rebel stronghold downtown."[1]

At about the same time this cable was going out, however, the OAS Council was meeting in emergency session to discuss the

* Note that this does not contradict my argument about the political intentions of the administration. As the constitutionalists were at that time considered to be under Communist domination, their military destruction would not necessarily have precluded a later democratic solution of the overall Dominican crisis.

crisis. At the suggestion of the Colombian representative, the Papal Nuncio in Santo Domingo (the dean of the diplomatic corps there) was sent an urgent request to negotiate a ceasefire pending the arrival of an OAS mission.[2] Perhaps in response to this development, new instructions were sent to Bennett to drop his discussions with San Isidro. Instead, he was informed, additional contingents of U.S. troops were on the way, the initial mission of which would probably be to cordon off the constitutionalist sector and establish an enforceable ceasefire as a prelude to an OAS-negotiated political solution.

The next morning, April 30, the Nuncio succeeded in negotiating a ceasefire, primarily because of Martin's and Bennett's pressure on the Wessin forces, who were told that the conflict was entering a political phase and that the United States did not intend to join in an attack on the constitutionalists. At about the same time, the OAS Council in Washington was passing a U.S.-sponsored resolution calling for the maintenance of the ceasefire and authorizing Secretary General José A. Mora to aid the Nuncio in his "peacekeeping mission."[3]

Despite the initial United States support for the ceasefire, though, there were numerous indications that later military action was far from ruled out. For example, at the same San Isidro meeting at which Bennett and Martin persuaded the Dominican commanders to accept a ceasefire, it was also pointed out to them that the deployment of U.S. paratroopers through the middle of Santo Domingo would allow the loyalists to regroup and would free them for possible later action against the constitutionalists; moreover, an American general was assigned to Wessin's forces to advise in the planning of military tactics and to arrange for any supplies and equipment they might need. Martin himself at several points admits to his dread that he might be about to preside over "another Hungary," a United States slaughter of the constitutionalists.[4] In fact, although he left for the Dominican Republic under orders to help the Nuncio and the OAS get a ceasefire, Martin's impression from his meeting with Johnson was that he had no more than a day or two to "find out what the facts were and influence our policy."[5] The ceasefire, in short, was apparently at first viewed as a temporary holding tactic, pending further developments in the Dominican Republic and a buildup of U.S. forces there.

Although the truce was precariously maintained in the next few days, pressures for a frontal U.S. attack on the constitutionalists continued to build. The U.S. military, under persistent sniper attack and persuaded that they were facing a Communist horde, wanted nothing more than to be allowed to "clean up" the constitutionalist zone. Moreover, Ambassador Bennett, who had earlier indicated his misgivings about the ceasefire and the prospect of negotiations, repeatedly complained that the ceasefire was protecting the constitutionalists from the rejuvenated military and was giving them an unwarranted political advantage, allowing them to consolidate their strength and improve their bargaining position.*

Gradually, though, the possibility of military action faded into the background. There is no doubt that the OAS involvement in the situation was a crucial restraining factor. The United States had at first supported and worked in behalf of the OAS Council's call for a ceasefire at least in part because the uncertain and rapidly changing character of the crisis made its military implications unclear—at the moment of the ceasefire the regular military was at least as much in need of a respite as the constitutionalists. Once the ceasefire was in effect, though, it took on

* "J. B. Bender" writes that Bennett and Mann wanted to "wipe out" the constitutionalists, but were checked by the OAS, the UN, Bundy, and Martin.[6] Szulc also notes that Bennett was "determined to see the rebels liquidated, pure and simple."[7]

a life of its own, so that even when it later became clear that the constitutionalists were its primary beneficiary, the United States could not blatantly violate it without enormous political costs, particularly in light of the frequent public warnings from the council (meeting in nearly continuous session in the first weeks of the crisis) against U.S. support for, or acquiescence in, military action.

Besides the OAS involvement, of course, a number of other factors acted to constrain the United States, including domestic criticism and international revulsion to what would surely have been seen as a Hungarian-type action; the presence of a UN mission in the Dominican Republic sympathetic to the constitutionalists; the diminishing U.S. fear, as the revolution was successfully contained in Santo Domingo, that a failure to take harsh action might lead to a new Vietnam; and the military estimate that a direct attack on the densely populated, well-defended constitutionalist stronghold would result in extremely extensive damage and in high casualties among noninvolved residents as well as in the U.S. and constitutionalist forces.

As a result, by the end of May a definite decision had been reached to seek a negotiated political settlement and to avoid not only direct military action (other than that already taken in mid-May against the smaller northern constitutionalist sector), but lesser measures as well, including a food and water blockade or the shutting-off of electrical power to constitutionalist-controlled sectors.* In turn, this decision necessitated the undercutting and eventual removal of Imbert's Government of National Reconstruction (GNR), for the refusal of the constitutionalists even to talk with Imbert (whom they regarded as just another front for the Wessin forces) and the increasingly

* This decision did not preclude the use of force for "self defense," which on occasion may have been rather broadly defined. (See Chapter 5, pps. 114-117.)

general hostility to him throughout the country made it obvious to U.S. officials that even as a transitional device the creation of the Imbert regime had been a serious mistake.

But what kind of political solution? Three paths were tried; in chronological order they were (1) an attempt to establish a coalition government between the constitutionalists and the conservative forces to rule until free elections were held; (2) the constitutionalism-without-Bosch formula—a PRD-dominated government to serve out the remainder of Bosch's aborted presidential term under the provisions of the 1963 constitution put into effect during the Bosch government; and (3) when the first two failed, the formation of a third-force provisional government to rule until the holding of elections.

The primary responsibility for negotiating a political settlement initially fell to the OAS, for by mid-May the U.S. Government had decided to withdraw to a less-prominent role in the crisis, reflecting its assessment that the Communists were fading from leadership positions in the constitutionalist movement* and that the general situation in the Dominican Republic had been stabilized. As a result, it was felt, the United States could now afford the luxury of a greater multilateral effort, which in turn might make a compromise settlement more palatable to the Dominican contestants as well as to domestic and international opinion.

Beyond the immediate political requirements of the Dominican situation, it is most likely that the belated effort to channel U.S. policy through the OAS also reflected Washington's desire to repair the damage done to the inter-American system by the flagrantly illegal unilateral U.S. intervention. Both of the two

* An official U.S. account later stated that on May 5 all three Dominican Communist and Castroite parties decided to withdraw their top leaders from open activity.[8]

key principles of the inter-American system, collective security and nonintervention, had been ignored in the crisis. Under the collective-security system institutionalized in the Rio Treaty of 1947, the United States had promised to refrain from unilateral military action except in the most urgent cases of self-defense, with all other hemispheric conflicts to be handled by multilateral measures. The nonintervention principle, considered by the generally weak and vulnerable Latin American states to be the heart of the inter-American system, proscribed the intervention of any state or, indeed, of the OAS itself in the internal affairs of any of the members.

During the forties and fifties the system generally worked well. In the early forties a series of collective actions were taken to insulate the hemisphere from Nazi infiltration and subversion and to build up hemispheric defenses in the event of an outright attack. In the late forties and early fifties, OAS peacekeeping operations succeeded in dampening down a series of local Caribbean skirmishes that could have escalated into more serious conflict.

The coming of the Cold War to the hemisphere, however, seriously strained the organization, as the United States began to reinterpret the principles of collective security and nonintervention in such a way that they directly clashed with each other. In the Guatemalan, Cuban, and finally the Dominican situations, for example, the United States argued that Communist threats in those countries (real or alleged) were really manifestations of an aggressive international movement that under the Rio Treaty required a collective response from the hemispheric states. A number of Latin American states, however, always unhappy with any U.S. tendencies toward intervention in Latin American domestic affairs, stressed instead the predominantly indigenous nature of the revolutions in question and invoked the nonintervention principle to inhibit any collective action.

Since the Castro revolution, this conflict has increasingly split the organization and prevented the development and implementation of a consistent and effective common policy. Probably it was with this background in mind, then, that the Johnson Administration initially decided to ignore its treaty obligations and completely bypass the OAS in the Dominican crisis.[9]

Later, the Johnson Administration was to claim that the OAS *did* "consider" the Dominican situation prior to the intervention. However, the sum total of OAS involvement to that point consisted of two vitriolic, anti-constitutionalist tirades by José Bonilla Atiles, the Dominican representative of the defunct Reid Cabral government. No collective action was asked for by either Bonilla Atiles or the United States; on the contrary, none was desired, for it was assumed that the constitutionalists were about to be crushed.

The other strand in the administration's official line was that in light of the urgent embassy cable calling for immediate action to save American lives, there was no time for OAS action. Moreover, it argued, the OAS ambassadors were notified of the U.S. action as soon as the decision to intervene was taken. The first argument is highly misleading at best and the second utterly irrelevant. While it is technically true that the actual presidential decision to intervene was a response to the famous Bennett cable, the far more significant point is that the administration had been intensively *considering* the possibility of intervening from the earliest stages of the revolution, had drawn up contingency plans in the event the decision was made, but yet had made no move to consult the organization. Anyway, as has been discussed earlier, there is considerable doubt that even the initial intervention was primarily a response to any alleged threat to American lives; certainly the wording of Bennett's cable suggested that the American Ambassador was more concerned with the Communist issue.[10] In any event, even if time was of the essence, the Cuban missile crisis had demonstrated that when the Latin Americans were genuinely convinced of the need for strong action the OAS could move very rapidly indeed, for the organization approved the U.S. blockade on the same day it was asked to do so.

As for post-intervention consultation, Senator Fulbright's acid remark hardly needs embellishment: "Advising the Latin American countries of our action after the fact did not constitute compliance with the OAS Charter or the Rio Treaty; nor, indeed, would advising them before the fact have constituted compliance. One does not comply with the law by notifying interested parties in advance of one's intention to violate it."[11]

Some further light on the bypassing of the OAS is shed by evidence that the Johnson Administration thought little of the organization (Johnson has been quoted as saying that "the OAS couldn't pour —— out of a boot if the instructions were written on the heel"[12]) if, indeed, it thought of it at all: according to Rowland Evans and Robert Novak, the initial draft of the President's statement announcing the landing of the Marines made no mention of the OAS; when Senator Mansfield noted the omission, the President said to the Secretary of State, "Dean, that's a good idea, now you make certain it's there."[13] Probably more fundamental was the State Department's undoubtedly correct assessment that there was little chance that a sufficient number of Latin American states, if asked in advance, would support an intervention in the Dominican revolution.* Thus, the reasoning undoubtedly ran, it would be easier for the United States to weather

* The Rio Treaty requires a two-thirds majority for any collective action involving the use of armed force.

the expected storm of disapproval if it acted first and asked later than if it asked first, was told no, and then acted anyway.

The first OAS body to enter the scene was the Special Committee of the Tenth Meeting of Consultation (SC), consisting of the council representatives of Argentina, Brazil, Colombia, Guatemala, and Panama. (The United States, which normally would have been assigned to the committee, had decided to allow a strictly Latin American mediation effort to be made, presumably as part of its new "low posture" strategy.)

On May 1, the council had authorized the Special Committee, by a 19-0 vote, to use its "good offices" in order to "obtain the re-establishment of peace and normal conditions."[14] This unanimous support for an OAS role in the crisis was the product of a variety of differing, but partially converging, Latin American motives. A number of states had little hesitancy about participating in the Dominican operation, even if they were somewhat miffed about its initial unilateral character, for they genuinely feared the constitutionalist uprising—it should not be forgotten that there are a great many conservative regimes and military dictatorships in the hemisphere which are only too ready to see a Communist menace in any revolutionary movement.

Nor was support for the United States's actions limited exclusively to the right; the relatively progressive and democratic governments of Venezuela and Costa Rica, for example, while initially bitter at the unilateral actions of the United States[15] and suspicious of its motivations, nonetheless are extremely sensitive to the possible spread of Castroism in the Caribbean. Venezuela resolved its mixed feelings by voting for the establishment of the SC but abstaining on a number of subsequent votes, while Costa Rica usually voted with the majority, explaining: "It is true that we cannot accept as good that the United

States decides for itself when it should send troops to prevent the triumph or defeat of a revolution . . . but neither can we accept as good that anarchy reigns in a brother country and . . . a tyrannical regime like that of Cuba [be established]."[16]

To be sure, the intervention itself was a *fait accompli*, but a number of Latin American states, anxious not to totally abdicate responsibility, supported an OAS role for precisely that reason. As the Colombian delegate put it, "If it were necessary we could be here for hours censuring the unilateral action of the United States, but that would not alleviate or remedy the situation in Santo Domingo."[17] A very painful dilemma had been presented: collective action might seem to legitimize the intervention, but a refusal to act on that account would leave the Latin Americans without influence either on U.S. policy or on the unfolding events in the Dominican Republic. Thus, Uruguay, Mexico, and Chile, the most bitter critics of the United States, reluctantly decided to vote for the SC because of its humanitarian mission, although they opposed later extensions of the OAS role. Others, led by Costa Rica, played an active role throughout the crisis, deciding that the logic of the situation left them no choice but to salvage what they could.

And what needed to be salvaged, it was felt, was both the reputation of the OAS and the future of democratic government in the Dominican Republic. The hope of "overcoming the action of a single state with collective action"[18] was reinforced by the traditional Latin American desire to close ranks and handle hemispheric problems without outside "interference," particularly after the UN became involved in the crisis. Thus, even the strong opponents of collective action were partially influenced by the argument that the existence of the inter-American system might be at stake if the Dominican crisis was not satisfactorily resolved.

A satisfactory resolution, in turn, would require the restoration of democracy in the Dominican Republic, and with twenty-two thousand troops on the ground, here indeed was an unprecedented opportunity to rid the country of the remnants of Trujilloism, especially in the armed forces. Gonzalo Facio put it this way:

> It may be that the government of the United States, in its anxiety to avert worse evils, has violated the principle of non-intervention. But that should not prevent us from acting to repair the wrong and to help our brothers. . . . In the face of an accomplished situation such as the one in which we find ourselves, the sane, the logical, the humanitarian thing is to find formulas which will permit us to correct the errors and to help a long-suffering people find the path to liberty.[19]

Unfortunately, however, many of the more democratic and progressive governments refused to participate *actively* in the search for a settlement, considering that the United States would continue to dominate the Dominican situation regardless of what the OAS did and fearing that their presence would tend to legitimize an outcome over which they would have little control. Mexico, Chile, Peru, and Venezuela, for example, all turned down opportunities to serve on the Special Committee. Understandable as the stance of the pro-democratic states was, their abstention from an active role strengthened the influence of the conservative states, assured that the Special Committee and later the IAPF would have a markedly rightist character, and seriously delayed and complicated U.S. efforts to achieve a democratic solution.

The Special Committee was almost a total disaster. First, it adopted an absurdly narrow and legalistic view of its role. Its mandate—to do "everything possible to get the reestablishment of peace and normal conditions"—had obviously been deliberately vague so as to allow the committee great leeway in arranging a settlement. Rather than using its influence and the weight of U.S. power tacitly behind it to mediate actively, however, the committee chose to interpret its function as strictly catalytic, limiting its political activities to ineffectual urgings to the two sides to sit down and negotiate their own solution. Moreover, there is nearly unanimous agreement among United States, Dominican, and Pan American Union officials that even in the go-between role it chose for itself, the committee was lackadaisical, easily aroused to petulance, and generally incompetent.

Not only that, but the committee seemed to go out of its way to antagonize the constitutionalists, and soon had so compromised its mediating status as to dissipate whatever chance it might have had to arrange a compromise. Ironically, the constitutionalists at first had insisted on an OAS presence as a precondition to negotiations, and they welcomed the committee with open arms in the hopes that it would counterbalance the United States and grant them at least tacit political recognition.[20] Within a few days, however, the committee had publicly accused the constitutionalists of tolerating Communist infiltration of their movement and had issued a report asserting that had the United States not intervened the Dominican revolution "could rapidly have been converted into a Communist insurrection."[21]

In response, the constitutionalists bitterly accused the committee of being partial to the Imbert junta and nothing more than a docile arm of United States policy.[22] These attacks were lent considerable credence by the way in which the committee ignored or even sanctioned massive violations of the military status quo it had been charged with maintaining. On May 2 the committee "authorized" the United States to create the so-called neutral zone of refuge in Santo Domingo by extending American lines directly across the middle of the city, thus creating an unbroken line of U.S. military power all the way to the San Isidro Air Base. (In a revealing indication of what *it* thought of the Special Committee, the State Department told the U.S. Embassy to proceed with the move even if the committee refused its permission and, according to Moreno, the United States began deploying its troops before the authorization was granted.[23]) As has been pointed out earlier, the real intention—and effect—of this move, as was immediately obvious to the constitutionalists, was to divide the rebel forces in two and cut off the main body of combatants from reinforcements from the countryside.

Similarly, the committee failed to prevent or even to condemn the Imbert junta's blatant violations of the ceasefire, including the major attack in mid-May on constitutionalist forces in the northern sector of the city, which resulted in the killing of hundreds of constitutionalists or innocent bystanders and the jailing of thousands of others. Indeed, there were reports that the chairman of the Special Committee, Ricardo Colombo of Argentina, personally favored military action against the constitutionalists, despite his explicit mandate to maintain the ceasefire.

To be fair, whatever the committee's inadequacies, in the last analysis it is questionable whether any OAS body could have done substantially better. The real power to arrange a settlement continued to remain in the hands of the United States, a fact that was not lost on the contending Dominican groups, who continued to deal primarily with Washington's agents rather than the Pan American Union's. Yet for several months a series of high-level U.S. representatives were able to do little better than the Special Committee in arranging a negotiated settlement. The crux of the problem, of course, was that the deep bitterness and polarization produced by the revolution made a settlement based on a coalition government impossible.

After about two weeks in Santo Domingo and with a settlement nowhere in sight, the committee resigned in a huff and returned to Washington, charging in its report that the appearance on the scene of the UN observer mission and, by strong implication, the Bundy mediating team undertaking discussions on the "Guzmán formula," had "greatly obstructed" their negotiations, inducing the constitutionalists to play one international group against another in hopes of getting better terms.[24] * The report was not unanimous, however. Panama pointed out that the primary objective of the committee, the reestablishment of peace and normal conditions, had hardly been accomplished and warned that the "dissolution of the Committee would seriously discredit the OAS, because it would imply an admission of lack of strength and of capacity to solve the problem."[25]

Panama's concern was widely shared, and so the OAS Council immediately directed Secretary General José A. Mora to go to the Dominican Republic and continue the search for a settlement. Although Mora's mission was tacitly understood to be only a temporary stopgap, pending the establishment of a new member-state committee, the step was of considerable significance in the development of the inter-American system, for it was the first time that the Secretary General had been authorized to play an important political role. His mission, however, was to prove no more successful than had the Special Committee's.

Whatever possibility Mora had to play an effective mediating role soon disappeared when the constitutionalists decided that he too was partial to Imbert and a front man for the United States. This judgment was almost certainly mistaken and unfair. While it is true that he dealt extensively with the Imbert gov-

* Another reason for the committee's resignation, however, may have been the traditional Latin American reluctance to become publicly involved on the side of the United States against another Latin nation. In particular, it appears as though the committee feared having to take a decision which would place Latin American contingents of the IAPF on the firing line, thereby risking a situation in which they might have been forced to join with U.S. troops in firing on Dominicans.

ernment and worked closely with U.S. representatives, this was not necessarily a function of his personal views but rather of the situation that had been imposed by the U.S. intervention. (In fact, there are indications that Mora's *opposition* to the GNR was one factor in Washington's decision to force out Imbert.) With the United States supporting Imbert at least until another provisional government could be established, the Secretary General had little choice but to deal with the existing centers of power in the country in the hopes of at least alleviating suffering and creating an atmosphere a little more conducive to settlement. Thus, any attempt Mora might have made to throw his weight on the side of the constitutionalists, even if he had been so inclined, would have been futile; he had no weight to throw. Within this framework of established facts and minimal personal or political leverage, Mora interpreted his authority broadly and worked long and hard to foster negotiations, maintain the ceasefire, and provide emergency economic relief to the residents of Santo Domingo. His ultimate political failure, then, as had been the case of the Special Committee, reflected the fact that none of the major actors in the situation—the constitutionalists, the Dominican military, and the Imbert junta—were interested in a compromise settlement based on a coalition government.

Beginning in mid-May, in fact, the United States had itself taken a new tack in its search for a solution. Imbert, it was decided, would have to go as soon as possible, for it was clear to the administration that he had no chance of gaining substantial Dominican support and was only a highly visible propaganda millstone around Washington's neck. Domestic criticism of U.S. policies was now sharply focused on the administration's support of what was rapidly developing into a new military dictatorship. In general, there is no doubt that the continuing opposition of crucial political leaders and organs of the mass media played an important role in the evolution of U.S. policy throughout the crisis. Senator Fulbright, the leading senatorial spokesman on foreign policy, had openly and eloquently broken with the administration; Senator Robert Kennedy, the leading political competitor of the President, for the first time had publicly criticized the administration; CBS and NBC television reporters were challenging Washington's versions of Dominican events; and at least six of the most influential U.S. newspapers—the *New York Times*, the Washington *Post*, the New York *Herald Tribune*, the St. Louis *Post-Dispatch*, the *Christian Science Monitor*, and even the *Wall Street Journal*—were highly critical in both their news and editorial columns.[26]

Other factors also played a role. It was increasingly evident, as embassy reports to the State Department grudgingly acknowledged, that there was considerable support for the constitutionalists or at least for their general cause throughout the Dominican Republic, even though there had been no uprisings outside the capital. Finally, and most important, intelligence assessments indicated that the strength of the Communist elements inside the constitutionalist zone was fading, and in any event the presence of United States troops made an extremist takeover impossible.

Accordingly, the administration shifted to a constitutionalism-without-Bosch formula. It will be recalled that the State Department had initially considered this strategy in early May; with the failure of the Imbert gambit and the inability of the OAS to find a solution, the Department now returned to this formula.

As if in desperation to at last find some competent representatives after the Bennett-Martin debacles, Johnson turned over the new round of negotiations to the all-star team of McGeorge

Bundy, Cyrus Vance, Thomas Mann, and Jack Hood Vaughn (then Assistant Secretary for Latin American Affairs). On May 15, after several days of secret talks in Puerto Rico, Bosch and Bundy agreed on the main outlines of what came to be known as the Guzmán formula. The key point, from the U.S. perspective, was Bosch's willingness to drop his earlier demand for the immediate withdrawal of U.S. troops, which would now apparently depend on Washington's satisfaction that the Communist danger was completely eliminated. In turn, Bundy offered some very significant concessions. At Bosch's suggestion, Antonio Guzmán, a close friend of the deposed President and a leader of the more moderate wing of the PRD, would serve out the remainder of Bosch's term under the provisions of the 1963 constitution. His cabinet would have a distinctly liberal cast, with most of the members coming from the PRD, although Balaguer and one conservative acceptable to the military would also be offered positions. Who was to be given control of the armed forces and what would happen to the present military leadership was somewhat more troublesome. Bosch and Guzmán initially insisted on a purge of the existing command, with officers from the constitutionalist ranks taking over. However, since this was entirely unacceptable to the United States, after some negotiating Guzmán agreed to a compromise under which Wessin would be ousted from his command and sent out of the country at the same time as a new Army Chief of Staff not associated with either side in the revolution would be appointed.

The only major sticking point in the Puerto Rican negotiations concerned the disposition of the Communists. The United States insisted that all "Communists and Trujilloists" had to be "separated from the Dominican community," either by internment in some isolated area (that is, presumably, concentration camps) or through deportation.* Perhaps surprisingly, Bosch was willing to go along with this, but Guzmán was not. Nonetheless, there seems to have been a general feeling on both sides that the issue eventually could be resolved, and after several days it was agreed to continue the talks in the Dominican Republic, where the United States would attempt to gain the support or at least the acquiescence of the Imbert junta and the regular military for the main outlines of the settlement, while Guzmán discussed it with the constitutionalists.

Predictably, Imbert, the military, and other Dominican conservative groups were very unhappy, not unreasonably seeing the Guzmán formula as in essence a victory for the revolution. Imbert's position had stiffened, especially after his successful mid-May drive against the northern constitutionalist sectors.† The military were even more of a problem, for while they had no great love of Imbert, they feared that Guzmán would eventually purge their ranks and turn over control of the armed forces to Caamaño and the constitutionalists. With their very survival at stake, as they saw it, they remained adamant, despite pressures by Vance and Mann, who alternated reassurances that the

* Defending his impartiality in his writings on the Dominican crisis, Theodore Draper cites his "careful investigation" of Sydney Lens's charge that Bundy had demanded the internment of Communist leaders in concentration camps, in which he concluded that the charge was "a disgusting and indefensible calumny."[27] However, it must now be stated with equal force that Lens was more nearly correct. "More nearly," because Bundy did include Trujilloists and did give Guzmán the alternative of deportation.

† There are several indications that Bundy, foreseeing just this problem, sought to have U.S. troops ordered to block the Imbert attack. If this is so, then he was apparently overruled at higher levels. In this connection, Szulc has written that Mann deliberately undercut the negotiations by encouraging Imbert to continue his military pressures on the constitutionalists.[28] An alternative interpretation might be that Washington tolerated a limited Imbert offensive in the hope that increased pressures on the constitutionalists would induce them to accept the Guzmán formula on U.S. terms. Mann himself has privately admitted to his personal lack of enthusiasm for the Guzmán solution, but vigorously claims that he not only loyally supported the administration's policy but used harsh and threatening language in his attempt to force Imbert and the military to go along.

United States would never allow their destruction with blunt warnings that once the Communist issue was resolved the United States would proceed with the settlement even over their opposition.

Meanwhile, though, both the State Department and the Bundy group were developing doubts about the viability and wisdom of the Guzmán formula. Conservative lobbying against Guzmán in both the Dominican Republic and the United States, stressing his alleged weakness and closeness to Bosch, may have been having an effect, and in any event Guzmán's continued refusal to go along with the Communist-control measures added to the growing distrust. If Guzmán balked now, ran the reasoning in Washington, how would we know he would stick to the rest of the agreement once U.S. troops were removed? In particular, what guarantees would there be that he wouldn't eventually turn the military over to the constitutionalists, just as the military were saying he would?

By the same token, there was serious concern over the consequences of imposing a settlement on the rightists and doubts that it would hold together very long once the United States departed. Imbert was not a crucial problem, for he had very little diehard support and was almost totally dependent on U.S. economic backing. But the military were another matter, for they were threatening to fight to prevent Guzmán from coming to office, raising the specter that the United States might be forced to crush the very force it had intervened to save. Even in the more likely circumstance that under heavy U.S. pressure the military reluctantly accepted Guzmán, there was concern that they would be so badly divided and demoralized that they would cease to be an effective and reliable anti-Communist bastion. All things considered, it was increasingly feared, U.S. troops might have to remain indefinitely in the country in an occupational role, an eventuality that Washington badly wanted to avoid.

Nevertheless, as the alternatives to a Guzmán government seemed equally bleak, the negotiations continued. On May 22, Bundy summed up the situation for the State Department. His report clearly emphasized the need for the United States to act massively to meet Dominican political, social, and economic aspirations, but it was balanced by a fear that major changes could open up a Pandora's box of potential dangers. The Guzmán formula, in effect, posed in microcosm a dilemma that had run through U.S. policy in Latin America (and, for that matter, in all the underdeveloped world) since the Kennedy days: which objective should the United States emphasize—change or stability?[29]

Specifically, the pros and cons of installing Guzmán, according to Bundy, were as follows: on the one hand, the Guzmán formula was far more likely to meet the real desires of the people than a continuation in power of Imbert, who was not only unpopular with the Dominicans but was distrusted by all major U.S. officials on the scene as well. On the other hand, though, there was no evidence that the PRD-constitutionalist slant of the Guzmán formula was the first choice of the Dominican people, for recent polls had shown Balaguer running well ahead of Bosch.

Of even greater concern was the survivability of the Guzmán formula. Though Bundy liked and trusted Guzmán himself, he considered the constitutionalist military leadership to be dangerous and unsavory and, even worse, suspected them of being under continuing Communist influence. To put a good but weak man up against a group of strong and determined men of dubious motivations and objectives was to provide a setup for a takeover, Bundy feared. Moreover, he wondered, what would happen to the Dominican military, a group for which he had no great admiration but which represented an organized authority; forcing them to accept the Guzmán formula would be a very messy affair that might well leave them shattered and fragmented, facilitating the possible spread of the revolution to the countryside. Seen from this point of view, it could be argued that Imbert was the least of the evils in a number of gloomy alternatives. In an ideal world no one would choose Imbert, Bundy conceded, but the U.S. situation in the Dominican Republic was about as far from the ideal as possible and at least, he thought, Imbert was a going concern.

After pointing to the potential dangers, though, Bundy quickly argued the other side too. It would almost surely be impossible to sell Imbert to the Dominicans and the outside world as the final result of the U.S. intervention. Moreover, once in office Guzmán might well pick up strength and keep extremist groups in his camp under control. And, most crucially of all, U.S. troops need not leave until Washington considered the situation to be safe; so long as they remained a collapse of the Dominican military was unlikely and a takeover by the Communists impossible.

The Bundy report would appear to belie the Szulc-Draper stories of a deep division in the administration, with Bundy failing because "other powerful officials in Washington had been able to paralyze his maneuvers."[30] To be sure, there are indications that there were some differences between what the State Department and the field negotiators considered acceptable, but they were differences of emphasis, not of principle.[31] What is more significant is that it was Bundy himself who provided all the arguments for discontinuing the negotiations or at least markedly stiffening the U.S. terms; indeed, the report ended with the assurance that the entire negotiating team would unanimously and unreservedly support whatever ultimate decision Washington reached.

On the following day, May 23, new instructions were sent to Bundy. Draper and Szulc have interpreted them as a sharp switch in policy or even a deliberate "torpedoing" of Bundy's efforts by the conservative Mann-Rusk forces in Washington,[32] but they are far better understood as an effort to meet Bundy's own primary concerns and yet keep alive the possibility of an agreement, though a substantially changed one. In response to the objections of those Dominicans and U.S. officials who had protested that a Guzmán government would amount to an external imposition on a Dominican populace that had demonstrated no clear majority preference for it,* the administration dropped its support for the initial formula providing for Guzmán to serve out the remainder of Bosch's term. Instead, a Guzmán government would be viewed as a provisional coalition government, which would have to have a base sufficiently broad to gain the support of as many Dominican groups as possible and which in any event would serve only until elections could be held.

Second, to meet Bundy's concern over a possible Communist takeover after Guzmán took office and U.S. troops were withdrawn, the negotiators were to stand on the initial U.S. position that Guzmán accept immediate measures against genuine Communists, including surveillance, detainment, and deportation, as deemed necessary by the United States. Moreover, Guzmán himself would have to publicly announce and decisively support

* Bennett, for example, had been continuously lobbying against the Guzmán formula, warning of the continued "extremist" influence in the constitutionalist camp. At one point, for example, he argued that constitutionalist violations of the ceasefire were deliberately designed to win UN sympathy; such well-planned tactics obviously sprang from minds much more versed in world affairs than that of Caamaño, he darkly hinted, raising the question in his mind of who was in behind-the-scenes control of the rebel camp. At another point the ambassador asserted that many (unnamed) Dominicans were telling the embassy that a pro-Bosch government could be forced on the country only by U.S. bayonets.

these measures, and the United States would maintain its intelligence operations in the Dominican Republic until satisfied the danger was past.*

Third, although these actions would apply only to hard-core Communist revolutionaries, not to leftists or constitutionalist activists in general, Bundy was instructed to demand that along with Wessin and perhaps some other rightist leaders, Caamaño, Montes Arache, and Héctor Aristy be sent out of the country. Here there apparently *were* some differences between the State Department and the Bundy group, for there are indications that Bundy was willing to settle for the Communist-control measures without pressing Guzmán on the emotionally charged issue of deporting the leading constitutionalists as well. But Bundy's own distrust of the constitutionalist leaders and his fear that they would continue to exercise major power under the nominal leadership of a Guzmán government had undercut the rationale for compromise, and the department insisted that Guzmán's support of strong action against both the Communists and the specified constitutionalists must be viewed as a test of his reliability and his willingness to maintain "safeguards" after U.S. forces were withdrawn.

As for the problem of the Dominican military, the new instructions provided that the military leadership were once again to be told firmly that the Imbert government was no longer acceptable and that a Guzmán government with strong anti-Communist safeguards guaranteed by the United States was the best achievable solution. No ultimatums or threats of force would be issued at the moment; reliance would be placed in-

* Draper is misleading in arguing that if the United States had been negotiating in good faith it would have presented these demands at a much earlier stage,[33] for they were substantially the same conditions that the United States had set out at Puerto Rico two weeks earlier. However, it is plausible that Bundy for a while had acted as if there were room for compromise.

stead on convincing the military leaders that the United States had absolutely no intention of allowing a Communist takeover or the destruction of the Dominican armed forces. A willingness to impose a solution on the military if that should ultimately prove necessary, however, was clearly implied. On the other hand, there was no hint of forcing Guzmán or the constitutionalists to accept the U.S. position; if the new conditions made a final understanding impossible, as the department recognized they might, then the OAS would be called back in to assume responsibility for pursuing other lines toward a negotiated settlement.

There are still ambiguities about the precise circumstances surrounding the final breakdown of the Guzmán negotiations on May 25 or 26, although the main factors are evident enough. It is not clear, for example, what significance should be assigned to a story appearing in the May 24 edition of the Washington *Daily News*, charging that Guzmán had been involved in financial irregularities when he was director of the Dominican Agricultural Bank. Subsequent investigation revealed that the story was totally false and had apparently been originated by a registered lobbyist for the Reid Cabral government. Draper and Szulc, however, link this event to divisions within the administration over Guzmán, clearly implying it was part of a concerted effort to undermine the Bundy negotiations. Draper, in fact, flatly asserts that the story "was a consequence . . . of the decision to abandon Guzmán."[34]

The timing of the story and the State Department's initial reaction to it, suggesting that it was now up to Guzmán to clear his name, obviously made such suspicions inevitable. Nonetheless, I am inclined to doubt this interpretation. As my analysis has suggested, no decision to "abandon" Guzmán had yet been made, and there is evidence that for that very reason the State

Department was genuinely concerned over the story, for it immediately requested Bundy to investigate and observed that the negotiating team would probably not be thanked by President Johnson if it opted for a man to lead the Dominican Republic who turned out to have a casual way with other people's money. Thus, while the initiator of the *News* story probably was hoping to sabotage the negotiations, there is no evidence linking him to high policy makers, and as I have already tried to demonstrate, the entire deep-division theory is sharply overdrawn.

On May 24 Bundy and Guzmán made a final attempt to reach agreement. Although no real meeting of the minds had been attained on the composition of the Guzmán cabinet, the prime points of difference apparently continued to be the disposition of the Communists and leading constitutionalists. Guzmán reminded Bundy that the 1963 constitution explicitly prohibited political deportations, and in any event it was his view that forcible repression in the past had only produced more Communists. As a result, even though Bosch had agreed to the detention or deportation of the Communists, he, Guzmán, would not. Even less would he agree to the removal of the top constitutionalists, who, he argued, had great popular support and had earned the honor and respect of their countrymen. Nor would he move from this stand even if Bosch or the constitutionalist leaders themselves asked him to do so. So ended the Guzmán formula, foundered on the honor and the principles of a man who would rather be right than President.

5

The Negotiations for the Provisional Government

THE FAILURE OF the Guzmán formula marked the end of the second approach toward a political solution—first, coalition government; second, constitutionalism without Bosch. Soon after the arrival of Ellsworth Bunker in the Dominican Republic, the third and final strategy emerged—a middle-of-the-road provisional government to hold free elections.

As Bunker saw the situation, it would be futile for the United States to continue to look for a solution based on the outright delivery of power to any particular individuals or groups, no matter how apparently neutral or apolitical they might be, for it was virtually impossible to imagine a formula which at once would meet Washington's requirements, be acceptable to the constitutionalists, and attract support of other key Dominican groups, particularly businessmen, the armed forces, and the Church. As a result, the impasse could be broken only through the formation of a provisional government to rule until elections could be held. Moreover, Bunker emphasized, for a settlement based on free elections to be credible to the Dominican people they would have to be held within a short time—six to nine months—and a major role for the OAS in supervising them and guaranteeing compliance with their results would have to be made very specific.

Evidently anticipating that this path might discomfort the more vigorous anti-Boschists in the U.S. Government, Bunker bluntly warned that the continuing OAS and UN roles, as well as the intense U.S. and international attention focused on the Dominican Republic, would make it impossible for the United States to manage the outcome of the affair as it might like. The best it could do, he concluded, was to insure that the solution met the basic requirements of the national interest, by which he clearly meant the avoidance of a Communist Dominican Republic.

Bunker's views in these and indeed in almost all subsequent matters were to become the established U.S. policies. A tall, erect, white-haired man in his early seventies, the New England mandarin was one of the most prestigious U.S. diplomats. For most of his career a successful businessman, he was the director of the National Sugar Refining Corporation when he was appointed Ambassador to Argentina in 1951. From there he moved up quickly, serving as Ambassador to Italy in 1952-53 and to India from 1956 to 1961. The high point of his relatively brief diplomatic career had come in 1962, when he successfully mediated the Dutch-Indonesian dispute over West New Guinea that had defied solution for years. Since 1964 he had served as the U.S. representative on the OAS Council.

After the failure of the Martin and Bundy missions, Bunker was given wide latitude and authority by President Johnson, with Bennett, the embassy, and even the State Department being relegated to a secondary role. While normally reporting to the State Department, Bunker also had open access to the White House and he did not hesitate to use it; such was Johnson's confidence in him that there was no important case in which disagreement between Bunker and Bennett or the department was not resolved in Bunker's favor.

THE OAS AND THE DOMINICAN CRISIS

IT IS LIKELY, TOO, that Bunker's other role, as de facto chairman of a three-man OAS committee in the Dominican Republic, added to his authority, for the Johnson Administration continued to be anxious to gain as much Latin American support, or at least acquiescence, as possible. On June 2, the OAS Council, responding to U.S. entreaties, had given a new Ad Hoc Committee (AHC) a tortuously phrased but sweeping mandate:

> to proceed with the work, begun by the Special Committee and now being continued by the Secretary General, of making its good offices available to all the parties with a view to creating an atmosphere of peace and conciliation which will enable the democratic institutions in the Dominican Republic to operate and make possible its economic and social recovery.[1]

There is a considerable difference of opinion among participants in the Dominican drama as to whether the committee, consisting of Bunker, Ilmar Penna Marinho of Brazil, and Ramón de Clairmont Dueñas of El Salvador, was a mere rubber stamp for Bunker or a genuinely collective body in which the Latin Americans had at least some impact on U.S. policy. There is no doubt that Clairmont and Penna Marinho played a fairly significant complementary role to Bunker in the negotiating process, by virtue of their diplomatic experience and familiarity with the Latin culture, language, and general style of operation. In particular, Clairmont is given credit by U.S. officials for being very effective in winning over elements of the Dominican military and other conservative groups to a more moderate view.

How much influence the Latins had in actual policy making is another matter. There were some differences of emphasis in the commission, with Penna Marinho, representing a military dictatorship, standing somewhat to the right of Bunker and Clairmont a little to the left. The bulk of observer testimony indicates that Bunker went to considerable lengths to consult with his colleagues and to resolve any differences through full discussion and give-and-take. Still, it is clear that Bunker dominated the committee, planned its general strategy, and was the source of almost all its initiatives. If nothing else, Bunker's position as the personal representative of the U.S. President assured his predominance, for Brazil and El Salvador were not anxious to incur the annoyance of the United States in a matter so crucial to it by undue shows of independence. Moreover, Bunker's experience, diplomatic skill, and powerful personality won genuine admiration and deference from all the participants in the crisis, even the constitutionalists. Finally, Clairmont and Penna Marinho, having less at stake in the outcome than did Bunker, frequently deserted Santo Domingo for the more pleasurable amenities of Washington, leaving the U.S. representative as the only committee member on the ground.

Although technically the Ad Hoc Committee was only a committee of the OAS Council, in fact it maintained but a nodding relationship with its parent body and was not accountable to it in any meaningful sense. It asked for no policy guidance and took action on its own authority, only afterward reporting back. Indeed, as a number of Council members observed, the AHC reports were frequently less informative than the U.S. press. A few delegates objected to the AHC's autonomy,* but most were content to remain on the sidelines and allow the committee

* The most strenuous objections were raised by Alfredo Vázquez Carrizosa of Colombia, whose continuous sniping at the AHC received considerable publicity in Latin America, especially in the Dominican Republic itself. After one particularly strong attack, the committee acerbically replied that "with the many and varied difficulties that face it each day, it would be much easier for the AHC to bring its work to a close,"[2] an unmistakable dig at the earlier withdrawal of the Special Committee, of which Vázquez Carrizosa had been a member.

sufficient latitude and flexibility to reach an early solution. Besides, many of them reasoned, there was little point in gratuitously offending the United States, which, willy-nilly, was clearly going to dominate the negotiations.

The overall role of the OAS in the Dominican crisis, then, was at best peripheral to that of the United States. In part this was a function of the unwillingness of the United States to give up control over the main lines of its policy, but it also reflected the refusal of the leading Latin American states to become involved, inhibited as they were by domestic opposition, the nonintervention doctrine, and a reluctance to be associated with an operation which might yet turn out disastrously.

Moreover, insofar as the OAS was involved in the crisis, its actions generally tended to bring discredit on itself. Not only in the Dominican Republic but all over the world the OAS was seen, whatever the oversimplification, as nothing more than a front for the United States, unable to muster up even a slap on the wrist for the country that had engaged in the most flagrant violation of the nonintervention norm, proclaimed *ad nauseam* by the Latin Americans as the "cornerstone" of the inter-American system.*

Beyond its failure to condemn the United States, a number of other OAS actions, especially in the early months of the crisis, were hardly calculated to convince anyone of the organization's impartiality and independence:

1. As has been noted, the OAS refused to allow such leading Latin American progressives as Rómulo Betancourt, José Figueres, and Luis Muñoz-Marín to mediate the crisis. On the contrary, at least two of the OAS bodies, the Special Committee

* Jottin Cury, the constitutionalist "Foreign Minister," put it this way: "Since that moment, it has not been possible to distinguish between the interventionists and the OAS."[3]

and the IAPF, were dominated by conservative, strongly anti-Communist states openly hostile to the constitutionalists.

2. The fourteenth vote necessary to obtain the minimum two-thirds required was frequently provided by the Dominican delegate on the Council, who was bitterly hostile to the constitutionalists and "represented" only the overthrown government of Donald Reid. When the Council's Credentials Committee, noting that the United States had repeatedly argued that there was no government in the Dominican Republic but only two struggling factions, recommended that the Dominican seat be declared vacant until a recognized government was in power, the Council majority (joined by the United States, of course) refused to act.[4]

3. In the name of establishing a "neutral zone," the OAS agreed to authorize the United States to extend its lines in such a way as to isolate the constitutionalists at the moment when it appeared they were on the point of defeating the Dominican military.

4. An official constitutionalist request for an OAS investigation of charges that their movement was under Communist influence was ignored, despite several attempts of Latin American states sympathetic to the revolution to get the majority to respond.

5. Despite its mandate to maintain a ceasefire, the OAS did nothing about the Imbert junta's repeated violations of the ceasefire, including the bloody mid-May drive against the constitutionalist sector in northern Santo Domingo. Nor did the OAS as such do anything to prevent a summer of repression, terror, and murder by Imbert's police and soldiers.*

6. Nothing was done to stop the IAPF itself from a series of apparent overreactions to sniping from the constitutionalist

* The Inter-American Commission on Human Rights, a semi-independent body of the OAS, did valiantly attempt to control the terrorism. See page 109.

zone, including a drive in June that resulted in the death of over sixty Dominicans.

The leverage of the OAS was thus diminished by the hostility it aroused in the Dominican Republic. Nonetheless, it would probably be incorrect to conclude that the outcome of the crisis would have in no way differed if the organization had not become involved at all. While the OAS played only a minor direct role in the evolution of U.S. policy, the repeated warnings of the more democratic states of the hemisphere that they would not be associated with any solution leading to the restoration of dictatorship in the Dominican Republic may have reinforced the Johnson Administration's determination to press for free elections.[5] In other ways as well, the very fact of official OAS involvement probably exerted an important restraining influence on Washington; as noted earlier, for example, if the inter-American body had not successfully pressed for a ceasefire in the early days after the U.S. intervention, Washington might well have ordered its troops to crush the constitutionalists.

Even more indirectly, the OAS played a fairly useful lightning-rod role. Both the rightists and the constitutionalists, fearing the consequences of a total break with Washington, typically attacked "the OAS," "Mora," or "the Inter-American Peace Force" for disliked actions that were clearly primarily or exclusively controlled by the United States Government, such as the seizure of the Central Bank, the military interposition between the two sides, and the semi-dictation of the terms of settlement.[6] Thus, though the fiction was apparent to all, the involvement of the OAS helped keep open the lines of communication between the United States and the contending Dominican factions.

Finally, the de facto diplomatic recognition by OAS bodies of the constitutionalists gave them a certain status and legitimacy. Once the situation had settled down and serious political negotiations had begun, the constitutionalists were accepted as being on at least an equal plane with the Dominican military and the Imbert junta—a contending party whose demands had to be accommodated if a settlement was to be reached. Moreover, the involvement of the OAS during the long political negotiations provided the constitutionalists with a forum for public pressure against the United States, thus giving them a degree of political leverage that partially offset their military weakness.

THE UNITED NATIONS AND THE CRISIS

THE OVERALL negotiating strategy of the constitutionalists, especially in May and June, was to play for time by stretching out the talks as long as possible, hoping thereby that world opinion and a buildup of other external pressures would eventually force major concessions from the United States. As a result, the constitutionalists were particularly delighted—and the United States annoyed—by the appointment of a UN observation mission in mid-May.

The Dominican situation had been brought before the Security Council on May 1 by the Soviet Union. In the ensuing debate most of the "third world" countries joined the Soviet Union (which throughout the crisis was to remain strikingly passive, limiting itself to rather pro forma verbal denunciations of Washington) in attacking the U.S. intervention. Aside from a few Latin American dictatorships, there was little support for the United States, but, as is always the case, there was considerable reluctance to engage in quixotic direct confrontations with a great power. As a result, after two weeks of inconclusive maneuverings, the council limited itself to authorizing the Secretary General to send a personal representative to the Dominican Republic to report on the situation. The United States had initially sought to exclude the UN completely, resorting to its traditional argument that the involvement of the OAS made UN action unnecessary. Although this strategy had been successful in the past—in the Guatemalan crisis of 1954, for example—this time the defection of a number of Latin American states would have made all-out resistance (i.e., a veto) too politically costly. With much grumbling about "outside interference in inter-American affairs," then, the United States reluctantly acceded to a minimal UN role.[7]

The head of the UN mission sent to the Dominican Republic by U Thant was José Antonio Mayobre, a former high official in Rómulo Betancourt's Acción Democratica party in Venezuela. Mayobre, by all accounts a highly intelligent and forceful man, was sympathetic to the revolution and did not limit his role to mere observation. Within a short period of time he had established very close contacts in the constitutionalist zone, thereafter acting as a communications channel between the revolution and the outside world and working vigorously behind the scenes to help bring about a political settlement acceptable to the constitutionalists.

Not surprisingly, there was a good deal of conflict for a while between Mayobre and the U.S. negotiators. As Washington saw it, Mayobre was raising false hopes among the constitutionalists and encouraging their "intransigence." Beyond that, there was a particular source of tension in what Washington considered to be Mayobre's "biased" reporting on the frequent exchanges of fire between the constitutionalists and the IAPF. The inevitable U.S. version was that the constitutionalists always began the firing and the IAPF returned fire only in self-defense. Mayobre, however, while noting the U.S. versions, also reported the diametrically opposed constitutionalist accounts. For a while, Mayobre and his military staff, headed by General Indar Rikhye of India, had attempted to conduct their own investigations, but as Rikhye was considered a Communist sympathizer by the IAPF commanders, he had received no cooperation from them. Given this situation, then, Mayobre had little choice but to report both versions. Occasionally, to be sure, he went beyond that to challenge the U.S. line directly, as when he noted the inaction of the IAPF during Imbert's mid-May offensive and pointed to the "unavoidable implication of United States involvement."[8] Although this was nothing but the merest common sense and, indeed, was far less damning than a number of leading U.S. newspaper accounts, it so infuriated the Johnson Administration that Adlai Stevenson was instructed to protest to U Thant and demand more "impartial" reporting from Mayobre. While there is no evidence that the Secretary General sought to curb Mayobre, the United States did succeed in blocking several Mayobre requests for the expansion of his staff to permit more extensive investigations.

Eventually, though, relationships improved, and in fact a number of U.S. officials came to appreciate and take advantage of Mayobre's considerable influence in the constitutionalist zone. With the establishment of the provisional government, the UN role effectively was terminated, although token representation was retained until the elections of 1966.

In light of the multiplicity of forces at work in the Dominican situation, it is difficult to isolate and assess the overall significance of the UN involvement in the crisis. It is probable that the world body had only a marginal restraining impact on U.S. policy but a considerably more important effect on constitutionalist policy, for there are indications that Mayobre's great prestige and broad contacts with the democratic left in Latin America enabled him to play an important role in bulwarking the PRD leadership against more radical elements and convincing the constitutionalists to accept a compromise settlement.

THE SETTING FOR THE NEGOTIATIONS

THE NEW ROUND of negotiations were extremely delicate and complicated, involving as they did a number of participants or constituencies and a great many highly significant, if not explosive, issues. The major matters to be settled included the nature and composition of the forthcoming provisional government, the constitutional framework under which it would rule, the manner in which elections would be held and the results guaranteed, the disposition and control of the Communists, the ending of political terrorism and the protection of human rights, the role and duration of stay of the Inter-American Peace Force, and the means by which the Dominican armed forces would be brought under political control.

Somehow, all of these issues had to be resolved in a way acceptable to the Johnson Administration, the Ad Hoc Committee, the constitutionalists, the Dominican military, key sectors of the Dominican polity at large, and the man soon tapped to be the provisional President, Héctor García-Godoy. At a slightly further remove, but still exerting a general influence over and setting the outermost boundaries of the ultimate solution were U.S. domestic opinion, the OAS as a whole, Latin American opinion, and, finally, world opinion, particularly as expressed through the UN.

The Imbert junta, though, was not considered by the Johnson Administration as an important actor in the negotiations, for it had a bad press around the world, very little popular support in the Dominican Republic, only the temporary, highly expediential support of the Dominican military, and practically no money. It was, then, nearly completely dependent on U.S. economic, political, and, in the last analysis, military support, all of which were to be withdrawn as soon as a settlement was reached.

It might be helpful at this point to outline briefly the positions of the major actors on the crucial issues, prior to a more detailed discussion later. As far as the nature of the provisional government was concerned, the United States sought to ensure that it would be clearly anti-Communist, yet sufficiently broad to attract the support of moderate Dominican opinion and at least the acquiescence of the constitutionalists. The military were primarily interested in retaining their own power and preserving their autonomy from civilian control, and thus would support only a government they assumed would tamper with neither. The constitutionalists continued to press for a Guzmán or Guzmán-type provisional government, in which the constitutionalists themselves or at least their sympathizers would predominate.

The nature of the constitution under which the provisional government would rule, while primarily symbolic in nature because of the short period of time the government would actually be in office, was nonetheless of considerable emotional importance to the Dominicans. The constitutionalists demanded the full restoration of the 1963 constitution promulgated under the Bosch government, which in addition to the usual guarantees of civil rights and liberties committed the government to an active role in economic and social development, limited the rights of private property, and sharply circumscribed the societal role of the Church. Conservative Dominicans, obviously enough, detested the Bosch constitution and pressed for a return to the 1962 constitution, which had been prepared by the rightist Council of State and was very similar to Trujillo's 1960 constitution.[9]

Because of the mutually exclusive Dominican positions on this issue, the United States was initially uncertain about what posture it should take. In early June, Bunker and the embassy summed up the situation for the State Department. On the one hand, they noted, not only the constitutionalists but their many nonextremist supporters throughout the country viewed the 1963 constitution as an expression of their hopes for a better life, genuinely believing that to give in on this point would set the country back to the Trujillo days. On the other hand, though, the conservative sectors and the armed forces would bitterly resist the reinstatement of the Bosch document, fearing that it would open the floodgates to an eventual Communist takeover.

By the end of June, the administration had authorized Bunker to seek a compromise solution in which the provisional government would rule under a temporary constitution, with the definitive one to be prepared by the government winning the forthcoming elections. In order to be palatable to the constitutionalists and their supporters as well as to U.S. and hemispheric public opinion, the transitional document should be as liberal and progressive as possible, although Washington would insist that the civil-liberties provisions could not be allowed to undercut the capacity of the provisional government to control Communist activities.

The question of holding free elections within a short period of time initially provided fewer problems, for the constitutionalists and Balagueristas enthusiastically welcomed them, and the military could not afford to oppose them openly. Later the rightists would attempt to disrupt the elections, but in the negotiating stage the only overt issue was the participation of the Communists. At first, the U.S. position was that none of the three Communist parties could participate. Later, though, as the weakness of the Communists became more evident, Washington relaxed its opposition, and the 14th of June movement was on the ballot in the elections. It was clear, though, that (as mentioned earlier) U.S. support for "free" elections was not unqualified, depending as it did on the assessment that the Communists could not win.

On the more general question of what to do about the Communists, at the start of the negotiations Washington's position remained as hard as it had been in the Guzmán discussions, and Bunker was instructed to insist that the provisional government must be committed to working closely with U.S. intelligence services in identifying and then deporting the Communist leaders to any country that would take them. However, this demand was later modified, since it was not only unacceptable to the constitutionalists but was firmly resisted by García-Godoy, who, like Guzmán, would not take office under such conditions.

Another issue in the negotiations was political terrorism. At the end of May, after Imbert's succesful drive against the northern constitutionalist sector, Dominican police began rounding up thousands of rebels, suspected rebels, and political enemies, many of whom were subsequently tortured and murdered.[10] On June 2 the constitutionalists asked the OAS to send the Inter-American Commission on Human Rights to the Dominican Republic,[11] a request that was promptly supported by the United States, which had already instructed Bunker to do what he could to offer the constitutionalists guarantees against reprisals.

The most crucial set of issues revolved around the control of the armed forces, for all sides in the negotiations understood that, whatever long-range efforts were made to create a nonpolitical military establishment, in the foreseeable future the military would continue to be a powerful influence in Dominican politics. For the constitutionalists the significance of the issue went beyond even that, as their very survival might well depend on how the question was resolved.

As far as Washington was concerned, there was general agreement within the administration that the ultimate objective should be the creation of an apolitical "professional" Dominican military, responsive solely to the will of elected governments. However, while it was well understood that this could be achieved only by a considerable restructuring of the existing military establishment, there were important disagreements or, at least, differences of emphasis over when this process should begin and how far it should go. Interestingly, the State Department was initially willing to consider a number of immediate steps. However, Bunker successfully argued that first priority had to be given to eliminating the vestiges of the Communist threat and putting together a provisional government that would be able to guide the country through free elections; for both of these objectives, he believed, the support of the military would be essential. Moreover, he argued, if the United States were to actually force changes on the military they would be so demoralized and embittered that the settlement might come apart at the seams as soon as U.S. troops departed. Once the provisional government was in office, he concluded, a start toward restructuring could be made, but for the moment the United States should support only changes at the chiefs of staff level, with the diehard anti-constitutionalists to be replaced by "moderates" who had not played an active role in the April events.

The constitutionalist position was quite straightforward: they wanted the appointment of one of their own—probably Caamaño himself—as Chief of Staff of the Army, the deportation of leading rightist military officers, and the incorporation of the constitutionalist military into the regular armed forces. Conversely, the regular military demanded the retention of the existing leadership, the deportation of the constitutionalist leaders, and the retirement of all military personnel who had "deserted" and rebelled against the government in the revolution. Not very surprisingly, then, the resolution of this entire issue was to be the stickiest in the ensuing negotiations.

THE NEGOTIATING PROCESS

TO SUMMARIZE the situation as it stood at the outset of the negotiating process, the problem for the Ad Hoc Committee was to find a formula that would meet the minimal U.S. demands and yet would be reasonably attractive to the constitutionalists, moderate Dominicans, and United States, Latin American, and world opinion. While the Dominican military also had to be brought to at least tacit acquiescence in the settlement, Imbert could be disposed of without great difficulty as soon as all the pieces had fallen into place.

Technically, the committee's mandate was only to mediate between the two contending factions, but in fact it would go far beyond that to initiate proposals, write the drafts of the major documents, choose the provisional President and, finally, induce the key Dominican groups to accept the compromise package that it had put together. In part the central role of the committee was necessitated by the nearly complete lack of communication and common interest between the constitutionalists and the Imbert group, but more importantly it reflected the fact that the United States, having ideas of its own as to what constituted an acceptable solution and the power to enforce its will, was in no mood simply to let the outcome be decided by the Dominicans alone.

In early June the Ad Hoc Committee began intensive discussions with the parties to the conflict as well as other Dominican groups, including businessmen, professionals, church leaders, union officials, students, and politicians. Its general strategy was to attempt to split the PRD and the constitutionalist military from more leftist groups in the revolutionary movement, split the regular military from the Imbert junta, and generate pressure on both sides from Dominican sectors not directly involved in the revolution. Military measures were definitely ruled out by Bunker, and even overt economic pressures were to be used only gingerly and as a last resort. On the other hand, from time to time oblique reminders of the ability of the United States to impose a military solution if it so chose were to be employed. The essence of this approach, then, was patience, persuasion, and pressure, and it would not bear fruit until the logic of the deadlock imposed by the IAPF had fully sunk in on all sides. It was a course that at times was also to create a good deal of exasperation and frustration among the U.S. military commanders and in the State Department, but Bunker's determination to wait it out and Johnson's trust in his judgment finally prevailed.

On June 18 the committee made public its proposed settlement. The main features included general elections for the Presidency, the national Congress and municipal authorities within a maximum of nine months; OAS assistance in preparing for and observing the elections; the presence of the Human Rights Commission in the Dominican Republic until an elected government took office; amnesty to all combatants who agreed to lay down their arms; the return of the armed forces to their barracks and their withdrawal from the political arena; the establishment of a nonpartisan, broadly-based provisional government to rule (until the elections) under the terms of an "Institutional Act" composed of provisions drawn from both the 1962 and 1963 constitutions; and an expanded OAS program of economic and technical assistance to help the country recover from the crisis.

Simultaneously, the committee released a "Declaration to

the Dominican People," calling on all Dominicans to support its proposals. The declaration adroitly played on the growing Dominican weariness with the conflict, stressing the need for peace, stability, and reconciliation. Moreover, the Imbert regime was deliberately treated as transitory—the "Government of National Reconstruction" was referred to only in quotes—and the tone of the document was distinctly conciliatory to the constitutionalists:

> We recognize the patriotism and valor that have gone into the struggle. We understand the causes and objectives which have brought Dominicans to take up arms. We know the price that has been paid in human lives. We appreciate the fact that those who live do not want to break faith with those who have died. . . . In making the foregoing proposals we do not ask the Dominican people to cease in their struggle to win political freedom. What we ask is that the solution not be imposed by force of arms.[12]

Both documents were released by the Ad Hoc Committee without consulting or forewarning either side, in order to force the pace of the negotiations by building up popular pressures for a compromise settlement. Pursuant to this strategy, the committee launched a massive propaganda campaign. Hundreds of thousands of copies of the documents were distributed throughout the Dominican Republic. The texts were reprinted in an "OAS" newspaper (actually financed and controlled by the United States Information Agency) and they were repeatedly read over three Dominican radio stations under USIA control or influence.* Within days the strategy bore fruit, as thousands of supporting telegrams and letters began to arrive at the committee's offices and a number of Dominican professional as-

* For a while, the United States had considered seizing all Dominican radio stations, in order to deny Imbert, the San Isidro Air Base, and the constitutionalists access to the Dominican public. When this was bitterly resisted by Imbert and the military, the United States settled for establishing its own station (nominally an OAS outlet) and feeding a barrage of material, normally unattributed, to other, supposedly independent stations.

sociations, labor unions, and other organized groups publicly announced their support of the Ad Hoc Committee plan.[13]

Just three days before the release of the committee's proposals, the most serious firefight between the IAPF and the constitutionalists since the inception of the crisis had broken out. Exchanges of fire along the border between the constitutionalist zone and the IAPF lines had been an almost nightly occurrence, but normally they had died down quickly before much damage had been done to either side. This time, however, the IAPF advanced deep into the constitutionalist zone and a major battle broke out. Before the firing stopped on June 16 the IAPF had occupied an additional fifty square blocks in Ciudad Nueva and sixty-seven constitutionalists or bystanders were dead. Even after the ceasefire was restored, the IAPF did not return to its former lines, as the force commanders were able to convince Bunker that the new positions were necessary to deny the constitutionalists the use of a number of high-rise buildings from which they had been sniping.

The chances are that the enchange had been initiated by the constitutionalists, for Caamaño frequently admitted that he didn't have complete control over all his forces and was unable to prevent snipers from taking potshots at U.S. troops.* In his report to the Security Council, Mayobre was unable to assign definite responsibility for the fighting but he noted that "some armed civilian groups in the Caamaño zone might not be fully under Caamaño's control," and he concluded that "it is quite probable that a minor incident escalated into a general outbreak."[14] In its own report to the State Department, the embassy stressed that the constitutionalist "attack" was unprovoked,

* Moreno notes that the constitutionalist ranks included a number of "cowboy commandos"—well-armed hoodlums and irresponsible teenagers—who did not accept the discipline imposed by the leadership and caused most of the trouble in the constitutionalist zone.

and pointed out that it had followed on the heels of a call by the 14th of June leadership for armed struggle against the imperialists.

Nonetheless, most neutral observers as well as the constitutionalists considered the overwhelming response of the IAPF as the latest and most serious action in a pattern of overreactions to the sniping, designed to remind the constitutionalists periodically of their helplessness and thus intimidate them into making concessions in the negotiations. Bosch later was to put it this way: "Every time the government of Colonel Caamaño refused to accept a point in the negotiations with the United States . . . the Dominican capital was subjected to an attack. . . . The slightest resistance to accepting these [U.S.] terms cost Dominican lives."[15]

These allegations are vigorously denied by U.S. officials, and the record seems largely to bear them out. The IAPF was under strict orders never to initiate firing, not to return fire unless absolutely necessary, and then to use the minimum force necessary to protect their lives. Several U.S. officials were assigned to oversee compliance with these orders, and they reported that although there were some instances of individual overreactions, for the most part the troops acted with great restraint.*

In short, I know of no evidence that there was any deliberate plan to pressure the constitutionalists through military displays, at least after U.S. acquiescence in Imbert's mid-May attack on the Northern constitutionalist sector. Nonetheless, the constitutionalists very definitely believed they were being pressured,†

* There is general agreement that the worst offenders were the small Honduran and Paraguayan contingents, who frequently got drunk and provoked incidents. Reluctantly, the IAPF command, which for propaganda purposes had hoped to keep some Latin American troops in the front lines, moved them out.

† Moreno writes that at the outset of the June 15th fighting the rebels feared they were about to be massacred.[16]

particularly when the Ad Hoc Committee proposals followed on the heels of the June fighting, and in fact they dropped some of their maximum demands shortly thereafter. Naturally this did not escape the attention of U.S. officials, and whatever their intentions they were not unhappy about the effects of the IAPF action. Indeed, a couple of months later, frustrated by the seemingly interminable negotiations, the State Department rather wistfully inquired of Bunker if there was a possibility that the IAPF might not again react to a constitutionalist ceasefire violation by occupying additional blocks in the rebel zone and thus tightening the screws still further. Bunker, however, firmly refused to follow this course, and there were no major outbreaks after June.

Regardless of what pressures the constitutionalists may have felt, the basic principles of the June 18th proposals—amnesty, a new provisional government, a nonpolitical or at least neutral military establishment, guaranteed free elections in which Bosch could run, and large-scale U.S.-OAS economic assistance—were acceptable to them. Within this framework, however, a number of crucial questions were yet to be negotiated: Who would serve in the provisional government and how much of the 1963 constitution would be preserved? How, precisely, were the military to be brought under control, and who would the new military chiefs be? What would happen to the military units that had defected to the constitutionalists in the revolution? How would the constitutionalists be disarmed without risking retaliation and terror from the military and police? What would be the role of the IAPF under the provisional government and when would it be withdrawn?

On June 23 the constitutionalists replied to the Ad Hoc Committee.[17] For the first time, the goal of a compromise settlement was accepted, at least implicitly: "In the face of the superior armed force of the interventionists, the Constitutional Government understands that it must negotiate an agreement that will bring a solution to the Dominican problem." Free elections were welcomed, provided they would be "totally free . . . [and] participated in by all parties." To that end, the constitutionalists accepted the committee's proposal that the Human Rights Commission and special OAS missions observe the entire electoral process. On the other hand, the committee's insistence that a reduced IAPF remain in the Dominican Republic to help "maintain the peace" until after the elections was rejected, the constitutionalists demanding the force's complete departure within a month after the installation of the provisional government. As for the composition of that government, it had to be made up "of men of recognized faith in the democratic process, selected . . . because of the confidence placed in them by the people." Moreover, to ensure both its temporary and its impartial nature, all the provisional government members should be prohibited from running for office in the general elections.

Retreating from their insistence on the permanent reinstatement of the 1963 constitution as the supreme law of the land, the constitutionalists accepted the principle of an "Institutional Act" to be in force only until a new post-election constitutional congress could be convened, but insisted that the provisional document be based "on all economic, ethical and social achievements . . . [and] the human rights and public freedoms of the Constitution of 1963." Somewhat surprisingly, beyond calling for the reintegration into the regular armed forces of the constitutionalist military (including a number of pro-Bosch officers who had been discharged from the Army under the Reid Cabral junta and "reinstated" during the revolution), the constitutionalists said almost nothing about the broader issue of the control of the military. Perhaps their silence on this crucial issue reflected their hesitancy to antagonize the armed forces by a public statement of their insistence on sweeping changes in the military command structure.

On the same day, the Imbert junta also replied to the June 18th Ad Hoc Committee proposal.[18] The GNR, it said, *itself* constituted the broadly based provisional government referred to in the proposal, and therefore, it implied, there was no need to look for a new one. Giving lip service to free elections, it nonetheless called for the immediate withdrawal of the IAPF, which in light of the prevailing situation and Imbert's manifest drive for power would have made an utter mockery of the elections. (Note that *both* sides had called for the withdrawal of the IAPF, which suggested either that the contestants made radically different assessments of the outcome of the renewed civil war which surely would have followed, or, as is more probable, that the constitutionalist position was purely for the historical record and adopted only in the certainty that the Ad Hoc Committee would reject it.) Almost as if to make sure that there was no ambiguity about Imbert's intentions, other GNR proposals called for, or added up to, the immediate disarmament of the constitutionalists, the cashiering of all the constitutionalist military from the armed forces, the deportation of all "Communists," and the "normalization" of Santo Domingo by the military elimination of the constitutionalist zone.

Unlike the constitutionalists, Imbert apparently was still deluded enough to think he could dictate his own terms, amounting to the surrender and/or slaughter of the constitutionalists and his own indefinite perpetuation in power. Such a posture was rather odd: operating from extreme weakness, Imbert was following an extremely obdurate line. A better formula for a no-win strategy could scarcely have been devised; ironically enough, his preposterous stance very probably had the effect of ensuring greater Ad Hoc Committee concessions to the constitutionalists than would have been the case if he had established a serious negotiating position from which he was prepared to bargain.

After receiving the replies to its proposal, the Ad Hoc Committee decided to give priority to the establishment of the provisional government, hoping that the resolution of that problem would pave the way for the later settlement of the others. The committee began by asking the two factions to submit lists of their preferred candidates for the provisional Presidency. After eliminating those who were clearly anathema to either the Dominican side or to the United States, the committee reopened intensive discussions with representatives of leading Dominican groups not directly involved in the revolution and with the leading candidates themselves. Out of this process emerged Héctor García-Godoy, the man who impressed the Ad Hoc Committee as being most capable of leading the country to elections and as having the best chance of getting the support or acquiescence of the constitutionalists, the Dominican military, neutral Dominicans, and the U.S. Government. Let there be no doubt, though, that the crucial factor in the choice of García-Godoy was that Ellsworth Bunker was greatly impressed by him.* In his reports to Washington, Bunker noted that García-Godoy was effective, moderate, reliable, and, certainly not least, a "good friend of the United States," deserving all the help in his forthcoming tasks that the United States could give him. Not that it took much persuasion, for practically everyone in the U.S.

* Dr. Abraham Lowenthal asks whether García-Godoy really "emerged out" of the series of discussions, or whether the discussions served only to legitimize his prior choice by the U.S. Government. It is a good question, and I'm not sure of the answer, though it is my impression that the consultation process was genuine. At the very least, constitutionalist acquiescence was essential, for García-Godoy had firmly conditioned his willingness to serve on their approval.

Government involved in the Dominican crisis was taken with García-Godoy; around the State Department it was *de modo* that the suave diplomat was the "only modern man" in the Dominican Republic.*

To be sure, García-Godoy *is* a most impressive man, with great personal charm as well as high intelligence, ideals, and integrity: the *summum bonum* of the Dominican oligarchy at its best.† The "oligarchy" in the Dominican Republic consists of a very small group of generally well-educated and socially prominent businessmen, landowners, and professionals, closely tied by birth and marriage and living mostly in or near the city of Santiago (the full name of which, appropriately, is Santiago de los Caballeros—Santiago of the Gentlemen). In the pre-Trujillo days, this group furnished a disproportionate share of the Dominican political leadership. Three of the best Dominican Presidents, for example—Ulises Espaillat, Ramón Cáceres, and Horacio Vásquez—were wealthy plantation owners from the Santiago area. Not surprisingly, Trujillo, who came from a lower-middle-class family, detested the oligarchy, and during his rule its political power was broken.‡ More than any other group, though, the oligarchy managed to remain relatively aloof from, and uncorrupted by, Trujillo's murderous regime.

* Earlier the State Department had suggested a list of seven potential Dominicans to head the provisional government. Significantly, like García-Godoy (who was one of the seven), all were liberal, able, and highly respected.

† Héctor García-Godoy died suddenly of a heart attack on April 20, 1970, just as this book was going to press. The tragedy of his death will long be felt, not only by his family and his friends, but by the entire Dominican people. Indeed, his loss will be felt by all men who look to their leaders for decency, compassion, and intelligence.

‡ Unlike other Latin American countries where, at least until recently, the officer corps of the armed forces have been composed primarily of sons of the upper classes, the Dominican aristocracy has no tradition of military service. On the contrary, under Trujillo the armed forces were recruited mainly from the peasantry and lower classes, and the officers were usually "persons of limited education and even more limited moral character."[19]

Today, far from being rapacious and reactionary, most members of the oligarchy seem to be civic-minded, anti-military, and moderately progressive.[20]*

García-Godoy stands at the center of the intricate web of the Santiago aristocracy. Born in the nearby town of Moca in 1921, his grandfather was a former Dominican President (Cáceres) and both his father and father-in-law were ambassadors to the United States. After earning a law degree at the University of Santo Domingo, he too became a career diplomat. At the time of Trujillo's assassination he was the Dominican Ambassador to Great Britain.

García-Godoy's early career under Trujillo can only be understood in the context of the nightmarish totalitarianism that prevailed under "El Jefe." If Trujillo wanted someone in his government, there was no choice for the appointee but to serve or flee into exile. And, as Crassweller has pointed out, exile "involved practical and psychological problems . . . and . . . left one's helpless family and friends to bear the hard consequences."[22] Given the situation, service in the diplomatic corps might well have seemed the most honorable way out of the problem for a prominent Dominican who might otherwise have been forced into a more compromising position. In any event, nearly all leading Dominicans of every political persuasion who remained in the country were linked in one way or another with the Trujillo regime, and as a result the Dominicans themselves consider only direct participation in the Trujillo terror apparatus as truly damning.

In 1963, Bosch appointed García-Godoy as his Foreign Minis-

* Martin points out that the Bosch government of 1963 had more support from the "Santiago oligarchy" than from any other group.[21] Also, a number of Santiago professionals and businessmen—though perhaps not "oligarchs" as the Dominicans use that word—were prominent in the PRD and constitutionalist leadership, notably Antonio Guzmán, Salvador Jorge Blanco, José Agosto Vega, and Anibal Campagna.

ter. Following the 1963 coup, he became Vice-President of Balaguer's Partido Reformista. When brought back by the Ad Hoc Committee into public service, then, he had broad support from the Santiago group, the Balagueristas, numerous independents, and the more moderate wing of the PRD.

On July 8 the constitutionalist leadership met to decide whether to accept García-Godoy as provisional President. The minutes of that meeting have since been published,[23] and they make fascinating reading, for they shed a great deal of light on the structure and internal balance of power of the constitutionalists, the position of the extreme left, the general perceptions of the constitutionalist leadership group, and the negotiating tactics of the Ad Hoc Committee.

The position of the radical left, represented primarily by the 14th of June movement and to a lesser extent by Héctor Aristy (constitutionalist "Minister of the Presidency"), Jottin Cury ("Foreign Minister"), and the left wing of the Social Christians, was that García-Godoy was a reactionary who was being imposed on them by the Ad Hoc Committee. Therefore, it was concluded, the constitutionalists should refuse to accept him, even if this should induce the Ad Hoc Committee to unleash Imbert's troops or the IAPF. While a full-scale attack could not be long resisted, the 14th of June leaders admitted, the UN could be relied upon to step in and block military aggression against the constitutionalists.

The constitutionalist negotiating committee, a five-man group composed of PRD leaders and former high officials in the Bosch government appointed in May to represent the revolutionary movement in all discussions with the OAS, led the opposition to this course. While they agreed that the Ad Hoc Committee had flatly rejected their own candidates (of whom Guzmán was still their first choice) and in effect had imposed García-Godoy, they believed, unlike the radicals, that García-Godoy was a good man, and certainly the best they were likely to get. Furthermore, they were not at all complacent about the possibility of renewed military pressures, fearing not so much that the Ad Hoc Committee would direct the IAPF to attack the constitutionalist zone as that the OAS body might resign in frustration, leaving Imbert and the Dominican military as the ultimate arbiters of the crisis. In such a situation, they argued, the UN would be powerless to help the constitutionalists.

The position taken by the negotiating committee reflected the success of the Ad Hoc Committee in dividing Bosch and the PRD from the more radical constitutionalist groups. As some of the leftist leaders bitterly but accurately charged at the meeting, in addition to its formal sessions with the negotiating committee the Ad Hoc Committee had been meeting secretly with the PRD leadership, and had convinced them of the wisdom of a settlement based on a García-Godoy government. The PRD leadership had then begun to work quietly within the constitutionalist movement, eventually gaining the support of most of the key elements for this course, providing that García-Godoy agreed to the following points: genuinely free elections; a general amnesty and the protection of all public liberties; the fulfillment of the economic and social principles of the 1963 constitution; no deportations and the return to the country of all Dominicans currently in exile, including Bosch; and the reintegration of the constitutionalist military into the armed forces. Upon García-Godoy's response that, subject to further negotiations on the form of reintegration and the implementation of the 1963 constitution, all of these points were agreeable to him, José Peña Gómez, the eloquent young PRD activist who had called the people into the streets on April 24, undertook to convince the July 8th meeting to accept García-Godoy. It was principles rather than men that were important, Peña Gómez argued, and in the prevailing circumstances the establishment of a García-Godoy government was as close as the constitutionalists could get to the realization of the principles they had fought and died for.

According to some of those present, the Peña Gómez speech tipped the balance. In the ensuing ballot, the constitutionalists voted 4-2 "not to oppose" a García-Godoy government. One vote each was allotted to the presidents of each house of the national legislature chosen in the 1963 elections, the cabinet of the constitutionalist (Caamaño) government, the constitutionalist military, the PRD, the Social Christians, and the 14th of June. The latter two groups voted in the opposition, and the military abstained, explaining that as the nonpolitical arm of the revolution they would support whatever position the political leadership took.

The negotiations over García-Godoy demonstrated that politically the extreme left was quite weak, despite its continued military control over many armed units only nominally under Caamaño's command.* The most radical groups were not represented on the constitutionalist negotiating committee, were unable to prevent a favorable vote on García-Godoy, and subsequently made no move forcibly to block the implementation of the agreement. In a candid self-assessment of their role in the movement, leaders of the Soviet-oriented PSP were later to admit that they had had little influence over the constitutionalist leadership, which, they complained, had increasingly fallen under the domination of "spokesmen of the Right."[24]

With the constitutionalist acquiescence in García-Godoy, there now remained a final obstacle—the armed forces. Imbert's op-

* For what it is worth, the embassy claims that it was told by Caamaño that there were sections of the constitutionalist zone in which it was actually unsafe for him to appear. This is vigorously denied by the constitutionalists.

position to García-Godoy (whom he referred to as the "English lord of the oligarchy") was of no consequence as long as the military could be detached from the GNR. As the regular officer corps had no particular love for or loyalty to Imbert,* the main problem was to convince them that the accession of García-Godoy would not lead to eventual constitutionalist control of the military.

In the next few weeks, the leading officers reluctantly became persuaded that they had no choice but to go along with the Ad Hoc Committee, and finally agreed, as had the constitutionalists, "not to oppose" García-Godoy. The stage was then set for the removal of Imbert, with the major leverage to be provided by the U.S. economic control of the GNR. As has been discussed earlier, the Dominican economy had been brought to the point of collapse by the revolution, and thereafter the Johnson Administration, operating through OAS institutions but retaining complete control in its own hands, had furnished nearly all the revenue for the Dominican public sector. Most crucially, the salaries of seventy thousand state employees, including the military and the police, were in fact paid for by the United States. Restive about this situation, Imbert at the end of May had made an effort to seize the revenues of the Dominican Central Bank, but before he could do so the Ad Hoc Committee surrounded the bank with IAPF contingents and notified Imbert that thereafter no withdrawals would be permitted without the written authorization of an OAS official.

From June onward, then, the continued functioning of the Imbert government was at the mercy of the United States, even short of the use of armed force. From time to time in the negotiations, just to remind the GNR of its weakness, the United

* Although Imbert was technically a general, the title was strictly honorific, having been awarded to him by the Council of State because of his role in the *ajusticiamiento*.

States briefly held up the payment of public salaries. Until final agreement was reached on the provisional government and other major issues, though, Bunker was unwilling to pull the rug completely from underneath Imbert, fearing that economic chaos, a further breakdown of public order, and the disruption of military and police morale would result. Moreover, keeping alive the possibility that the United States might in the end decide to stick with Imbert if the constitutionalists proved too recalcitrant was a useful way of maintaining pressure in the negotiations. When, however, the constitutionalists and the military finally agreed to the Ad Hoc Committee's package settlement in mid-August, the time had come for Imbert. On August 14, the committee publicly announced that the OAS aid for government salaries and other expenditures would shortly be terminated and would not be resumed until the installation of the provisional government. Still, the GNR hung on for a few more weeks until, at the request of Bunker that Imbert be "leaned on" a little more, President Johnson sharply demanded that the junta accept the OAS plan, adding that "any who continue to oppose the OAS solution are not friends of peace."[25] Thus, with the handwriting not merely written but emblazoned on the wall, Imbert resigned the following day and the García-Godoy government took office.*

THE SETTLEMENT PACKAGE

IN THE FINAL WEEKS of the bargaining process García-Godoy had emerged as a central figure whose importance was no less than that of Bunker. Not only did he work closely with the Ad

* There is some reason to believe that Imbert's departure may also have been facilitated by a financial token of Washington's esteem for his not, after all, completely useless role.

Hoc Committee and act as mediator and channel of communications between the committee and the contending forces, but his own views were a major factor in the shaping of the final agreements.

The heart of the settlement, formalized in an "Act of Reconciliation" as well as in the "Institutional Act," was the firm promise that there would be free elections within nine months. To ensure that the preelectoral process would be genuinely open and the results of the elections accepted, the Ad Hoc Committee, the Human Rights Commission, and, most crucially of all, the IAPF, would remain in the Dominican Republic to support and, if necessary, enforce the agreement.

Until the elections, the country would be headed by the García-Godoy provisional government. Once García-Godoy was accepted as President, the makeup of the rest of the provisional government was not much of a problem. The State Department initially had instructed Bunker to insist that all members of the cabinet be men of clear-cut anti-Communist convictions, as verified by U.S. intelligence. During this period the CIA maintained files of all leading Dominican figures, dutifully noting all "evidence" of possible Communist leanings. Given the agency's propensity to take no risk whatever, it is highly probable that a government composed only of CIA-certified Dominicans would have been dominated by the extreme right. García-Godoy, however, warned that he would refuse the Presidency unless he was given a free hand in choosing his associates; faced with his insistence on this point, Bunker convinced Johnson to go along.

Final resolution of the constitutional issue was somewhat thornier, although it had been eased by the rebels' reluctant agreement (after the fighting of June 15-16) to drop their demand for the full reinstatement of the 1963 constitution. The new Institutional Act, drafted by Pan American Union officials working in conjunction with GNR and constitutionalist lawyers, combined the 1962 and 1963 constitutions, preserving the major political provisions of the latter document but dropping most of its more controversial economic and social provisions, particularly the right of government nationalization of private property, the right of divorce, and the nullification of Trujillo's concordat with the Vatican. Within four months after the election, the new government would call a constitutional convention to draft a permanent document.

In a major concession, the United States agreed to drop its earlier demand that known Communists be jailed or deported. As will be recalled, the administration's adamancy on this issue in May had been a major factor in the collapse of the Guzmán negotiations. But, when García-Godoy proved to be no less immovable than Guzmán had been, Bunker finally persuaded the State Department to accede to his wishes. There were three key differences between the García-Godoy and the Guzmán negotiations on this issue. First, by August the isolation of the Communists and their fundamental weakness was clearer. Second, García-Godoy was trusted by Washington more than Guzmán had been, and Bunker was reasonably confident that the provisional government would keep the Communists under close surveillance, take internal measures to cope with subversion if that should prove necessary, and generally exclude the extreme left from positions of influence. Third, Bunker was increasingly impressed with the breadth of the Dominican consensus against deportation, and on several occasions he pointed out to Washington that because deportation had so often been used in the past to expel non-Communist political opponents it was a widely detested measure.

Perhaps the most difficult and, in the long run, the most critical issue was the future of the Dominican military. Once the constitutionalists and the armed forces leadership had resigned themselves to the need for a compromise settlement, this issue had dominated the summer negotiations. There was a considerable amount of genuine agreement between the U.S. Government and García-Godoy on general principles. Both were convinced that the Dominican military had to be substantially restructured, taken out of the political arena, and brought under civilian control. To do so, it was further agreed, there would have to be major changes in the existing leadership of the armed forces. On the other hand, García-Godoy shared the Johnson Administration's concern that the military not be treated in such a way as to unnecessarily fragment, weaken, or demoralize it. In particular, both agreed that to turn over control of the military to the constitutionalists would be unwise and in any event so unacceptable to the armed forces as to be unenforceable without an indefinite U.S. occupation that no one in either country wanted.

There was, however, some difference of opinion between García-Godoy and Bunker on the timing of the reform process. García-Godoy, naturally enough, wanted the United States to impose immediate changes before he took office, in order to avert a certain crisis if he later had to move against the armed forces on his own rather limited authority. As was mentioned earlier, the State Department initially shared García-Godoy's views, and on a number of occasions during the summer negotiations felt it necessary to remind Bunker of the administration's continuing commitment to military reform. But Bunker's first priority was to break the post-revolution stalemate and establish a new government, and he therefore continued to resist any move that might endanger the emerging but tenuous settlement.

As in the other disagreements with the State Department, Bunker's views finally prevailed. With the general understanding that the Ad Hoc Committee and the United States would strongly support military reform after the establishment of the provisional government, García-Godoy reluctantly agreed to shelve the issue and convince the unhappy constitutionalists that significant changes would shortly be forthcoming. At the same time, however, both García-Godoy and Bunker were reassuring the nervous and suspicious generals that the "basic integrity" of the armed forces would certainly be maintained. As a result of these vague promises, a temporary modus vivendi was reached.

Technically, the commitments to the constitutionalists and the military were not incompatible, but the emphases and the general tone were quite different. No doubt such tactics were necessary to gain the minimal acquiescence of the combatants, but as García-Godoy had foreseen, the arousing of mutually incompatible expectations and, more generally, the failure to resolve the issue cleanly only exacerbated the later inevitable crisis.

The related set of issues dealing with the future of the constitutionalists was also handled in an inconclusive manner. A general amnesty covering civil war "crimes" was agreed upon easily enough, but the problems of disarmament of the civilian activists and the reintegration of the constitutionalist military into the armed forces were far more difficult. The original Ad Hoc Committee proposal called for the immediate withdrawal of the constitutionalists from Ciudad Nueva upon the installation of the provisional government, with IAPF forces to move in after them, exercise general police functions, and preside over the demilitarization of the area, including the collection of arms. The constitutionalists strenuously objected to this arrangement, not wanting to be cut off from their supporters and reduced to impotence—and certainly not before they were satisfied that all provisions of the settlement, particularly political control of the military, were being complied with. Nor did the fact that strong elements in the armed forces were still calling for a military "cleanup" of the rebel zone help convince the constitutionalists to surrender their means for self-defense. Finally, to have to turn their arms in to the hated IAPF was, psychologically, asking too much of the constitutionalists.

Bunker and García-Godoy proved to be flexible and understanding of these points, agreeing to modifications under which the constitutionalist military itself would be responsible for the collection of arms and the gradual demilitarization of its zone. More importantly, no time limits were set, and it was understood on all sides that effective compliance would depend on García-Godoy's success in bringing the armed forces under control.

A final resolution of the reintegration issue was also postponed. This was a crucial matter to the constitutionalists, for it involved not only the immediate question of the safety and continued livelihood of the thousand or so constitutionalist military defectors, but also the future political orientation of the armed forces. Specifically, the constitutionalists pressed for the reintegration at their current ranks of their entire officer corps, which included not only men on active duty at the moment of the revolution but also a number of former officers who had joined the constitutionalist ranks and had been restored to their previous ranks or given "battlefield commissions" by Caamaño. Spread out through the ranks of the armed forces, these majors and colonels could constitute an important balance of power to the "loyalists." Reluctant to go this far, García-Godoy and Bunker agreed only to stipulate formally that "those members of the armed forces who have participated in the present conflict will be reincorporated in the armed forces without discrimination or reprisal,"[26] thus leaving unanswered the question of whether constitutionalists not on active duty on April 24 would be considered "members of the armed forces." There was a general understanding, however, that García-Godoy would handle the matter on an individual basis, looking with sympathy primarily on those constitutionalists who had been career officers purged by the Reid Cabral government for their pro-Boschist inclinations.

The three remaining points of the settlement caused little difficulty. Only the timing of the withdrawal of the IAPF was at all controversial. The constitutionalists, it will be recalled, had initially "demanded" that the IAPF be withdrawn within a month after the installation of the provisional government. Neither the United States nor García-Godoy, though, had the slightest intention of leaving the provisional government at the mercy of the military, which almost certainly would not have allowed a free election in which Bosch was a participant; even the constitutionalists, of course, privately understood the importance of IAPF support for the realization of their objectives. Formally, the Act of Reconciliation provided that the withdrawal of the IAPF would be determined by the OAS in conjunction with the provisional government; informally, Bunker and the constitutionalists accepted García-Godoy's position that the IAPF should depart shortly after the elections.

At the request of García-Godoy and the constitutionalists, the Human Rights Commission was also to remain in the Dominican Republic until the elections. The commission had performed excellently since it had arrived in the country in June. With Bunker's close cooperation and encouragement, it had investigated thousands of complaints of police harassment, political imprisonments, and outright murders of constitutionalist sympathizers throughout the country. Its vigorous activities and forthright public reports, which received widespread publicity in the Dominican Republic and the hemisphere at large, were undoubtedly instrumental in deterring worse atrocities, securing the release of political prisoners, and bringing about a significant lessening of terrorism by the end of the summer of 1965. Moreover, by thus contributing to the improvement of the general atmosphere in the country, the work of the commission probably helped facilitate accord on the political settlement.[27]

A final García-Godoy and constitutionalist demand was for large-scale United States and OAS support of economic recovery and development programs. This was no problem, for it was well understood in Washington that the U.S. commitment to Dominican stability made such assistance mandatory. An agreement in principle was easily reached, with the details to be worked out later.[28]

In review, of the factors that made the settlement possible several emerge as of crucial importance. The situation had been stabilized by the firm IAPF-imposed military stalemate, which had gradually undercut the positions of extremists in both camps and strengthened the hand of more moderate and pragmatic elements, particularly the PRD leadership. Both sides, too, had come under growing pressure from the general populace to come to terms, and even among the militants morale had flagged and weariness with the fruitless deadlock had set in. As has been described earlier, the Ad Hoc Committee had adroitly played on these feelings, and with the vast propaganda apparatus of the U.S. Government at its disposal had effectively mobilized Dominican sentiment behind its proposed settlement. In the background, too, was the fear that a military solution might yet be imposed by the United States. Too much obstructionism, the constitutionalists believed, could eventually lead to an IAPF attack on Ciudad Nueva. Alternatively, the OAS might give up in disgust and withdraw, leaving the constitutionalists at the mercy of the reconstituted Dominican military. While there is no evidence that either the United States or the OAS was ever close to either course, Bunker nonetheless occasionally had alluded to such possibilities. In mid-August, for example, when the constitutionalists were still insisting on outright control of the armed forces, Guzmán and other PRD leaders were warned by Bunker and García-Godoy that time was running out on a solution favorable to the PRD, which would ultimately be the loser if the "diehards" and "extremists" continued to insist on "impossible" conditions. Similarly, the Dominican military had been repeatedly warned that they would not be allowed to obstruct a reasonable settlement, and they too were left to wonder at what point the IAPF might move against them. Finally, the key to the settlement was the provision for free elections, for it not only had the support of the constitutionalists and their sympathizers throughout the country, who anticipated a Bosch victory, but it was also acceptable to many middle-of-the-roaders and moderate conservatives, who had high hopes that Joaquín Balaguer would be elected.

This is not to suggest that the settlement sought simply to split the unbridgeable differences between the left and the right, for it was far more acceptable to the constitutionalists than to Imbert, the military, and the general Dominican right.* The man chosen to head the provisional government, Héctor García-Godoy, was an independent, progressive democrat, and his mandate was to provide a liberal transitional government that would make it possible to hold genuinely free elections, thus giving the moderate forces within the constitutionalists a real chance to attain their primary objective, the return of Bosch to the Presidency. Indeed, perhaps the best evidence for the progressive nature of the settlement was that by midsummer the most bitter Dominican criticisms of the United States and the OAS were coming from the right rather than the left, with Bunker and the Ad Hoc Committee accused of being pro-constitutionalist, if not pro-Communist!

* Note that this assessment differs markedly from Stanley Hoffmann's, who has written that the U.S. "prevailed" in the Dominican Republic "because the insurgents preferred a peaceful solution *unfavorable* to them to a bloody battle [with U.S. troops]."[29]

The reasons for this gradual U.S.-AHC shift to the left have been suggested earlier and need only be briefly summarized here. First, the U.S. Government had become increasingly impressed with the widespread support for the constitutionalist movement throughout the country and, on the other side, the almost universal contempt for, and fear of, Imbert and the old-line military.* Second, Bunker, Bennett, and the Latin Americans on the Ad Hoc Committee personally had become angered and disgusted with Imbert's manifest desire to establish a new dictatorship and hold on to power at any cost to his country. Third, once García-Godoy had been accepted, he exerted an important liberal influence in the negotiations. Fourth, the very weakness of the constitutionalists ultimately had proven to contain real strengths. The Imbert junta had pretensions to being a national government, responsible for administering the entire country; thus, being dependent on the support of the public bureaucracy, the police, and the military, it was highly vulnerable to economic pressures. The constitutionalists, however, contained as they were in a tiny zone, were beyond the reach of nonmilitary pressures, short of a food and water blockade to starve them out. Moreover, they could and did threaten to commit suicide—to resist any United States attack to the last man; the elaborate house-to-house defenses and open urban guerrilla training exercises in the constitutionalist zone testified to the credibility of the threat. Thus, given its unwillingness to be responsible for a massacre, the Johnson Administration had no option but a negotiated settlement. Finally, of course, the Dominican crisis was not confined to that small unhappy island but was played out on the world stage, with the reputations of the United States and the OAS dependent upon a reasonably democratic and peaceful outcome.

* Juan de Onis has written: "Interviews with scores of persons in this capital [Santo Domingo] and in towns in the interior disclose a desire that the United States use its power and influence to 'get the military off the country's back.' "[30]

6

The Provisional Government

GARCÍA-GODOY TOOK OFFICE on September 3, 1965. In less than nine months he had to create the conditions under which free elections could be held and their results accepted. To do this he had to bring the military under control, reincorporate the constitutionalists into the body politic and, in general, bind up the wounds opened by the civil war. Moreover, García-Godoy also saw his task as including a start on some of the longer-range problems, particularly the recovery and development of the Dominican economy and the restructuring of the Dominican military establishment and public bureaucracy. Finally, his own sense of nationalism and, perhaps, his future political needs, required what he called the "recovery of Dominican sovereignty"—the withdrawal of the foreign occupying forces.

The prevailing circumstances could hardly have been less promising for such ambitious objectives: a rebellious military that was still very much a product of the Trujillo era, a well-armed and bitter constitutionalist camp, and, perhaps worst of all, a society shattered and demoralized by decades of brutal tyranny and civil strife. On top of all this, the provisional government took office with the national treasury exhausted; tax collection paralyzed; the banks closed; a series of public and private strikes and labor disorders further crippling the almost bankrupt economy; the major newspapers and radio stations destroyed or not operating; the University of Santo Domingo, the country's only public institution of higher education, closed down and under military occupation; and shooting incidents, revenge killings, and outright terrorism nearly daily occurrences.

Without Washington's strong support, García-Godoy's task almost surely would have been impossible. That support was forthcoming—the United States was prepared to use its economic, political, and, if need be, even its military power to keep the provisional government in office and to ensure the holding of the elections. On September 6, General Palmer, commander of the U.S. contingent in the IAPF, told his troops that they were no longer neutral but would support the García-Godoy government.[1] To minimize further the extreme rightist threat, now considered by the Johnson Administration to be a greater source of concern than the radical left, the Dominican armed forces were informed in even more direct terms that the IAPF would be used to prevent a military coup.

Yet U.S. support of García-Godoy was not unlimited. It was well understood that the provisional President would have to maintain a strong anti-Communist posture and that planned reform of the military would have to be designed not to destroy it but to preserve it as a force for the maintenance of internal order. Within these limits, however, García-Godoy had a great amount of independence, and was certainly in no sense a "puppet" of the U.S. Government. On the contrary, the very depth of the Johnson Administration's commitment to his government and to the holding of free elections left him with a considerable amount of latitude to make his own political decisions, for he was well aware that the United States would have little choice but to continue supporting him. Thus, he frequently ignored

Washington's advice and took a number of important steps that overrode Bunker's misgivings or even, on occasion, outright opposition.

The first clash, or at least disagreement, developed over Bunker's proposal to the OAS that the Ad Hoc Committee be disbanded and replaced with a high-level special representative of the inter-American body, someone with the prestige and stature of Galo Plaza Lasso (now OAS Secretary General) or Alberto Lleras Camargo, the former Secretary General and President of Colombia. The function of this official, ostensibly, would be to supervise and coordinate all OAS technical and economic assistance programs in the Dominican Republic, but García-Godoy understandably suspected that such a super-representative would inevitably come to exercise considerable political power, whether or not that was the intention of the Bunker proposal. The new President would have none of this potential dilution of his own authority and threatened to resign if it should be imposed over his opposition. It was the first of several occasions on which he was able to make effective use of this threat; with reluctance, Bunker withdrew his proposal and settled for a compromise under which the Ad Hoc Committee would continue to play an important, though vaguely-defined role in the Dominican situation.*

In the ensuing weeks García-Godoy continued to move vigorously to establish his independence from the United States and his own military. There was considerable chagrin in both Washington and Santo Domingo, for example, over his cabinet appointments, which included a large number of constitutionalists or their sympathizers (as well as some "loyalists"). Moreover,

* To be sure, the Ad Hoc Committee itself exercised great political power in the Dominican Republic, but García-Godoy had come to trust in Bunker's judgment and discretion, whereas the proposed special representative would be an unknown quantity.

as part of his program of reconciliation, García-Godoy issued a decree providing that all former government officials who had lost their positions during the Reid government or the revolution because of their political views could immediately resume their posts. The effect of the decree was to open the government bureaucracy and the state economic enterprises to a sudden influx of constitutionalists. In a number of instances there was considerable tension and even violence, as the ebullient constitutionalists physically took over government buildings and unceremoniously removed the former occupants.

The manner in which García-Godoy handled the university crisis was even more controversial. Hundreds of students had fought with the constitutionalists, and on returning to the campus —usually with their guns—they had demanded the ouster of the heavily right-wing university administration. Although the existing authorities had been elected by the appropriate university bodies only a few years earlier, the students were in no mood to be deterred by formal due process, and even threatened to kill administration officials if they appeared on campus.* The outraged officials, supported by conservative groups throughout the country, demanded that García-Godoy crack down on the students and support the official establishment, not retreating even when the President pointed out that nothing less than a military operation and probably even the indefinite closing of the university would be required.

García-Godoy, however, had no intention of provoking such

* In this respect, the reader will note, Dominican students are still somewhat in advance of their compatriots in the United States. But not nearly as much as they used to be; writing in the dear, departed days of 1966 (in *Overtaken by Events* (!), p. 98), Martin made the following observation: "Watching the students riot, I remembered wryly that in Washington I had dreamed of inviting Adlai Stevenson and others down to lecture at the University. We in the United States, more concerned with our children's marks or morals than their politics, are often puzzled by student riots abroad. Latin American university traditions are wholly different from ours."

a crisis. As he saw the situation, the university problem was a microcosm of the national problem and could only be resolved in the same manner: by a negotiated political settlement. With considerable difficulty, the President managed to talk student leaders and their faculty supporters into allowing new university elections, subsequently swept by the leftist forces. Since then, the university has been the focal point and nerve center for Dominican radicalism, and has been in a state of continual turmoil. However, it is hard to see what other course García-Godoy could have followed, for the only alternative was to capitulate to the groups that were perfectly willing to sacrifice the educational process itself in the name of law and order.

The U.S. reaction to the provisional government's early moves was one of considerable trepidation. At the end of September the State Department warned Bunker that it was seriously concerned over what it saw as García-Godoy's unwillingness or inability to strike a greater balance between the left and the right, and his failure to act decisively against the strong-arm methods of "extremists" in the government bureaucracy, state economic enterprises, and the university. In response, Bunker, who had developed a considerable respect for García-Godoy over the course of the summer negotiations, pointed out that by giving the constitutionalists positions of responsibility the President was attempting to relieve their alienation and frustration and guide their energies into productive channels. While this approach might be risky, Bunker conceded, it might also pay large dividends; in any event, he believed it was worth waiting to see. Moreover, in his view García-Godoy's vigor and decisiveness were admirable, and it was far from undesirable that the Dominican President demonstrate his independence from the United States. According to several U.S. and Dominican officials close to the situation, Bunker's trust for García-Godoy's judgment continued to deepen as time passed, and he came to believe that even his own doubts over some of García-Godoy's actions were ultimately proven to be unwarranted.* As a result, then, of Bunker's key position in the U.S. policy-making structure, the embassy's and the State Department's objections continued to be overruled, and while Bunker played a very active role in consulting with and advising the provisional President, it was García-Godoy who made all the final decisions, even those that required full U.S. support to be successfully implemented.

One such decision was his resolve to get rid of General Wessin. As might be expected, García-Godoy's cabinet appointments and general conciliatory policy toward the constitutionalists caused considerable unhappiness in the military. The focal point of the unrest was Wessin's Armed Forces Training Center at San Isidro. Both García-Godoy and Bunker had felt for several months that Wessin would have to go, not only because of his known proclivities for military coups, but also because he had become the prime object of hatred of a good part of the Dominican population after he had ordered the bombardment and strafing of Santo Domingo during the revolution. On several occasions during the summer, García-Godoy had tried to persuade Wessin to resign and leave the country. To sweeten his departure, U.S. agents had offered to buy Wessin's modest home for $50,000, or so Wessin has testified.[2] When he refused, the United States had given serious consideration to more direct measures, such as using the IAPF to force him out of the country, but had finally decided to hold off on any drastic action in order not to jeopardize military backing of the negotiated settlement.

Shortly after the installation of the provisional government,

* According to a story told to me by a high U.S. official, months later Bunker confided to García-Godoy that he had frequently been disturbed and even angered by the latter's actions, but events had shown, he had to admit, that "you were right and I was wrong."

however, matters came to a head. With Radio San Isidro—calling itself the "Voice of the Armed Forces"—attacking the government and implying it was pro-Communist, García-Godoy moved to muzzle the station and to abolish Wessin's private shock troop unit at San Isidro. Within hours after the presidential decree of September 5 was issued, Wessin had mobilized a tank force and begun moving toward the city, ostensibly on "maneuvers." That was the final straw for both García-Godoy and Bunker. At the President's request, and with the support of the military chiefs of staff, the Ad Hoc Committee ordered IAPF units to block Wessin's force and to remove Wessin from his command. Wessin then agreed, "with a bayonet at my back,"[3] to "accept" a consular position in Miami, and shortly thereafter he was escorted to a U.S. military plane by an impressive "honor guard" of the IAPF.

Following Wessin's hasty departure, García-Godoy moved decisively to implement his program of reconciliation and military reform. On September 28 he issued a decree ordering the reintegration of the constitutionalist military into the armed forces and the transfer of the ten-thousand-man Dominican police force from the armed forces to the civilian-headed Ministry of Interior. The chiefs of staff had sought to dissuade García-Godoy from removing the police from their control, but they were even unhappier about the reintegration decree, which canceled all separations from the military after April 24, 1965, and thereby paved the way for the return to active service of units that the majority of the regulars considered as treasonous.

The final blow, as the military saw it, was the return of Bosch to the Dominican Republic at the end of September. Shortly before Bosch's scheduled arrival on September 25—the anniversary of his overthrow two years earlier—the military high command had demanded that García-Godoy refuse to allow the former President in the country, but were bluntly told that the provisional government intended to comply with its commitment to guarantee the free participation of all party leaders in the election campaign. On the appointed day, Bosch made a triumphant reentry into Santo Domingo, his route from the airport heavily guarded by the same U.S. units that five months earlier had been landed to block an uprising intended to restore him to office. To complete the irony, Bosch devoted his first public speech to an all-out attack on the United States and the Dominican military.

By the end of September, the Dominican political system was once again torn by a civil-military crisis, as the military sought by increasingly direct and even murderous methods to block civilian control of the armed forces and elections which could result in the return of Bosch to the Presidency. The first major crisis occurred in mid-October, when García-Godoy was forced to ask the IAPF to occupy Ciudad Nueva in order to forestall an apparently imminent military attack on the remnants of the constitutionalist forces there. For several weeks tensions had been rising and there had been a number of exchanges of fire between the constitutionalists and military patrols, as a result of which the military had been pressing García-Godoy for permission to conduct a house-to-house arms search. Under the terms of the Act of Reconciliation, it will be recalled, the constitutionalist military leadership was to have taken responsibility for the collection of arms from all civilians in the constitutionalist zone. The agreement, however, had been premised on a general reconciliation, and with military hatred of Bosch and the constitutionalists continuing unabated, there was understandably little disposition on the part of the constitutionalists to hurry the process of unilateral disarmament. With the somewhat reluctant support of Bunker, García-Godoy decided not to allow a forced disarmament, and refused to let the military go into Ciudad Nueva. On October 15 the President learned of a military plan to ignore his orders and move downtown in force, and so, with Caamaño's private consent, he asked the IAPF to take over the policing of the constitutionalist stronghold. (This was to be the first of a number of peacekeeping actions of the IAPF, which developed a system for the rapid movement of mobile units into trouble spots.)

Meanwhile, rightist civilian forces were also beginning to coalesce in opposition to the provisional government. In mid-November, García-Godoy and the U.S. Embassy learned of a rightist plot (apparently involving Antonio Imbert), to seize the city of Santiago, proclaim a new government, and attempt to rally Dominican military support behind it. At García-Godoy's request, an IAPF unit was flown to Santiago and with considerable fanfare occupied the airport and other key points; at the same time Bunker was issuing a warning that any attempt to overthrow the government would be in clear defiance of OAS efforts to restore democracy in the Dominican Republic. In the face of this show of force, the Santiago police and military units refused to cooperate with the conspirators and the plot collapsed.

Following this minicrisis, the overall Dominican situation seemed to improve. By the end of November, the commercial institutions of Santo Domingo had reopened, the major newspapers had resumed uncensored publication, the port of Santo Domingo was once again in full operation, and as shooting incidents diminished, the IAPF was gradually withdrawing to its barracks. On November 25, José Mayobre submitted his first optimistic report to U Thant, noting that the economy was nearly back to its prerevolutionary levels and that the return to normalcy was proceeding steadily.[4] On December 19, however, the short-lived peace was shattered by "the Matúm incident," and in the next three months the fate of the provisional government and, indeed, of democracy in the Dominican Republic, hung in the balance.

On the morning of December 19, ignoring García-Godoy's counsel, Caamaño and about one hundred of his followers set out in a heavily-armed automobile caravan for Santiago, ostensibly to celebrate a mass for one of their comrades killed in the revolution, but probably also as a show of force and of defiance against the military. During a ceremony at a Santiago cemetery, several shots were exchanged with local police or military units. Shortly after the constitutionalists arrived at the Hotel Matúm, several hundred soldiers attacked the hotel. For a while the constitutionalists successfully held off the surrounding forces, but as tanks began to move into position Caamaño telephoned García-Godoy for help. Within a few hours an IAPF unit, sent by helicopter at the President's urgent request, had arrived at the hotel, obtained a ceasefire, and transported the constitutionalists back to their base outside Santo Domingo.* But by that time about twenty men were dead, all but one of them from the attacking forces.

The battle generated severe pressures on García-Godoy to take decisive action. On the one hand, the military were humiliated at being outfought by the small constitutionalist force and were threatening vengeance if the government did not "punish" the constitutionalist leaders. On the other hand, the constitutionalists and their supporters were convinced that the military had deliberately planned to ambush and massacre the Matúm group. With tensions at the breaking point, shooting incidents again flar-

* A number of the constitutionalists believe that the IAPF deliberately dragged its feet in getting to the battle, hoping that the beleaguered Caamaño forces would be killed before they arrived. This is highly improbable, however, particularly as a number of civilians, including sixteen Americans and the U.S. Consul General at Santiago, were trapped in the besieged hotel.

ing up in Santo Domingo, and the PRD, Social Christians, and labor leadership threatening a general strike, García-Godoy temporized by ordering an investigation into the affair. A week later the results were released—the presidential commission was unable to assess responsibility for the fighting. Personally, García-Godoy to some extent shared the U.S. Embassy's feeling that the constitutionalist trek to Santiago had been provocative, but he placed greater emphasis on the irresponsible reaction of the military and suspected that the whole affair may have been planned by the military, just as the constitutionalists charged.

The President's most important conclusion, however, was that the battle had demonstrated the impossibility of proceeding toward free and peaceful elections so long as the top leadership on *both* sides remained in the country and in positions of responsibility. Accordingly, on January 6, García-Godoy announced on nationwide radio that he was ordering out of the country Caamaño, Montes Arache, and a number of other major constitutionalist leaders, on the one hand, and Minister of the Armed Forces Rivera Caminero, Chief of the Air Force de los Santos, and Army Chief Martínez Arana, on the other. For several days prior to this dramatic announcement García-Godoy had been consulting with the Ad Hoc Committee. Although Clairmont Dueñas agreed with García-Godoy's projected move, Penna Marinho and Bunker wanted the President to limit his decree to the constitutionalists and to secondary military figures, fearing that the chiefs would refuse to obey the orders and that the eventual use of the IAPF against the military might thereby become necessary. However, García-Godoy refused to modify his position, probably fearing an open break with the left if he failed to move as even-handedly against the military as against the constitutionalists. Without further consultation, then, he issued his decree, confronting the Ad Hoc Committee with a *fait accompli.*

Two days before García-Godoy's dramatic announcement to the nation, as rumors of impending military changes spread through the capital, the chiefs of staff had announced that all members of the police and military would be required to "solemnly swear they will not permit the enthronement of atheistic Communism in the Dominican Republic, against which they will fight with whatever means are necessary, against any person without regard to what may be the consequences."[5] At the same time, García-Godoy learned that this public "Pact of Honor" had been accompanied by the secret establishment of a specially-trained military unit charged with overthrowing the provisional government if any leading officers were removed from their positions!

It was therefore no surprise when the January 6th announcement triggered an open rebellion of the military. On the evening of the 6th, army units were ordered by Rivera Caminero to seize the government radio and television stations to prevent García-Godoy from explaining his decree to the nation. Meanwhile, Radio San Isidro, referring to the Pact of Honor, proclaimed that the military would not accept the changes because they endangered the "institutional integrity" of the armed forces at a time when they were severely threatened by "Communism."[6] The next morning, "Operation Honor" was launched—a military roundup of "Communists" in all parts of the country.

With his government in imminent danger of being overthrown, García-Godoy turned to the Ad Hoc Committee. In accordance with previously agreed-upon arrangements, the President submitted a formal request that the IAPF remove the armed forces from the radio and television stations and establish patrols in the vicinity of the National Palace. The committee, which had already spoken to Rivera Caminero about the day's events and demanded that the armed forces observe and maintain the law, immediately "transmitted" García-Godoy's letter to General Hugo Alvim, the commander of the IAPF, and "requested the cooperation" of the IAPF in carrying out the provisional government's request for assistance. But, perhaps taking advantage of the Ad Hoc Committee's failure to give him a direct order, Alvim balked, arguing that he could not order the IAPF to "attack" the stations and "establish the dangerous precedent of use of the IAPF against the Dominican armed forces, which would be a decision producing unforeseen political and psychological consequences." Instead, he suggested, the crisis should be handled by "political" methods.

It was not the first time that Alvim and the Ad Hoc Committee had clashed. The rigid and simplistic Brazilian general had the typical military man's contempt for "politicians" and for negotiated political solutions. After being frustrated in his desire to "clean up" the constitutionalists in the summer of 1965, he became increasingly close to the Dominican chiefs of staff and openly shared their view that García-Godoy was, at best, a dupe of the Communists, whose real purpose was to destroy the Dominican armed forces.

Meanwhile, García-Godoy had learned of the IAPF's refusal to take action, and he angrily notified the Ad Hoc Committee that he was about to demand an emergency meeting of the OAS Council and publicly denounce the failure of the committee to help him. But by now Bunker himself was infuriated at Alvim's insubordination and reiterated in stronger terms his demand for immediate IAPF action, warning Alvim that if he continued to delay he would be bypassed and General Palmer would be ordered to use U.S. troops to comply with the Ad Hoc Committee's orders. At the same time, the committee publicly announced that under the mandate of the provisional government García-Godoy had the right to make any military changes he deemed necessary. The President, the committee added, would have its full support and cooperation in carrying out this mandate, and any attempt to overthrow the government would be treated as direct defiance of the OAS. That evening the OAS Council met in secret session in Washington, preparing to order the use of force in defense of the provisional government.[7]

Faced with these pressures, Alvim reluctantly dispatched an IAPF unit to the radio station, whereupon the Dominican troops abandoned it without a fight. In fact, García-Godoy and Bunker had all along expected the matter to be resolved without bloodshed, for the President had been informed by a loyal officer that the unit at the station was under orders to leave at the first IAPF show of force. With the U.S. position now clear, Rivera Caminero also complied with Bunker's demand that "Operation Honor" be discontinued.

The stress of the Dominican civil-military crisis had forced to the surface a steadily building parallel crisis between the OAS political authorities and their military arm—i.e., between the Ad Hoc Committee and the IAPF. Back in early May, when the United States, concerned with deepening the involvement of the Latin Americans and legitimizing the presence of its own troops, was pressing for the early establishment of an inter-American military force in the Dominican Republic, the Johnson Administration had tried to persuade some of the more democratic Latin American countries to participate in the proposed force. For a while, it appeared that Argentina, Colombia, and Venezuela would make significant contributions and that the force would be headed by a Venezuelan general closely associated with Rómulo Betancourt. But, as the debates in the OAS Council proceeded, the liberal and even the centrist states became increasingly wary of any involvement in the affair: there were conflicts about which Latin American states would predominate in the force; concern that the United States would continue to exercise operational control over the force regardless of its formal structure;* and, most importantly, rising doubts about the wisdom of participating in a collective effort whose ultimate purposes and effects were unclear—the debates on the IAPF had spanned the period in which the United States established, and then almost immediately thereafter appeared about to disestablish, the Imbert government. Not knowing against whom or in behalf of what objectives the IAPF might be used, then, several states, notably Colombia and Panama, decided against participation in it. Finally, growing domestic opposition in Argentina and Venezuela to any involvement in the Dominican crisis forced those governments to reconsider their tentative commitments to the force.

In the end, the sole democratic state to participate in the IAPF was Costa Rica, which sent only a token unit of twenty policemen. The major Latin American contingents were provided by the military dictatorships of Brazil, Honduras, Nicaragua, and Paraguay. As a result, the political orientation of the force commanders was rightist and strongly anti-Communist, a general perspective, indeed, that was shared by most of the U.S. officers as well. The IAPF assessment of the crisis was perhaps stated most succinctly by a U.S. colonel, in a reported remark that caused a considerable storm in the OAS Council: "Those are Communists we are fighting in there, and the only way to deal with a Communist is to kill him. The sooner and quicker it is done, the safer the civilian population will be."[9]

Until the January crisis the OAS civil-military conflict had remained predominantly below the surface. Bunker's powerful

* In early June, in fact, the commander of the U.S. contingent in the IAPF was quoted as remarking that in the event of conflict between the United States and the OAS, he, of course, would follow the orders of his government. Although Secretary of State Rusk quickly asserted that it was firm U.S. policy that its force would operate under the direction of the commander of the IAPF, the continuing U.S. effort to multilateralize the force was not assisted.[8]

position had ensured that it was his views, not the IAPF's, that determined policy, although he was forced to spend a good deal of time explaining, persuading, and cajoling. In the final analysis, though, political control of the IAPF had remained assured only because, just as the OAS states had suspected, the United States was prepared to bypass the Latin American contingent in the IAPF. (After September, 1965, the IAPF consisted of 9400 U.S. troops, 1,100 Brazilians, and 700 from Honduras, Nicaragua, Paraguay, and Costa Rica.)[10] And while there was doubt about whether Alvim might obey even a direct order to, say, arrest the Dominican chiefs of staff or attack a Dominican military unit, there was none about the responsiveness of the U.S. troops. The U.S. commander, General Bruce Palmer, shared Alvim's dislike for the constitutionalists and aversion to any action against the Dominican military, but he was first and foremost a professional soldier who obeyed orders. From time to time, just to be sure, Palmer was reminded by Washington that Bunker was in complete charge. In any event, according to close observers Bunker's long effort at the political education of the U.S. commanders eventually in part paid off, as Palmer's views were said to have become more moderate and sophisticated.

Thus, the Dominican crisis had put to a test the system of political control of the military, not only within the OAS but in the U.S. Government structure itself. All in all, the system worked quite well: despite persistent and frequently deep differences between U.S. political authorities and their military commanders in the field,* at no time was the fabric of civil-military relations severely strained.

While in extreme circumstances Alvim could be bypassed, then, as long as he had nominal authority over the IAPF he could

* According to "J. B. Bender," in private the military were given to "scathing denunciations" of Bunker.[11]

complicate the work of the Ad Hoc Committee and do considerable damage in the Dominican Republic. The January events made it clear that he was supporting the military revolt against the García-Godoy government and very probably was encouraging the armed forces to believe that the IAPF would never be used against them. In fact, though, Bunker now foresaw the distinct possibility that the IAPF might have to be so employed, and he therefore decided that Alvim could no longer be tolerated. Accordingly, at the end of January, Bunker made a secret trip to Brazil to talk over the matter with General Castelo Branco, head of the military junta that had taken power in 1964. Alvim had been an embarrassment to the junta as well, especially in light of its anxiety to retain U.S. support. Thus, Castelo was disposed to cooperate, and he soon agreed to a face-saving formula under which both Alvim and Palmer would be removed, ostensibly as part of a normal rotation of duty. The new Brazilian commander, General Alvaro Braga, was a more compliant man, and he was instructed by his government to be responsive to whatever orders the Ad Hoc Committee issued. With his appointment in February, the civil-military crisis within the crisis ended.

It should be noted that the whole affair illustrated that sometimes there may be an unrecognized price to be paid for funneling national policies through international organizations. "International organization," "multilateral," and "collective action" tend to be honorific words eliciting favorable connotations, especially among the generally liberal and internationalist elite sectors of public opinion. Thus, behind the frequent exhortations to policy makers to allow international organizations to play a greater role in national policies lies the implicit assumption that collective bodies will exert a moderating, liberalizing, or enlightening influence. That this is not invariably so was amply demonstrated by the Dominican crisis, in which the conservative, nondemocratic majority in the OAS occasionally made it more difficult for the United States to follow relatively liberal policies than if it had acted entirely unilaterally.

Although the strong support of the Ad Hoc Committee for the García-Godoy government had made an outright military takeover impossible, the chiefs of staff remained in a state of insubordination and refused to comply with García-Godoy's decree removing them from their positions. On January 23, however, most of the top constitutionalist leaders, including Caamaño and Montes Arache, announced their decision to comply with the decree, pointing out that they had fought a revolution dedicated to restoring constitutional rule and political control over the military. Their compliance had been facilitated by a formal Ad Hoc Committee guarantee to protect the remaining constitutionalist military; pending their reintegration into the armed forces, the constitutionalists would be stationed in a special camp outside Santo Domingo to be guarded night and day by strong IAPF contingents under strict orders to repel any attack on it.*

Following the departure of the constitutionalists, García-Godoy and the Ad Hoc Committee increased their pressures on the chiefs of staff to comply with the January 6th decree. With the new IAPF commanders now adding their weight to this concerted effort, in early February the chiefs finally proposed a compromise: Minister of Defense Rivera Caminero would leave if the Army and Air Force chiefs—Martínez Arana and de los Santos—could retain their positions and the President would promise not to make any further changes in the armed forces

* There were also indications that the constitutionalists' decision to leave the country had been encouraged by Bosch and the PRD, perhaps in part because Caamaño represented a potential political threat to Bosch.

command. García-Godoy, however, refused to give any such unconditional guarantees, agreeing merely to refrain from further changes after Rivera's resignation as long as "those in command shape their conduct to complete obedience to the Government and absolute impartiality in the forthcoming electoral campaign."[12] Under heavy pressure from Bunker, the military leaders reluctantly acceded to this arrangement, although not before soliciting a formal letter from the Ad Hoc Committee "noting and endorsing" García-Godoy's qualified concession.

The deal did not last long. On February 9 a large student demonstration was held in front of the National Palace to demand the removal of all the military chiefs. Suddenly, the police fired into the crowd, killing five and wounding thirty others. In retaliation, mobs of students and workers coursed through the city, attacking isolated soldiers and policemen and killing two of them. On the next day, PRD and trade union leaders announced their support for a general strike, to remain in effect until all the chiefs of staff had been stripped of their commands and a new police chief appointed. The strike was extremely effective. Within a few days the entire country was deeply affected and Santo Domingo was almost completely paralyzed. At the same time, violence between the police and the strikers was increasing.

For over a week the provisional government made no attempt to bring the strike to an end. García-Godoy's attitude toward it was ambivalent: on the one hand, he was seriously concerned about the violence and economic chaos it was producing, but on the other he was fully in accord with the need to make further major changes and thus he probably in part welcomed the added leverage the strike gave him. As the situation worsened, the President decided to avail himself of the escape clause in his earlier agreement with the military and to insist on the departure of all the chiefs of staff, as originally stipulated in the presidential decree of early January. Moreover, he warned both the military and the Ad Hoc Committee that he was prepared to resign from office if the armed forces continued their refusal to comply with his authority.

Within a few days the military had provided its answer: García-Godoy's earlier letter and its cautious endorsement by the Ad Hoc Committee were released to the press, amidst the standard charges that further "tampering" with the armed forces would lead to their destruction and a surrender to "Communism." Accordingly, García-Godoy discussed the possibility of his resignation with his cabinet, which unanimously decided that in that event it would also resign.

On the afternoon of February 16 García-Godoy reported these events to Bunker and informed him that he would announce the resignation of the provisional government that evening on nationwide radio. Bunker pleaded with him not to do so, warning that the resulting chaos, if not outright anarchy, would surely lead to a new influx of U.S. troops and the occupation of the entire country. To underline his point, Bunker asked for at least a twenty-four-hour delay, if the President should decide to go through with his resignation, in order that the U.S. fleet could be brought closer to shore and readied for action.

But before taking precipitate action, Bunker urged, García-Godoy should consider some other alternatives. The United States and the Ad Hoc Committee fully sympathized with the need to bring the military under control, he told the President, and supported even García-Godoy's decision to disregard his earlier deal with the chiefs of staff and make a clean sweep of them. Indeed, Bunker promised, if the President asked the IAPF to remove the chiefs directly, à la Wessin, he, Bunker, would see to it that the IAPF did so. Once that was accomplished, García-Godoy could declare the general strike illegal if he chose (he didn't), with the inter-American forces standing prepared to ensure that orderly conditions necessary to allow the resumption of economic activity would prevail.

The course of action proposed by Bunker had, in fact, been under U.S. consideration for some time. Although initially Bunker had been cool toward García-Godoy's decision to remove the chiefs and had flatly opposed Clairmont Dueñas' repeated suggestions that the IAPF be used to enforce the presidential decree, he had become increasingly convinced that García-Godoy was right in his insistence that the military crisis had to be satisfactorily resolved if the elections were to be genuinely free: a military still acting as a law unto itself, it could no longer be doubted, would never permit Juan Bosch to return to power.

Another factor in Bunker's change of heart, apparently, was his growing revulsion at the tactics of the military, some of whom, true to their Trujillo heritage, did not shrink even from the attempted murder of García-Godoy. In one plot, a high military leader asked the President to provide about $5,000 for "civic action" projects, in order, ostensibly, to improve the "image" of the armed forces. Pleased with the military's apparent new concern with its public relations and its responsiveness to the latest U.S. ideas on the proper role of the armed forces, García-Godoy provided the money. His pleasure was somewhat dimmed, however, when he later learned that the money was used to hire a group of men to kill him! In another remarkable incident, one which seems to have been instrumental in Bunker's hardening posture toward the armed forces, García-Godoy learned of a military plot to have him machine-gunned as he left the National Palace. Calling Bunker to the Palace, the President asked for IAPF protection. Although he complied with the request, Bunker was skeptical of García-Godoy's information, but only until he was provided with a tape recording of the telephone conversation in which the order for the assassination was given.[13]

Another consideration was the considerable restiveness in the OAS at the Ad Hoc Committee's seeming impotence to help García-Godoy resolve the military crisis. Venezuela and Costa Rica, for example, whose support Washington considered very important, were openly calling for direct IAPF action in support of the provisional government.[14] As a result of all these factors, then, the Johnson Administration, albeit with some reluctance and trepidation, authorized Bunker to utilize the IAPF against the Dominican chiefs if García-Godoy so requested. In anticipation of this eventuality, contingency plans were drawn up to reinforce the IAPF on short notice if the situation so required.

García-Godoy, however, was not willing to call on the IAPF to enforce his orders. A dedicated nationalist, he had no stomach for using a foreign occupation force against his own compatriots, no matter what the justification, especially since he considered his problem to be not with the military as a whole but only with a few high officials. Moreover, he feared, direct IAPF action might so embitter the armed forces as to destroy whatever chance remained that they could be brought under genuine and lasting political control; sooner or later the inter-American force would have to depart and there would then be nothing to prevent the military from wreaking its revenge, particularly if the beneficiary of IAPF action was Juan Bosch. Even short of that, the President reasoned, the use of force would certainly demoralize and humiliate the military and perhaps even destroy their capacity to maintain internal order, thereby creating a dangerous vacuum of power in the country. Yet another factor, to be sure, may have been García-Godoy's own political future, which would hardly have been helped by resort to the IAPF. In any event, though, the entire provisional government, liberals and conservatives alike, was in agreement that the problem had to be resolved not by foreign forces but "*como Dominicanos*"—as Dominicans.

Be that as it may, all the alternatives seemed grim. As García-Godoy himself has put it, "every door I looked through, I saw chaos." If he turned to the IAPF in desperation, his hopes for stable democracy over the long run might well be dashed. If he did not, though, there probably could not be genuinely free elections in the short run. And, if he resigned, anarchy would reign and the foreign occupation would be extended and prolonged indefinitely. As a result, the President decided not to resign but to make a final effort to gain control over the military.

Fortunately, at this point the tide began to shift. Taking as his model Rómulo Betancourt's post-1958 course in Venezuela, García-Godoy for months had been visiting military bases and outposts all over the country, seeking to break the monolithic military front against his government. Painstakingly, the President sought to convince the armed forces that (in his own formulation) his aim was not to destroy them but to save them, and that their own best interests required subordination to political authority. Gradually, his persuasiveness and patience had paid off, as key officers declared their allegiance to him. Particularly crucial was the role of the new Minister of Defense, General Enrique Pérez y Pérez, who was cut from a different mold than his predecessors. Pérez y Pérez was apparently a true professional soldier, genuinely dedicated to the creation of an honest, respected, and nonpolitical military. For some weeks the new military commander had been supporting García-Godoy's struggle to clean out the old guard, and his own efforts to build support among the officer corps were also beginning to pay off.

By the middle of February, then, pressures on the recalcitrant chiefs to resign were coming not only from García-Godoy,

Bunker, and the IAPF commanders, but were beginning to develop from within the Dominican armed forces themselves. In late February, two events finally tipped the balance. First of all, perhaps seeking to allay persistent military suspicions that he was a front man for Bosch, García-Godoy removed from office about ninety government officials, the overwhelming majority of whom were constitutionalists or PRD members. Second, Bunker's ploy of moving the fleet close to Dominican shores convinced the waverers that time was running out. On February 26, Martínez Arana and de los Santos accepted a face-saving formula under which they resigned as heads of the Army and Air Force to accept meaningless positions as "vice-ministers" of the armed forces. Rejecting a last-minute military effort to dictate the choice of the successors, García-Godoy appointed two officers in whom he had confidence.

With these actions the military crisis ended. But the costs had been great. For one thing, the continuing bitterness between the constitutionalists and the military had undercut the efforts of the provisional government to disarm the civilian population. While most of the heavy armaments captured by the constitutionalists during the revolution were recovered, tens of thousands of small arms, machine guns, and explosives were never turned in. The price of continuing political tensions in a heavily armed society is reckoned in the almost daily gun battles that still rend the Dominican scene.

Also, the long revolt of the police and the military made it impossible for the provisional government to stem the terrorism that took the lives of perhaps several hundred constitutionalists. Some of the killings may have been individual acts of revenge for incidents arising out of the revolution, but it is quite probable that a good many were a consequence of a deliberate military effort to discredit the provisional government and generally to exacerbate the prevailing instability and tension. Not a single murder was ever punished, for even when the killers could be identified the insubordination of the police and the military left the provisional government helpless to act.

Similarly, the crisis undercut plans for the implementation of the reintegration decree of September 28. On December 11, just a few days before the Matúm affair, García-Godoy had announced that all constitutionalists who had been on active duty when the revolution broke out would be reintegrated by the end of the month.* By then, fewer than seven hundred of the original fifteen hundred military constitutionalists were to be affected, as some had drifted back to their regular posts shortly after the initial revolution, some had quit the military or were unwilling to expose themselves to retribution by returning to their former units, and some had been cashiered by the constitutionalists themselves. The government plan called for the dispersion of the constitutionalists throughout the military structure, rather than their retention in one unit. While the former procedure perhaps increased the risk that individual constitutionalists would be harassed and persecuted, neither the United States nor García-Godoy was willing to accept the problems that the continued existence of a cohesive constitutionalist force might entail. Moreover, the constitutionalists themselves were willing to take their chances as part of the regular military structure, in the hope that they would be more able to exert influence over the military than if they were isolated in one small group.

In the climate prevailing after the Matúm battle, however,

* As for those who joined the constitutionalist ranks *after* the revolution, only those who earlier had been removed from the regular military for political reasons were to be reintegrated; without fuss, Caamaño agreed that his civilian militia and former soldiers who had been retired from active service because of incompetence, corruption, or criminal behavior would not be included.

the reintegration of individual constitutionalists would obviously have jeopardized the lives of all or most of them. For the rest of the tenure of the provisional government, therefore, the matter had to be put aside. After the Balaguer government took office, most of the remaining constitutionalist leaders were sent abroad as "military attachés," and about three hundred of the enlisted men, including most of Montes Arache's frogmen, accepted offers to come to the United States for retraining in civilian skills. Many of them found jobs in the States and remained here. Ultimately only about one hundred constitutionalists were actually reintegrated, with most being assigned to meaningless guard-duty tasks. According to PRD charges, two years later even those few were still being harassed or had been forced to resign.[15]

By far the most serious cost of the crisis, though, was that it ended without any profound changes in the nature of the Dominican armed forces. Once again, the presumed exigencies of the immediate crisis undercut the initial U.S. commitment to begin the process of a major restructuring of the military. To cautious U.S. officials the time never seemed quite ripe. In the summer of 1965, it will be recalled, priority had been given to winning military assent for a political settlement, with projected reforms to be postponed until after the establishment of the provisional government. Once that government was in office, though, the civil-military crisis again focused attention on the short-term problem of neutralizing the military in the forthcoming electoral process. And the price for that was a general understanding that once the shifts at the top were effected, García-Godoy would make no further changes.

As Bunker now saw the problem, basic military reform had to be treated as a continuing rather than an immediate program; it could not really be accomplished merely by changing the chiefs, for their attitudes were shared by most of the officer corps as a whole. As a result, Bunker thought, fundamental changes could be brought about only by the virtual liquidation of the existing military establishment, a course precluded by the need to preserve a bulwark against Communism. For the present, he concluded, the appropriate U.S. aim should be the building of confidence between the military and the provisional government, with major changes postponed until the next government took office. Accordingly, at the end of February, Bunker insisted to García-Godoy that he must treat the compromise de los Santos-Martínez Arana formula as the definite resolution of the immediate military problem and warned that for the duration of the provisional government the United States would not be disposed to support any further personnel shifts, let alone more far-reaching reform.

7

The Elections and After

ALTHOUGH VERY LITTLE has been written on the Dominican crisis since the elections of June, 1966, there appears to be a fairly widespread assumption that the failure of Bosch to win the Presidency can be explained only by rightist intimidation of the Bosch vote and/or various forms of rigging which the United States acquiesced in or, indeed, deliberately instigated.[1] (A widely repeated story in the Dominican Republic has President Johnson exploding on being informed of a pre-election poll showing Bosch in the lead and warning that he would certainly not stand for that.) Such speculation is natural and logical enough. After all, the United States *had* intervened in order to prevent the victory of a revolution dedicated to the return of Bosch to the Presidency. Would not a Bosch electoral victory represent such a humiliating Dominican repudiation of the intervention as to be totally unacceptable to the Johnson Administration?

In fact, as has been pointed out earlier, the United States had decided on genuinely free elections shortly after the intervention. While the assessment that Bosch could be beaten by Balaguer played a role of some importance in that decision, the administration did not waver from it even after a pre-election embassy assessment pointed to a probable Bosch victory. On the contrary, all available evidence indicates that the United

States applied persistent and sustained pressures to ensure that the elections would be free and that a Bosch victory would be accepted by the Dominican armed forces.

To be sure, it is unlikely that U.S. policy was a mere reflection of an abstract commitment to free elections—Vietnam alone demonstrates the ease with which proclaimed values can fall before what are thought to be the sterner requirements of *Realpolitik*. Of far greater importance, it may be suspected, was Johnson's well-known yearning for the accolades of posterity.* Whatever distaste and trepidation administration officials felt at the prospect of a Bosch victory—and there is no doubt that Johnson himself as well as other important members of his administration felt exactly that way—far greater weight was given to the desire that the intervention be seen, in retrospect, as legitimate and successful, regardless of the initial criticisms of it. That could not happen, the administration knew, unless the elections were universally accepted—in the Dominican Republic, the United States, and in world opinion—as genuinely free. And, with the Dominican Republic swarming with OAS observers, U.S. and Latin American journalists, labor-union missions, and representatives of private groups, nearly all of them pro-Bosch, suspicious of U.S. policy, and assiduously on the lookout for signs of tampering, there was little prospect of U.S. shenanigans, or even a too-obvious preference for Balaguer, going unexposed. In short, for the elections to be seen as free, they *had* to be free.† Moreover, they could not be made farcical by a routine post-election coup.

* Cf. Johnson's earlier reported remark on Imbert: "I'm not going down in history as the man responsible for putting another Trujillo in power in the Dominican Republic."[2]

† Even José Peña Gómez, the fiery and strongly anti-American Secretary General of the PRD, recognized this, at one point explaining his pre-election confidence that Bosch would win with the observation that U.S. policy needed free elections.[3]

As a result, the Johnson Administration went to great lengths to convince Bosch, the Dominican military, the IAPF, and even the U.S. Embassy that U.S. policy in the elections would be scrupulously neutral. Indeed, the very number of times that this policy was pointedly emphasized to the embassy, and by the embassy to Dominicans, constituted an implicit recognition of the doubt and skepticism about Washington's policy that reached into the U.S. Government itself. In early March, for example, a guidance sheet was distributed to all members of the U.S. country team in the Dominican Republic (aimed particularly, no doubt, at the military mission) setting forth U.S. neutrality and warning against any deviation from this policy, even casual, supposedly unofficial statements of personal preferences. Similarly, at the same time Bunker sent a letter to the IAPF commanders reiterating that their mission was to support the efforts of the provisional government in preparing for free elections and directing them to avoid any actions or statements that would appear to be designed to influence the outcome of the elections; all IAPF officers, the directive continued, would be responsible for insuring that both the letter and spirit of this policy would be fully observed by all men under their command.

Meanwhile, Bunker and the new U.S. Ambassador-designate, John Crimmins,* were meeting regularly with Dominican political leaders in efforts to persuade them of the sincerity of U.S. policy. Understandably enough, it took considerable persuasion to convince the military and conservative groups that the United States would not only demand free and honest elections and use its power to assist the provisional government toward that goal, but would fully support whoever won the elections. Even

* Crimmins did not officially assume the post of Ambassador until after the elections. However, after the reassignment of Bennett in early April, Crimmins, as Deputy Chief of Mission, was the key embassy figure.

after repeated assertions of U.S. neutrality, for example, the worried conservatives were surprised at the embassy's refusal to exercise even informal influence to try to persuade several splinter rightist candidates to withdraw from the race in order to avoid splitting the Balaguer vote.

Most skeptical of all, of course, was Bosch himself. In fact, as the campaign wore on the primary concern of U.S. officials was not so much that Bosch would win, but that his deep depression about his prospects of successfully governing if he should win would induce him to drop his candidacy and thus, by making an apparent mockery of the elections, greatly complicate prospects for the restoration of peace in the Dominican Republic. To allay Bosch's concern, Bunker and Crimmins repeatedly met with him and sought to convince him that the United States would make every effort to work with and support him.[4] Moreover, Bosch's charges that rightist intimidation of PRD activists and organizers was making it impossible for him to campaign outside Santo Domingo were taken with great seriousness. On several occasions the State Department asked the embassy for detailed assessments of these charges and recommendations on ways in which the United States might apply influence and pressure to keep the police and military under control. Although the embassy (and other observers as well) believed that Bosch was exaggerating and that the overall political climate was reasonably good, it did confirm that terrorist acts were occurring and conceded that Bosch had some reason to be concerned for his personal safety and that of his followers. Several actions were taken: García-Godoy was urged to intensify his efforts to arrest terrorism; Imbert and other Dominicans known or suspected to be behind rightist actions were told in strong terms of U.S. disapproval; the Human Rights Committee and other OAS observation teams were encouraged to tour the country-

LEFT: *Juan Bosch* (City News Bureau) MIDDLE: *Ambassador William Tapley Bennett, Jr., and Dr. José A. Mora.* (Pan American Union) BOTTOM: *John Bartlow Martin (right) and General Imbert—"Like the sparrow mesmerized by the snake, Martin was to be undone by his peculiar, somewhat reluctant fascination for Imbert."* (Photo by Lynn Pelham, LIFE Magazine © Time, Inc.)

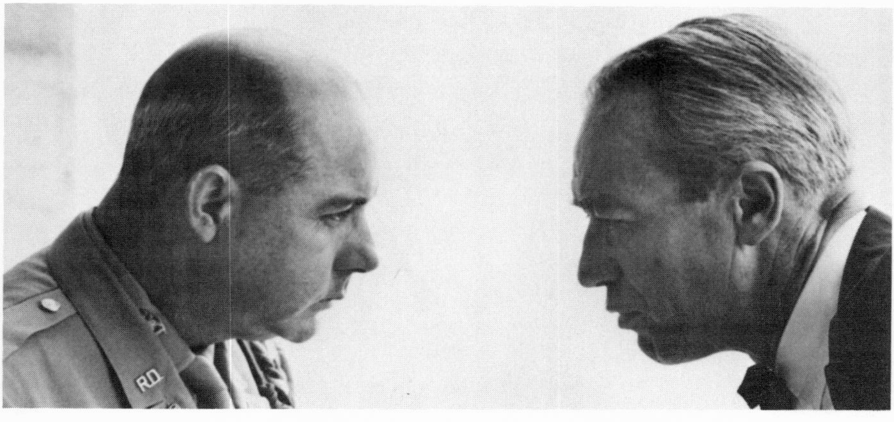

Ambassador Ellsworth Bunker (right) and Dominican Ambassador José Antonio Bonilla Atiles at OAS meeting in Washington, May 1. (Pan American Union)

Dominican citizens reading the "Declaration to the Dominican People" issued by the OAS Ad Hoc Committee, proposing a peaceful solution to the crises. (Pan American Union)

Colonel Francisco Caamoño Deñó, the rebel leader, greets Ambassador Bunker. (Pan American Union)

The IAPF command (left to right): Major Cibulars; General Hugo Alvim, Commander of the IAPF; Dr. José A. Mora, Secretary General of the OAS; General Telmo O. Vargas, military adviser to Mora; Lieutenant General Bruce Palmer, Jr., Deputy Commander of the IAPF. (Pan American Union)

Hector Garcia-Godoy. (Foto Fernandez)

The OAS Peace Mission (left to right): Frank Morrice, Jr., of Panama; Dr. Ricardo Colombo of Argentina; Dr. Carlos Garcia Bauer, of Guatemala; Dr. Alfredo Vazquez Carrizosa, of Colombia; and Ilmar Penna Marinho, of Brazil. (Pan American Union)

side continuously in order to exercise the strongest possible psychological deterrent; and, most importantly, the leaders of the armed forces were again informed that the United States was firmly committed to supporting a Bosch government and would not hesitate to use its influence and power to that end.

I am convinced that the embassy's assurances to Bosch of U.S. support were completely genuine.[5] On the very eve of the elections, the embassy and the State Department once again concurred on this policy, with Bunker and Crimmins advising that the government avoid any statements indicating either jubilation or disappointment over the results. This was not just a matter of public posture, for most U.S. officials expected a Bosch victory and were reasonably optimistic at the prospects of working with him. A number of concrete steps had already been decided upon. Detailed plans for a large-scale economic-assistance program, to be put into effect regardless of who won the elections, had been prepared and were ready for immediate implementation. Second, in addition to making public appeals to the Dominican people to accept the results of the elections and privately urging García-Godoy not to hesitate to use the police and even the armed forces to quell possible rightist violence in the event of Bosch's election, the United States was prepared to order the IAPF into action if necessary to restore order, particularly if the armed forces themselves should try to overturn the results. Most importantly of all, by late spring the Johnson Administration had in principle decided to keep the IAPF in the Dominican Republic for a limited time if so requested by the incoming government.

The question, however, of when, how, and under what circumstances the IAPF would be withdrawn was extremely sensitive and fraught with a number of pitfalls. Reflecting the rising tide of Dominican nationalism, the public posture of every Dominican candidate, even the rightist Rafael Bonnelly, included the demand for the immediate withdrawal of the IAPF. Moreover, García-Godoy, no doubt with an eye toward history if not his own political future, was pressing for at least a start toward withdrawal before the elections. To this end, the provisional President in early April sent an emissary around the hemisphere to seek Latin American support for the early removal of the inter-American force. The mission infuriated Crimmins, who considered it an unconscionable grandstand ploy that might even so discomfort Bosch as to lead to his withdrawal from the election. In fact, though, García-Godoy was quite prepared to modify his position if Bosch would clearly and publicly indicate a desire to have the IAPF stay on, but without such a statement he was concerned—in my view quite understandably—that Bosch would play the double game of privately asking for an IAPF extension while publicly denouncing García-Godoy's "failure" to live up to his promise to restore national independence before the elected government took office.

As matters developed, both Balaguer and Bosch, despite their public positions, were strongly opposed to an immediate IAPF withdrawal. For some time, PRD leaders had been reevaluating their position, and most of them now were prepared temporarily to swallow their nationalistic pride and bitterness over the intervention, recognizing that IAPF support would provide an essential underpinning to a Bosch government. By mid-May, Bosch had indirectly but quite concretely made it known to the embassy and to García-Godoy that he wanted the IAPF to remain in the Dominican Republic for at least eighteen months after the elections. Balaguer, meanwhile, was talking about a six- to nine-month stay.

Thus, the Johnson Administration was caught in a squeeze play, for whatever the private positions of the leading Dominican candidates and its own assessment of the proper course, pressures in the OAS as well as from Dominican and U.S. public opinion were building for a quick withdrawal after the June elections. To delay settlement of the matter any longer would inevitably look as though the United States was planning an indefinite occupation of the Dominican Republic, particularly if Bosch should win.*

Accordingly, the State Department proposed to the embassy that, in order to emphasize U.S. neutrality in the elections, a pre-election statement should be issued, announcing the OAS intention to withdraw the IAPF promptly after the elections unless the new Dominican President should formally request otherwise. Crimmins, however, an extremely able and liberal career diplomat who was increasingly moving into a position of equality with Bunker, took vigorous exception to this course. Reaffirming that there was no doubt that both Bosch and Balaguer wanted the IAPF kept on, he pointed out that it would be politically almost impossible for either of them to make a formal public request to that end. In that case, ironically enough, a U.S. initiative might well be interpreted as a handwashing exercise or even a green light for a rightist Dominican movement against Bosch. As for the department's worries that the United States would take a political beating by keeping the force on, Crimmins argued that Washington could "live with" uninformed criticism so long as the new President refrained from public calls for withdrawal for the three months or so that Crimmins thought should be the maximum extension of the occupation.

* To illustrate: even *after* the facts were in, a year later John Gerassi was able to write that "Balaguer's election was dominated by the popular desire to get rid of the U.S. Marines, something that was most unlikely if Bosch won."[6] This, despite the fact that before the elections the United States had publicly committed itself to withdraw.

The differences were resolved by a compromise. On May 27, a few days before the elections, the six hemispheric states with contingents in the IAPF (the United States, Brazil, Paraguay, Honduras, Nicaragua, and Costa Rica) formally requested that the OAS initiate steps to bring about the withdrawal of the IAPF after the elections. The actual decision to do so, the note went on, would be made in consultation with the forthcoming President and only "in orderly fashion and as soon as conditions permit."[7] The escape clause reflected the administration's decision to work out the actual details of withdrawal after the elections, in consultation with both García-Godoy and the President-elect. At that time, Bunker and Crimmins would try to find a formula that would meet García-Godoy's political needs but would be compatible with the main objective of assuring the new government a reasonable degree of security at the outset of its term. The main lines of such a formula, administration thinking ran, would be a public announcement of a staged withdrawal plan, which would nominally begin while García-Godoy was still in office, but which could be stretched out for a number of months if the new President would agree to pass the private but definite word to OAS members that such a course met with his approval.

All of these relatively minor differences within the U.S. Government should not obscure the main point: the Johnson Administration was unmistakably prepared not only to accept an elected Bosch but to use military force for some months to come if necessary to keep him in office. To be sure, U.S. support could not really be unlimited. Obviously Bosch would not be permitted to make deals with, or in any other way strengthen, the position of the Communists. As, under the circumstances, Bosch would hardly do so, the more likely test of the outermost parameters of U.S. tolerance would have been Bosch's handling of the military. On the one hand, so high State Department officials claimed, the United States fully expected and was prepared to support further substantial changes in the armed forces while the IAPF was around to make them stick, and just before the elections the embassy warned the Dominican military against equating any and all forthcoming Bosch economic, social, or military reforms, no matter how moderate, necessary, or gradual, with a "Communist threat." On the other hand, however, it is extremely unlikely that the United States would have acceded to a Bosch attempt to complete the April revolution by political means, for example by making Caamaño Chief of Staff of the Armed Forces and installing other constitutionalist military leaders in command positions. Apparently Bosch understood this quite well, for he reassured Crimmins that if elected he would proceed cautiously and would certainly not put Caamaño or anyone else who would arouse such strong military opposition in charge of the armed forces. The practical problems aside, there were indications that there was growing friction between Bosch and Caamaño, so that in any case Bosch would not have been likely to strengthen further a potential political rival.

On June 1, 1966, in an atmosphere of remarkable order and tranquillity, the Dominicans went to the polls. With the turnout exceeding that for the 1962 elections by more than 300,000, Balaguer won by a margin surpassing nearly everyone's expectations, receiving 770,000 votes (57 percent) to Bosch's 525,000 (39 percent). Five splinter parties on the far right got a total of 3.5 percent, and the extreme left, represented by the 14th of June movement, less than 1 percent. Balaguer carried 22 of the country's 27 provinces, with a better than 2-1 margin outside

Santo Domingo. In the capital, the Bosch vote was down to 60 percent (from 77 percent in 1962), and even in Ciudad Nueva, the constitutionalist zone, Balaguer got 33.6 percent.

Aside from the scores of journalists from all over the world, no less than five different groups had officially or semi-officially monitored the electoral process to ascertain if it was genuinely free: the UN mission, the Inter-American Commission on Human Rights, an OAS Electoral Assistance Mission, an OAS Electoral Observation Mission, and a group of seventy American liberals, headed by Norman Thomas and Bayard Rustin. Most of these groups were overwhelmingly pro-Bosch or at least liberal in their sentiments, particularly the Thomas group and the forty-two-man OAS observation mission, headed by Gonzalo Facio of Costa Rica and made up of Latin American Council representatives, former diplomats, national electoral officials, jurists, academicians, and journalists. Many members of these groups apparently fully expected to find signs that the elections would be rigged; at one point Bunker reported to the State Department that his contacts with the Thomas mission indicated that many were prepared to believe the worst of the United States and the best of the constitutionalists in all situations.

Yet there was unanimous agreement among all these groups that the elections were remarkably free, open, and fair. The OAS Electoral Assistance Mission reported that there had been no discrimination against any political group in the use of the mass media and no "undue limitations" on party campaigning, meetings, or demonstrations. Beyond that, according to the mission, the general atmosphere throughout the campaign had been very good, with no significant disruption of peace and order: "The occurrence of one or another isolated incident of no importance does not change the general picture."[8] On election day itself, according to the official report of the Facio group, all was in order at the polls. There were no complaints received by any member, and direct observation at various polling places throughout the country revealed no cases of police or military interference. Voting was in closed booths and the secrecy of the ballot was observed everywhere.[9]

The OAS reports were verified by the Thomas group, which had made several trips to the Dominican Republic during the campaign and on election day had been out in force in the countryside. Thomas and Rustin made several statements to the press praising the elections, and according to Bunker, Allard Lowenstein, later one of the leaders of the 1968 McCarthy movement in the United States and presently a Congressman from New York, privately congratulated the Ad Hoc Committee on the success of its efforts to bring about genuinely free elections and conceded that he had found nothing to criticize.

Nonetheless, one can still find considerable feeling in the Dominican Republic, and to some extent among liberal or leftist journalists and writers in the United States, that the elections were rigged by Dominican rightists or the United States itself or, at least, made meaningless by military intimidation in the countryside.* Most of this appears to stem from shock at the size of Balaguer's margin and a face-value acceptance of Bosch's post-election charges of fraud and terror. For several weeks after the elections, Bosch and some PRD leaders kept up a steady drumfire of denunciation, although on June 14 Bosch publicly conceded defeat and admitted that he could not prove the existence of enough fraud to have altered the overall

* For example, Richard Barnet asserts that the elections were held in a "context of continued intimidation of the military."[10] Similarly, Norman Gall and Ruth Shereff claim that the elections were characterized by widespread fraud, forgery, terrorism, and intimidation, with hundreds of Cuban exiles expert in voting fraud imported during the campaign.[11] None of these writers provide any evidence or cite any sources.

result. According to embassy reports, Bosch and PRD officials were privately telling Balaguer and the embassy itself that they knew they had lost fair and square, but were "forced" to denounce the process in order to placate the more radical and emotional elements in the party. In my own interviews as well, most PRD and constitutionalist leaders minimized fraud as a significant factor in their defeat.

It is my own view that the issue of fraud or deliberately rigged elections can be dismissed as unfounded. The García-Godoy government, under whose auspices the campaign was run, the balloting held, and the vote counted, was beyond any reasonable doubt completely neutral and committed above all to honest and free elections. And, as for the United States, given the saturation of the country with outside observers it had neither the motivation nor the ability to tamper with the elections, even if it had otherwise been so disposed. While Barnet, again citing no evidence, casually charges that "strong U.S. support for Balaguer (behind declarations of neutrality) strongly influenced the outcome against Bosch,"[12] in the Dominican Republic itself even those most suspicious of the United States can point to nothing concrete and say only that they think that Washington funneled large amounts of money to Balaguer, especially in the closing weeks of the campaign. It is true that in late April Balaguer told Crimmins he was so concerned over his shortness of campaign funds that he was beginning to fear his defeat. It is also true that by the end of May the Reformistas had found new sources of funds. According to the Reformistas' own explanation—and it is certainly plausible—conservative money that initially had been going to the splinter rightist parties shifted to Balaguer as the prospect of a Bosch victory began to loom larger. However, one former high U.S. official (not connected with Dominican policy), told me he had "heard" that

CIA and FBI money *was* spent on behalf of Balaguer, especially to get out the vote in areas in which Balaguer was strong. On the other hand, he was unable or unwilling to provide any evidence or direct me to anyone who could confirm his story. In pursuing this charge further, I have found no supporting evidence. Thus, while the possibility that U.S. money went to Balaguer (perhaps even without the knowledge of the embassy) cannot be ruled out, I am strongly inclined to doubt it, not simply because I was unable to find proof of the practically unprovable but because such action would have run a high risk of exposure and was thus quite inconsistent with what I have argued to be the Johnson Administration's main concerns and policies. In any event, it would be extremely unlikely that U.S. funds could have accounted for any but the smallest part of Balaguer's very large margin of victory.

Nor can it be argued that the electoral machinery worked against Bosch. If anything, the converse is true, for to win the election only a simple plurality of the total popular votes cast was required. Thus, since the 14th of June and the Social Christians as well as the PRD nominated Bosch, he had a considerable advantage over Balaguer, some of whose conservative strength was drained off by Bonnelly and other rightist candidates.

The extent to which there was military intimidation of PRD campaigners and potential voters is somewhat more difficult to assess. As the campaign began, Garcia-Godoy took a number of steps aimed at eliminating any military influence over the electoral process: the armed forces and police were formally prohibited from playing any political role whatever, even from voting; small units composed of officers known to be honest and apolitical were formed within the armed forces and charged with rooting out military terrorism; the provisional President personally traveled throughout the country, visiting all military bases to urge the armed forces to remain neutral; and most importantly, the new commanders of the armed forces and the police, Generals Enrique Pérez y Pérez and José Morillo Lopez, moved vigorously and efficiently to comply with civil authority. Within a few weeks, the police were substantially reorganized and a number of men forced by Morillo into retirement.

By the end of April, there was general agreement that the whole atmosphere for elections had greatly improved. Most PRD leaders were at that time prepared to admit that the incidents of violence and harassment were few and generally not important,* and the OAS missions were reporting that since March 1 there had been few denunciations of serious police or military abuse.[13]

Bosch himself, however, made no such concessions and, indeed, his charges became increasingly bitter. "How can we have elections when people are beaten and shot every day?" he was reported to have said. "You know that 70% of Dominicans live in rural isolation subject to constant intimidations by anyone with arms."[14] At the end of April, Crimmins reported, Bosch was describing himself as a "cow headed for the slaughterhouse." Finally, on May 18, Bosch made a public speech detailing alleged incidents of military terrorism and concluded with a threat to withdraw from the elections unless the repression was immediately ended. Two days later, though, after strong public statements by Morillo and Pérez y Pérez promising to investigate Bosch's charges and guaranteeing free elections, followed by a presidential decree confining all members of the

* See the interview with Peña Gómez in the Dominican magazine *Ahora,* April 11, 1966, in which he took a highly optimistic posture on the elections, praising the attitudes of high military and police officers and noting the diminishing terrorism since the appointments of Pérez y Pérez and Morillo.

military to their barracks until after election day, Bosch announced that the crisis was resolved and that the PRD would participate in the elections.

After the elections, however, as perhaps was inevitable, Bosch and other PRD leaders charged that the various restrictions had been evaded and that police intimidation in the campaign had been a crucial factor in the electoral outcome. First of all, they argued, PRD organizers and activists had been so severely harassed outside Santo Domingo that in many parts of the country only the Reformistas were able to campaign. Second, it was claimed, subtle or not so subtle threats had deterred many *campesinos* from casting their ballots for Bosch.

It would be indeed surprising, given the entire history of the Dominican Republic as well as the prevailing situation in 1966, if there hadn't been *some* military role in the elections. Even short of outright intimidation, the military and police are an important source of influence and channel of communications, especially in the small towns, where the local chief of police or barracks commander has traditionally been the most powerful and frequently the most prestigious man in town. Moreover, in a society in which the military have long been so powerful, the mere fact that they were known to hate Bosch could have had a psychological effect, even in the absence of a direct military role. Beyond this unavoidable impact though, the PRD charges are not generally supported by most Dominican or foreign observers of the electoral process (and it is significant that, whatever the post election charges, *before* the elections the PRD fully expected to win). Not only was the extent of intimidation generally thought to have been retrospectively exaggerated by the PRD, but all observer reports stressed, and the PRD does not deny, that the secrecy of the ballot was everywhere implemented, so whatever threats the police or military may have made, they could safely be ignored once the voter was inside the closed booth.

To be sure, one cannot completely rule out the possibility that some *campesinos,* accustomed to thirty years of Trujilloism, simply did not trust the secrecy of the process, regardless of the manifest safeguards. That is an argument, however, that at least to some extent cuts two ways. What the PRD understandably does not stress—and sympathizers with its position ignore or fail to understand—is that the Bosch forces themselves had a considerable potential for intimidation, for in large parts of Santo Domingo and in several other cities as well the heavily armed constitutionalists were more powerful than the local police and military units. Moreover, the PRD controlled the extremely important government sugar mills as well as most local government bureaucracies, sources of employment for thousands of Dominicans. In fact, on several occasions Balaguer strongly protested that government funds and vehicles were being used by the PRD, and that goon squads were intimidating and attacking his organizers and campaigners. In its reports to the State Department during the campaign, the embassy confirmed many of these charges and worried that the net balance of extra-legal pressures each side could bring to bear to influence the electorate would heavily favor Bosch.

All in all, the general consensus among most official and unofficial observers of the 1966 electoral process, foreigners and Dominicans alike, is that, while some violence and intimidation occurred, there was less coercion than in most Latin American campaigns and in any event not enough to have altered the outcome.

If the electoral outcome did indeed reflect the genuine will of the Dominican electorate, why, then, did Bosch lose, especially by a far larger margin than anticipated by anyone?

More generally, what did the vote signify about Dominican attitudes toward the revolution? The easy answer to the latter question, of course, is that the Balaguer sweep demonstrated that most Dominicans opposed the revolution. On further reflection, however, the matter is far more complicated. For one thing, Balaguer, while considerably more conservative than Bosch, had (from exile in New York) spoken out against the anti-Bosch coup of 1963 and had not opposed the 1965 uprising. Indeed, as was pointed out earlier, many of the constitutionalist military and other early high-level participants in the uprising were Balagueristas.* Also significant was the fact that the only clearly anti-constitutionalist candidate, the far rightist Bonnelly, received only 3.5 percent of the vote. On the other hand, one certainly cannot simply add the Balaguer to the Bosch vote to determine the percentage of Dominicans who supported the revolution, for, as shall be argued shortly, Balaguer did indeed represent "law and order" to many Dominicans who nonetheless were unwilling to vote for Bonnelly. In short, there *are* no reliable statistics on the numbers of Dominicans who supported the revolution or, if they supported it, on what they perceived the revolution to represent.

As for Bosch's poor showing, one factor considered very significant by many Dominican observers was the PRD leader's failure to campaign actively. Bosch had been quite reluctant to run in the first place, apparently believing that he could not govern even if he won, and had accepted the PRD's nomination only under pressure. For the rest of the campaign, Bosch literally did not leave his home for fear he would be assassin-

* Moreover, U.S. questioning of 170 *working-class* Dominicans detained by or surrendering to U.S. troops in May, 1965, revealed that half of them supported Balaguer rather than Bosch. To be sure, it is possible that under such circumstances the Dominicans told American officials what they were presumed to want to hear.

ated, and reached his countrymen only through radio speeches. Balaguer, by contrast, ranged widely throughout the country.[15] In fact (for what such second-hand anecdotes are worth), according to a high Dominican political leader, a very close friend and confidant of Bosch informed him that the former President had confessed his desire to lose the elections, so that he would not have to face an inevitable coup. Bosch's refusal to leave his home also may have further diminished the prestige he lost because of his unwillingness to return to the country in the early days of the revolution. In a culture placing a high value on *machismo,* such apparently excessive timidity could well have been a significant factor in Bosch's defeat.

Beyond these negative factors, Balaguer had a high degree of genuine popularity. Despite his long subservience to Trujillo, he had managed to escape opprobrium after the downfall of the dictator, and in his brief term as President in the post-assassination period he had won many friends by effecting price reductions and creating public employment projects. Balaguer was particularly strong in the countryside, where 70 percent of the Dominicans live, for the *campesino* in the Dominican Republic, as in other Latin American countries, tends to be conservative. Moreover, it is among the *campesinos*—and among women, who were also considered to be strongly pro-Balaguer—that the influence of the Catholic Church is most strong; a majority of parish priests strongly opposed the anticlerical Bosch, even considering him a "Communist," and it is known that many of them ignored the high clergy's call for political neutrality and urged their parishioners to vote for Balaguer.[16]

Finally, the vote for Balaguer was very probably a vote for a return to peace and order after six years of violence, conflict, and instability. No doubt many Dominicans agreed with Bosch's own assessment that he would not be able to govern and feared that a Bosch victory would only reopen the civil war. Moreover, Bosch's campaign strategy appears to have exacerbated these feelings: while Balaguer was running on a platform of reconciliation, the embittered ex-President was making a series of speeches that many Dominicans considered to be inflammatory.* On the eve of the balloting, in a final tactical blunder, Bosch publicly called on his supporters to defend themselves on election day by taking sticks and stones with them to the polling places.

It is in this general context that, plausibly, the United States may have played a significant though indirect role in influencing the electoral outcome. Whatever Washington's determined neutrality and whatever its willingness to support a Bosch government, it is very likely that most Dominicans thought of Balaguer as the candidate of Washington, and therefore far more likely to get U.S. economic assistance and general support than Bosch. Moreover, it is a casual article of faith among many Dominicans that their own armed forces are really controlled by "the Pentagon," which, presumably, would order the military to overthrow a Bosch government. Thus, those who wanted to vote for peace and stability may have seen additional reasons not to vote for Bosch.

On the other hand, there are many Dominicans who dismiss such speculation, arguing that on the contrary the U.S. intervention, by arousing nationalistic hostilities, must have helped Bosch. In 1962, they point out, the United States was thought to be in favor of the conservative Fiallo, and yet Bosch won in a landslide. In the absence of attitude studies it does not seem possible to resolve this question, though it is interesting that the

* It is noteworthy that in Bosch's winning campaign of 1962, *he* was the candidate of "reconciliation," while his major opponents were calling for the rigorous "de-Trujilloization" of the country.

U.S. Embassy's own assessment was that even with the revolution and the continued presence of U.S. troops, Washington's presumed preference for Balaguer remained an advantage rather than a kiss of death.

The election of Balaguer precipitated an immediate conflict between the State Department and the embassy on the broad outlines of future U.S. policy in the Dominican Republic. In response to a Crimmins request for the immediate initiation of a new economic-assistance program, the department responded in a manner interpreted by Crimmins as reflecting a business-as-usual attitude, in which detailed justifications meeting rigorous standards would be required for all economic-aid programs, just as with any other Latin American nation. Angrily admonishing Washington, the blunt-spoken Ambassador warned that a tight-fisted attitude entailed the serious risk that the United States would lose what he believed to be the very considerable progress so painfully and expensively achieved until then. The elections were only a first step, he argued, and no matter how they had come out the United States would have been faced with the necessity, dictated by its own interest, of imaginatively and determinedly helping the elected government meet the great problems of political stability and economic and social development that would confront it. Indeed, Crimmins continued, the election of Balaguer in a sense placed an even greater burden on the United States than a Bosch victory would have, for Balaguer was widely thought to be Washington's boy, whose success or failure would reflect directly on the United States. Balaguer himself and the persons around him, Crimmins noted, had given many indications that they too believed that in winning they had gained a victory for the United States, which in turn imposed substantial obligations on Washington. This general opinion, he acidly remarked, was not in any way weakened by press comments out of Washington that Balaguer's election was regarded in official circles as a vindication of U.S. actions since the revolution.

As Crimmins saw the matter, the embassy was not advancing grandiose schemes nor seeking a blank check, but simply trying to maintain a prudent regard for U.S. interests. Niggardliness and rigor, he believed, did not represent the course of prudence, when after so much travail the United States and the Dominicans had another chance, and one which, if lost, might not come again. In the coming Balaguer Administration, then, the United States should encourage and support the following programs:

1. Economic development and social reform. The defeat of Bosch, Crimmins warned, should not be interpreted as a rejection of the PRD's general position, for the Reformistas had also promised reform and in fact their program was quite similar to the PRD's. Balaguer's election should thus be understood as a sign only that the average voter had opted for a less-dangerous and less-turbulent way of obtaining reform. Indeed, the United States should try to help Balaguer overcome the resistance of some of his own supporters who saw the vote as a mandate for a return to the "ordered past." All of this would require not only political support but relatively large-scale economic and technical assistance.

2. An end to terrorism and gradual structural military reform. The United States must help Balaguer maintain control over what Crimmins termed the hard-nosed unreconstructed types who appeared to be only too ready to view the election results as a hunting license against the left. Beyond that, the United States must help Balaguer build on and continue the progress in military reform made under the García-Godoy government.

3. Finally, the key U.S. interest, as Crimmins saw it, was the establishment of a working consensus between the amorphous Balaguerista center and the non-Communist left, which, if control of the military was maintained, would facilitate the gradual evolution of a stable democratic system in the Dominican Republic.

The embassy-department clash was resolved at the presidential level. The decision went to Crimmins, very probably because of his sharp reminders of how much the Johnson Administration had at stake in the Dominican Republic. For the rest of the administration, the Dominican Republic had a very high priority (in part reflected in the unusually large size and high quality of the U.S. mission in the country), and Crimmins emerged, as Bunker had before him, as the key man in the U.S. policy-making machinery for the Dominican Republic.

The first order of business after the elections was the working-out of the details for the withdrawal of the IAPF. As will be recalled, the task was to find a formula that would at once meet García-Godoy's wishes for at least some troop reductions in the month remaining in his term but would leave sufficient forces in the country to support the Balaguer government in its early months. In the initial discussions Balaguer was reluctant to see the IAPF depart before his government was solidly established, reintegration of the constitutionalist military was accomplished, and the civilian population was disarmed. While there could be some token withdrawals in the near future, the bulk of the force should be kept on for at least ninety days, Balaguer argued, with the possibility left open of a presidential request for a further extension if the situation in his view so required. Bunker and the other members of the Ad Hoc Committee, however, were not willing to wait for disarmament, which could take years, and pressed Balaguer to agree to the complete withdrawal of the force by the end of September, barring a serious breakdown of internal order. On June 10, García-Godoy, Balaguer, and the Ad Hoc Committee reached agreement on a compromise formula: there would be a gradual withdrawal of troops, beginning just before the end of García-Godoy's term and ending September 30. Only the least-important units would be withdrawn in the early months, however, and Balaguer retained the option of requesting the Ad Hoc Committee either to delay or to speed up the process. On September 21, no crisis having occurred, the last of the IAPF units departed.

THE BALAGUER GOVERNMENT

ALMOST FOUR years after the withdrawal of the IAPF, the Dominican Republic was again on the edge of a new explosion. Initially, the prospects for establishing progressive democracy under Balaguer seemed reasonably promising. In its first few years in office, the Balaguer regime instituted a number of important economic and social-development programs, with substantial U.S. encouragement and assistance. The gross national product rose seven percent in 1969, one of the highest growth rates in Latin America; a number of new lower-income housing projects have been built; some government-owned land has been distributed to poor *campesinos;* the education budget has been increased and many new schools have been constructed;* the crucial sugar industry, after years of marginal operation, is functioning well; agricultural production is increasing; foreign investment is rising; and, as a result of a severe austerity pro-

* The proposed 1970 budget, for the second time under Balaguer, allotted more money to education than to the armed forces.

gram, the chronic balance-of-payments deficit is easing.[17] From the inauguration of the Balaguer regime through November, 1968, the United States had disbursed over $132 million in economic assistance to the Dominican Republic, some of it in grants and the rest in loans with very mild repayment terms. Measured either since the 1965 revolution or in 1968 alone, the U.S. aid program was higher, on a per capita basis, than to any other Latin American country. Moreover, the United States was buying over 700,000 tons of Dominican sugar a year, more than from any other country in the world. Since the United States pays a premium on sugar of two cents a pound above the world market price, the Dominican quota amounted to a disguised subsidy of over $28 million a year.[18]

Balaguer at first also moved, under gentle U.S. prodding, toward military reform. Shortly after the elections Bunker and Crimmins expressed their hope to the new President that he would continue the progress initiated by García-Godoy, and made available to him a detailed study of the problem recently completed by the U.S. government. The heart of Washington's program was a reduction in the size of the armed forces, primarily by incremental cuts in the budget and gradual attrition through decreased reenlistment incentives and the retraining of military personnel in civilian skills. The program was to be instituted slowly and cautiously, not only because of the obvious political problems but also to minimize the potentially disruptive social effects of relatively large numbers of men suddenly coming onto a domestic labor market that was already severely over-manned. Other features of the program included the breaking-up of elite units in the armed forces that represented threats to civilian control; the inevitable civic-action programs that would involve the military in "nation-building" tasks as well as, hopefully, improve their public image; and a long-range "reeducation" program designed to create a more-professional, nonpolitical force.

Balaguer has indeed moved cautiously, as he has been extremely wary of taking any action that might antagonize the the military, particularly since for several years a substantial number of extreme rightist officers, rallying around the banner of General Wessin,* posed a considerable threat to the government. Ironically, one of the main counterforces to a possible pro-Wessin military coup has been a core of ex-Trujilloists personally loyal to Balaguer, many of whom had been forced out of the armed forces after 1961 but were reinstalled by the President.

Nonetheless, some steps have been taken, in line with the broad outlines of the U.S. program. By modestly cutting the military budget and not filling new positions opened by retirements, Balaguer has begun to allow the armed forces to dwindle; according to U.S. officials, the goal is the eventual reduction of the present force structure by 40 percent. Second, the President has retained the generally respected General Pérez y Pérez as Minister of Defense and Chief of Staff of the armed forces. Third, the Armed Forces Training Center at San Isidro, Ramfis Trujillo's and Wessin's old power base, has at last been broken up and put under the control of the army. Finally, the armed forces have been encouraged to become involved in civic-action projects—scarcely a day goes by without a picture in the Dominican newspapers of soldiers distributing food packages, inoculating babies, teaching literacy classes, or building roads.

The most crucial question, however, is whether or not basic military attitudes have begun to change, and on this matter there

* In January, 1969, in response to rightist pressures, Balaguer allowed Wessin to return to the country from his Miami exile. At the same time, however, he began to weed pro-Wessin officers out of the armed forces.[19]

is little ground for optimism. It is increasingly apparent that the military's present acquiescence in civilian rule is far more a matter of personal loyalty to Balaguer than to the general concept of a nonpolitical military, and thus might well not survive the present administration. Indeed, as the 1970 elections approached, many high officers were openly supporting Balaguer, if not condoning or actively engaging in harassment and repression of his political opponents.

Meanwhile, others of the nation's most fundamental problems remain acute, or have even worsened. The economy is still in the process of recuperation from the wrenching instabilities of the past decade, with the overall growth rate barely matching population increases; as of 1969, in fact, per capita income was still not as high as it was in 1960.[20] As a result of the stagnant economy (until 1969, at any rate) as well as Balaguer's stiff austerity program, there is an extremely severe unemployment problem—somewhere between one quarter and one half of the labor force are jobless (depending on who does the estimating), and many more are underemployed.[21] With the population growth rate at 3.6 percent a year, one of the highest in the world, and rural migration to the cities continuing, the problem threatens to grow even worse.

Perhaps even more ominous is the steadily worsening political terrorism, which has recently reached crisis proportions. Scarcely a day goes by without a political murder, a "suicide" of a jailed political prisoner, the disappearance of a political activist, or, at the very least, a case of police harassment of the political opposition. Most of the victims are Communists or Castroite radicals, PRD activists, or former constitutionalists, although recently even anti-Balaguerists on the right have been attacked. While there has also been a rise in leftist counter-terror, with machine-gunnings of isolated police and soldiers increasingly common, the main culprits appear to be unregenerates in the police and, to a lesser extent, the armed forces. It is not clear what Balaguer's role is in this, but although he has frequently condemned what he calls the "uncontrollable forces" behind the violence and on several occasions has shaken up the police leadership, there is a growing feeling among moderate Dominicans that he is encouraging the rightist terrorism or, at best, has been inadequate in his response to it.

This explosive combination of high unemployment and continued political violence is once again producing sharp polarization. As in so many other countries, the generation gap has become acute, with many observers considering that Balaguer has lost touch with the youth. In a nation in which over 50 percent of the population is under twenty, that is a major problem indeed. One manifestation of the alienation of the younger generation is the increasing power in the University of Santo Domingo and in the public high schools of well-armed Castroite and Maoist groups.

The same polarization process is at work in the political arena. On one side, the Wessin "movement," the latest vehicle for the powerful extreme right, has made sufficient progress so that on several occasions in recent years Balaguer and the U.S. Embassy were seriously concerned about an imminent coup or the assassination of the President. While the threat recently seems to have eased, largely because of the anti-Wessin purge within the armed forces, the potential for disruption or even the imposition of a new rightist dictatorship is not inconsequential. On the other side of the political spectrum, the PRD has splintered and ceased to be an effective democratic opposition, with many of its most influential leaders following Juan Bosch in his sharp turn to the left. The embittered former President, until recently in self-imposed exile (for some years, ironically enough, in Franco

Spain), has proclaimed his abandonment of electoral politics and democracy in favor of revolution and an undefined "dictatorship with popular support." Following Bosch's latest dictum that representative democracy has failed in Latin America in general and the Dominican Republic in particular, the PRD has refused to participate in recent Dominican elections and now considers itself a revolutionary movement.

As this book went to press, the political crisis was coming to a dangerous head in the 1970 presidential campaign. Balaguer was constitutionally entitled to run for re-election, but because of the Dominican Republic's long history of "*continuismo*," there was great opposition to even the democratic form. Balaguer, who clearly considers himself to be a Caribbean de Gaulle, mystically "destined" by history to exercise power, was adamantly insisting on defying this sentiment. Meanwhile, growing military and police intimidation on behalf of Balaguer, with or without his encouragement, had made the prospects for genuinely free elections increasingly remote.

While Bosch's despairing pessimism was not yet fully justified, given the continuing existence of a critical press, vigorous trade unions, a functioning legislature, and active opposition parties, there seemed little doubt that many of the portents in the Dominican Republic were grim. Once again, the ill-starred Caribbean nation seemed poised on the edge of massive violence, civil war, or outright military dictatorship.

8

Conclusions

ONE OF THE MAJOR PURPOSES of this book has been to correct what I consider to be a number of important misconceptions and oversimplifications about the nature of the Dominican revolution and the U.S. response to it. Because of these errors of fact and interpretation, almost all the writing on the crisis—at least all worth taking seriously—has been excessively critical of U.S. policy. But that is not to say that a number of serious criticisms are not warranted, and it is to that task of criticism that I would now like to turn, focusing on the role of the United States in the period immediately preceding the military intervention of April 28, the manner in which the intervention was handled, and the development of U.S. policy after the intervention.

THE PRE-INTERVENTION PERIOD

THE MOST CRUCIAL pre-intervention error of the U.S. Government was its failure, or more precisely its refusal, to use its considerable influence to aid the moderate, non-Communist PRD leadership within the constitutionalist movement, vis-à-vis both the rightist military and the Castroite forces. As Senator Fulbright has put it: "On the basis of ambiguous evidence, [the United States] . . . assumed almost from the beginning that the revolution was Communist dominated, or would certainly become so. It apparently never occurred to anyone that the United States could also attempt to influence the course which the revolution took."[1] Had the United States exerted such influence, there was at least the possibility that control of the movement would have been retained by the moderate leadership, the Communist threat (whatever its magnitude) averted, and Juan Bosch peacefully returned to the Presidency with at least the acquiescence of a divided and confused military. To be sure, the argument should not be overstated, for it would be foolhardy to be *confident* that events would have taken such a course. Although the United States had considerable influence, it was certainly not in a position to control an explosive situation; in particular, it is plausible that in the face of an imminent Bosch return the military would have rallied its forces and continued to fight, regardless of the U.S. position. Be that as it may, the United States deliberately let pass at least four opportunities in the April 24-28 period in which it might have exerted a constructive and liberal influence. The first occurred during the morning of April 24, the first day of the revolution, when the U.S. Embassy in the Dominican Republic received a report that Donald Reid had offered to turn over the government to the PRD, with the PRD leaders agreeing to acept only if it was done in the presence of a U.S. representative.* Chargé d'Affaires William Connett, however, offered no encouragement to the PRD and advised the State Department against any dealings with the constitutionalists at that time, fearing that the United States could become associated with a government that was not to its liking—it will be recalled that from the very outset of the revolution Connett was concerned with Communist

* Reid has since denied he made such an offer; it is irrelevant to my point whether he did or not.

participation in it and his assessment was that even the PRD was in the hands of its more extremist element. The State Department accepted Connett's advice.

Second, the United States could have thrown its support behind the moderate constitutionalist "provisional government" of José Molina Ureña, instead of urging the military to continue resisting the movement. On Sunday morning, the second day of the revolution, an embassy official had gone to the National Palace to talk with Molina and assess the situation; he reported back that the situation was chaotic, that the provisional government seemed to include a number of Communists or Castroites, and that Molina was not in control of the unfolding events. Apparently on little more than this rather flimsy evidence, the embassy decided against backing Molina, reporting to Washington that he was a weak man with no personal support whose government was simply a front for Bosch or, at worst, "the Communists."

Third, the United States might have dealt with Bosch *before* the intervention and even offered to bring him back to his country, so as to assure his continued leadership over the constitutionalists and preclude the possibility that Castroite groups would fill a leadership vacuum in the revolutionary movement. A final opportunity was lost when Ambassador Bennett refused the PRD leadership's April 27th request for U.S. mediation and assistance in obtaining a ceasefire. Following that famous embassy meeting, a number of PRD leaders went into hiding, the *combatientes* at least temporarily became the dominant force in the movement, and events moved swiftly toward the U.S. intervention.

Months later Thomas Mann sought to explain why the U.S. had not followed any of these courses. A policy of supporting the Boschists in the revolution would have been "intervention" in the internal affairs of the Dominican Republic, he argued, and thus the U.S. had refused to support either side, working instead for a ceasefire![2] This astonishing statement hardly needs extended refutation: not only had the U.S. Embassy stopped working for a ceasefire after it thought that the regular military had gained the upper hand, but it had been vigorously intervening *against* the constitutionalists from almost the first hours of the revolution. The real explanation, of course, was the embassy's repeated playing on the Communist theme, compounded by the almost universal disdain and distrust for Bosch throughout the U.S. Government.

THE INTERVENTION

BY APRIL 28 the opportunities for constructive U.S. action were past history. Given this, was the United States in some sense justified in its military intervention? The answer to this question depends in turn on the answers to two other questions: how much risk can the United States afford to take on a Communist takeover in another Latin American or at least Caribbean country, and how much risk in fact was there in the Dominican Republic? Turning to the latter question first, it is my view that the intervention was a mistake even within the framework of the established No Second Cuba policy. Not that the fear of a successful Communist takeover in the Dominican Republic was a figment of the Johnson Administration's paranoiac imagination,[3] for (as I have earlier sought to demonstrate) by April 28 there was indeed some risk that out of an uncontrollable revolutionary upheaval Castroite forces might emerge victorious. My case, rather, is that the risk was not yet sufficiently great to justify the predictably enormous political and moral costs that the intervention entailed. Even without challenging (at this point) the underlying policy premises on which the intervention was based, I would argue that the more appropriate response would have been to do nothing until the situation had sorted itself out, while announcing in strong terms that the United States would not allow a Communist government to come to power in the Dominican Republic.

To be sure, this course of action itself might have posed serious risks, as State Department officials are quick to point out. The longer the delay, the more resistance a later intervention would be likely to meet. Even worse, the longer the delay, the greater the likelihood that the whole crisis would become entwined in the larger Cold War conflict. The Cuban scenario of 1959-60, very much present in the minds of U.S. officials, acted as a powerful deterrent to a policy of "watchful waiting." As the State Department saw the matter, in Cuba the United States *had* delayed firm action until, by the time the political orientation of the Castro government was unmistakably clear, it was too late to do much without risking a major confrontation with the Soviet Union.

This argument is by no means entirely implausible or indefensible. Nonetheless, I remain persuaded that on April 28 the balance of costs and risks was still clearly on the side of nonintervention. The prospect that the Soviet Union would have committed itself to the protection of a radical government in the Dominican Republic, especially in the teeth of a firm U.S. threat to take military action to prevent a new Cuba, was seriously exaggerated. It is, of course, easier to be confident of such an assessment in retrospect, for, as was pointed out earlier, the Soviet Union did in fact remain on the sidelines throughout the crisis. But even at the time, it seems to me, previous Soviet cautiousness in the Cuban missile crisis strongly indicated a noninterventionist course in any future Caribbean crisis that the United States again defined as critical to its national interests, just as cautious U.S. behavior in the 1956 Hungarian revolution allowed the Soviets correctly to predict similar behavior in the Czechoslovakian crisis of 1968.

The reader will have undoubtedly noted that until this point my argument has apparently accepted an assumption that is far from self-evident—that a U.S. intervention if *really* necessary to prevent a Communist revolution from succeeding in another Latin American or, at least, Caribbean country would have been justifiable. Put a little differently, I have not challenged the No Second Cuba policy itself, but simply its misapplication in the Dominican Republic. This assumption must now be squarely faced. In what way, it may fairly be asked, would another Communist government in the Caribbean threaten U.S. security, threaten it so massively as to require military intervention against a genuinely indigenous revolution? On what basis, other than brute force, does the United States arrogate to itself the right to determine the future of small and helpless nations? In short, even if the revolution in the Dominican Republic had been *unmistakably* Communist, would the United States intervention have been defensible?

The answers to these questions are complicated, but, put briefly, it is my view that further indigenous Communist revolutions in the Caribbean would *not,* per se, be a threat to the United States, that the United States certainly has no general moral right to intervene in the internal affairs of other countries, but that nonetheless in the prevailing domestic and international context of 1965, decent, intelligent, and reasonable men might well have reached the conclusion that the consequences of nonintervention in a Caribbean Communist revolution could be worse than the consequences of intervention.*

* Note that this kind of argument separates me from radical critics of U.S. foreign policy like, for example, Noam Chomsky, who would deny legitimacy to intervention under any circumstances. As the distinguished religious philosopher

To elaborate: economically the Caribbean is of trivial significance to the United States, as its products are not of great importance to our economy and in any event could, if necessary, be supplied from other parts of the world. As for geopolitical factors, whatever strategic significance the area once had has radically diminished in the age of nuclear weapons and intercontinental missiles. Traditionally, the islands of the Caribbean were thought to be important because they lay astride important trade routes and the approaches to the Panama Canal as well as, simply, because of their physical proximity to the United States—conceivably they could be used as forward bases and stepping stones in an attack on the mainland. Ever since the end of the Second World War and the development of a massive U.S. military machine, though, the possibility of a conventional invasion of the Western Hemisphere must be counted as considerably less than remote. Nor can one easily imagine a scenario in which an aggressor would attempt an assault on the Panama Canal, except, perhaps, as part of an all-out general war, in which case defense of the Canal would not seem to rank among the higher priorities.* All this is tacitly recognized by U.S. officials, who, when pressed, can cite only the necessity of denying the Soviet Union possible missile bases in the hemisphere. Undoubtedly, a good case for this can still be made. Even so, however, it hardly follows that a blanket policy of intervention against new Communist revolutions is necessary:

Paul Ramsey has argued, in an anarchic, bipolar world military intervention is sometimes politically and even morally justifiable. In such a world, one *can* speak of the "responsibilities of power," however badly they have been recently abused by the United States. In Ramsey's words: "No moral theory or sound political doctrine can, from any general principle, rule . . . [Johnson's Dominican] intervention to have been an illegitimate decision; in fact, sound theory must open and hold open possibilities such as this as well as contrary acts of nonintervention. Then statesmanship must bear the burden of having been prudent and wise."[4]

* This is not to deny that the area still is militarily *convenient* to the United States, for example as a site for antisubmarine technology, but simply that it is not any longer *crucial*.

(1) the Cuban missile crisis and the further Soviet development of long-range and submarine-launched nuclear missiles have reduced the chances of a new Soviet adventure to nil; (2) if the Soviets should act irrationally and confound this prediction, they still, presumably, have Cuba; (3) and if Cuba should deny the Soviets new bases, the same minimal rationality of self-preservation would almost certainly persuade other governments to do the same. In short, a simple declaration of the continued U.S. intention to prevent the establishment of Soviet military bases would meet the requirements of U.S. security in the Caribbean.

A different kind of argument is based on a variant of the domino theory: the importance of preventing the establishment of another Communist government in the Caribbean is not geopolitical or related to the intrinsic strategic significance of any particular state in the area but stems, rather, from the possibility that a successful new revolution could trigger a wave of revolutions throughout Latin America. A Communist Dominican Republic or Haiti might not be very troublesome, the argument runs, but a Communist Brazil, Argentina, Chile, or Venezuela would be considerably more serious. The flaw in this logic, of course, is in the assumption of mechanistic linkages between revolutions in one country and potential revolutions in others. A full refutation of the domino "theory" would take too much space here, and in any event has already been accomplished many times;[5] in brief, however, whether revolutions occur and whether, more importantly, they succeed, depends overwhelmingly on the internal economic, political, and social conditions of each individual country and hardly at all on the "example" set by other countries. Indeed, we have already had a test of the domino theory—in the ten years since the Castro revolution no other radical movement has come to power in Latin America.*

Despite these arguments, however, in 1965 a failure to act against a new Castroite or openly Communist government in the Caribbean might well have had very severe domestic and international repercussions. It is quite clear, in fact, that domestic considerations played a crucial role in the Johnson Administration's decision to intervene in the Dominican Republic—the President has been quoted as remarking: "When I do what I am about to do, there'll be a lot of people in this hemisphere I can't live with, but if I don't do it there'll be a lot of people in this country I can't live with."[6] † Thus, like the underlying No Second Cuba policy itself, the Dominican intervention was based in good part on the premise that the American people would not stand for U.S. passivity in the event of a new hemispheric Castro. And in the climate of opinion prevailing in 1965, it seems to me, that premise may very well have been correct; while the continued existence of the Castro government has now all but ceased to be a domestic issue, one need only recall the hysteria of the early 1960's over the Cuban revolution—"Cuba is a dagger pointing at the heart of America" and all that—to understand the Johnson Administration's concern. With the Cuban missile crisis still a very live memory, and with the rise of the radical right, culminating in the Republican nomination of Barry Goldwater only a year earlier, still a major factor in American politics, reasonable men could and

* However, Joseph Nye suggests that the domino theory may not be refuted by the Cuban case *alone*, because of the exceptional U.S. efforts at isolation which might have become more difficult if more than one country was "lost."

† Cf. also another Johnson statement: "You can imagine what would have happened . . . if I had not [intervened] . . . and there was an investigation and the press got hold of [Bennett's] . . . cable."[7]

in fact did fear that a successful Communist revolution in the Dominican Republic might well jeopardize the future of the Democratic party in the United States, if not of American liberalism in general. Even short of that, a new Communist revolution in the hemisphere could certainly have made impossible a more flexible and relaxed policy vis-à-vis the entire Communist world.

Similarly, a failure to act against an unmistakably Communist revolution in the Caribbean might have produced serious de-stabilizing consequences in the rest of the world. While a new Communist government in the hemisphere would not in fact threaten U.S. security, since the Castro revolution the United States had been proclaiming that it would. While a genuinely indigenous revolution in fact was a far cry from "international Communist aggression," the United States had been loudly denying such a distinction. While an indigenous Communist government in the Caribbean would in fact almost certainly be independent of Moscow or Peking, the United States had been minimizing the significance of pluralism in the Communist world. Thus, in the white heat of crisis, the government could not suddenly reverse itself and deny the manifest implications of its proclaimed policies without inviting dangerous consequences elsewhere in the world. If one assumes, as I believe we must, that there are at least as many militant cold warriors in the Kremlin as in Washington, the price of non-action in the Caribbean might have been more aggressive Soviet behavior elsewhere, say in Berlin or the Middle East. If Washington refused to act in the Caribbean, which the United States itself had insisted was essential to its national security, why would it live up to its commitments in areas outside its immediate sphere of influence? To be sure, internal revolutions are quite different from external pressures on Berlin, but the United

States had been steadfastly (and obtusely) obscuring the distinction.

Put differently, in 1965 the United States was a prisoner, both at home and abroad, of its own oversimplifications, myths, and outmoded policies, particularly the Monroe Doctrine and its ramifications. Indeed, one of the more revealing aspects of the Dominican crisis was the way in which it highlighted the inflexibility and obsolescence of the operating framework of assumptions of so many U.S. policy makers. So far as can be determined, prior to the crisis there had been no reexamination of the underlying premises of American policy in the Caribbean, despite the disappearance of any external military threat (as traditionally conceived of) to the area, despite the revolutionary developments in weapons technology since 1945, and despite the fragmentation of what officials were still calling the "international Communist movement." Instead, it was simply taken as axiomatic that not merely the presumed exigencies of public opinion but the "national interest"—that empty phrase that so often has served to conceal intellectual poverty if not to excuse outright immorality—continued to require the maintenance of "friendly" governments in the Caribbean. Still, while U.S. policies badly needed changing, perhaps this could safely be done only in relatively quiet periods. To do so under severe pressure might be seen not as a courageous act of statesmanship but as a powerful indicator of irresolution and timidity that could well invite far more serious challenges and *real* aggression elsewhere.

Or so it could be reasonably argued. I do not want to load this discussion too much. To reiterate the major points of my argument: (1) the overall No Second Cuba policy was an error, based on obsolescent premises, which should have been abandoned before the crisis ever arose; (2) that having not been done, though, it is arguable that in the domestic and international environment prevailing in 1965 the United States had trapped itself into the necessity of intervening against a *genuine* Communist revolution; (3) *but* in the Dominican crisis itself, the evidence of Communist influence in the constitutionalist movement was insufficient to justify the predictable political and human costs of the intervention—indeed, it was very lucky that the costs were not far higher, for the intervention might have met with major resistance and entailed a large-scale loss of life; the appropriate course, even within the framework of existing policy, would have been to act only if an unmistakably Communist government had actually come to power.

In addition to the intervention itself, the United States made a number of serious errors in the post-intervention period. To begin with, the landing of U.S. troops should have been directed not only at forestalling whatever danger there was of a Communist takeover but also at curbing the Dominican military, strengthening the PRD elements in the constitutionalist movement, and restoring Juan Bosch to the Presidency. As the troops landed the United States might have made the following announcement: "In view of the possible threat of a Communist takeover of a revolutionary movement in the Dominican Republic, as well as the serious dangers to U.S. and Dominican lives, the United States has been forced to send troops to that country. The purpose of this intervention, however, will be not only to prevent a new Castro in the Western Hemisphere but also to end the fighting, restore order, prevent a military takeover, and restore the rightful President to his office." Once the troops were on the ground, it would not have been difficult to isolate completely the Communist elements within the constitutionalist movement and ensure that they would not be in any position to dominate a Bosch government.

To be sure, such a course would not have been beyond criticism, either. As U.S. officials are quick to point out, to a considerable extent it would have amounted to an imposed, even an undemocratic solution, for the diverse nature of the constitutionalist movement, its failure to spread to the countryside, and the poor showing of Bosch in the 1966 election suggest that the revolution did not necessarily reflect a nationwide consensus for Bosch's return. Nonetheless, Bosch was still the constitutional President and the dominant leadership within the constitutionalist movement clearly were fighting for the direct return of Bosch to the Presidency without new elections. Had the United States thrown its weight behind Bosch and the restoration of the 1963 constitution, the intervention would have been joyously welcomed by the constitutionalists and by much of Dominican public opinion, and it would have been viewed far differently in the United States and Latin America.

Second, the United States used an excessive amount of force against the constitutionalists and, more importantly, failed to use enough force to curb the terrorism of the Dominican police and military. Although the Johnson Administration had proclaimed as one of the main purposes of the intervention the need to save Dominican lives in a bloody civil war, in fact most of the estimated three thousand Dominican deaths occurred after the intervention, some of them in clashes between the constitutionalists and U.S. troops, and the rest at the hands of a Dominican military that the United States had rescued from probable annihilation in April and thereafter had helped protect and rebuild.

It may be recalled that during this period the policy-making style in Washington was one which exalted the virtues of "pragmatism," "realism," and "tough-mindedness," especially in opposition to "fuzzy-minded idealism." So it is perhaps not surprising that the United States on several occasions in the crisis departed from adherence to international law, respect for fundamental civil liberties, and even, to speak plainly, from simple moral decency—always, of course, in the name of "the national interest." The long-run costs of such behavior, as I shall shortly argue, are not merely moral but political, a fact that the "pragmatists," uninterested in any but the most short-term consequences of national actions, are blind to.

The most completely inexcusable U.S. action during the entire period of the intervention, in my view, was its acquiescence in and probable support of Imbert's May military attack on the constitutionalist sector in northern Santo Domingo, ending in the brutal slaughter of hundreds of constitutionalists and innocent civilians.[8] In large part for narrow political purposes (additional pressures on the constitutionalists in the forthcoming negotiations), American policy makers had demonstrated a shockingly callous willingness to expend other people's lives.

Later, the IAPF itself killed sixty-seven Dominicans in the course of occupying fifty additional blocks of constitutionalist territory. While the main purpose of this action probably was the protection of IAPF positions rather than further political pressures on the constitutionalists, the amount of force employed appeared to be greatly excessive.

All through the summer of 1965, the Imbert government—a U.S. creation—and its military and police forces—equipped and paid by the United States—continued their reign of terror, jailing, torturing, or murdering thousands of Dominicans throughout the country. The U.S. goverment was certainly opposed to these actions, but it did nothing effective to block them, except in areas actually under IAPF occupation.

ism continued, although on a substantially diminished scale.

It was apparent that Washington was deeply concerned, fearing that the long-term beneficiary would be the Communists, and U.S. intelligence operatives in the Dominican Republic were directed to make a major effort to identify the terrorist leaders. These actions, however, continued to prove insufficient, and neither García-Godoy nor the United States was able to prevent the murder of perhaps several hundred constitutionalists or their sympathizers.

To be sure, even stronger U.S. efforts might have proved unavailing. Given the magnitude of the problem, it is possible that nothing short of a nationwide occupation and the complete dismantling of the military and police structure would have ended the terrorism. Thus, without radically modifying its overall policy, which sought to control the military but gave much higher priority to preserving it, the United States was relatively powerless to affect the course of events.

This brings us to a crucial point. In the long run, perhaps the most serious criticism that can be made of U.S. policy after the intervention itself is that, having intervened, it refused to use the opportunity to effect really sweeping military reform, thereby creating the essential prerequisite for major political and social change in the Dominican Republic. While there is no doubt that the United States was, and is, committed to *gradual* military reform, its policy is conditioned on the very explicit premise that, whatever its faults, the Dominican military is an essential force for "order" and "stability" and that, therefore, nothing must be done that would seriously weaken it. This is a long-standing policy, applicable not only to the Dominican Republic but to all Latin America; it was profoundly reinforced by the near collapse of the Dominican armed forces in the early days of the revolution (so reminiscent of the disintegration of Batista's armed forces in late 1958), which left Washington greatly shaken and extremely reluctant to take any actions that might undermine military morale.

Had fundamental change rather than essential preservation been given priority, there were a number of points throughout the crisis at which decisive action, or non-action, could have been taken. First, of course, the United States could have refrained from military intervention at the moment when the armed forces were apparently on the verge of defeat at the hands of the constitutionalists. Second, and much less drastically, in the summer negotiations the United States might have acceded to the constitutionalist demand that one of their own be made chief of staff of the armed forces. Third, if García-Godoy had been so disposed, the United States might have taken advantage of the military revolt against the provisional government to institute deep-rooted changes in the military structure, using the IAPF if necessary to enforce its will.

This latter suggestion, however, points to another complication—from September onward the President of the Dominican Republic was himself opposed to the use of the IAPF against the Dominican military if it could possibly be avoided, preferring the moderate reform of the armed forces (primarily by the removal of what he referred to as the "bad apples") to their radical restructuring.

The United States–García-Godoy position was by no means obviously untenable. In a very real sense the armed forces, if they could be kept under political control, *were* the major force for a minimal order and stability in a society that could have quite easily slipped into a terrible fratricidal chaos. Moreover, the military was united in its bitter opposition to further changes after the chiefs of staff were eased out in the winter of 1966. In early March, for example, the entire Dominican middle-range officer corps (lieutenant colonels and colonels) signed a letter to García-Godoy warning that if any further changes were made at the top of the armed forces, none of them would step into the vacancies. Just as U.S. officials argued, then, any attempt to have forced further changes might have ended in a head-on clash with, and even the possible destruction of, the Dominican armed forces. At a minimum, it almost certainly would have required the prolonged stay of the IAPF in the country—a prospect that appalled Dominicans and Americans alike—lest after its departure an embittered military once again turn against the government.

It is only with extreme caution and full awareness of the severe risks that the alternatives entailed, then, that one can criticize the middle-of-the-road course that Bunker and García-Godoy chose. Nonetheless, despite undoubted reforms (the total size of the armed forces continues to be whittled down through attrition and retraining, and military expenditures are down to under 18 percent of the national budget, from a high of 36 percent in 1961),[9] recent events in the Dominican Republic make it evident that genuine political control of a disciplined, honest, and constructive military establishment is far from a reality. The approach of the United States has been to attempt to educate the military into accepting the concept of an apolitical "professionalism," while at the same time emphasizing the military's role in counterinsurgency and civic-action programs. It is the same approach that the United States has been following throughout Latin America for the last decade, and the results to date have not been exactly encouraging. In the last few years alone there have been eight military coups in Latin America, often led by officers recently returned from U.S. military schools, and the military have established themselves as the major political institution in several other countries. It is very probable, indeed, that U.S. policies have *exacerbated* rather than diminished the traditional tendency of the Latin American military to intervene in political affairs, for civic action and counterinsurgency are highly political roles, tending to strengthen and legitimate the military's posture as the ultimate arbiters of what political movements will be deemed acceptable.[10]

In sum, the United States, García-Godoy, and, perhaps, Balaguer have all favored the course of gradual rather than radical military reform. It is still very much an open question, however, whether the military will permit the far-reaching social and economic change that is the necessary (if not sufficient) condition for long-range stability and meaningful democracy in the Dominican Republic. If not, gradualism will have failed dismally, and the opportunity that existed in 1965-66 for once-and-for-all drastic surgery will probably have been permanently lost.

THE DOMINICAN CRISIS IN RETROSPECT

THERE IS NOW a widespread tendency, particularly among government officials but even among outside observers, to concede that the United States may have erred in intervening in the Dominican Republic and made further mistakes afterward but that, nonetheless, the overall operation must be counted, somewhat surprisingly, as a success. Samuel Huntington has summed up the dominant view: "Whether or not there was a threat of communist takeover on the island, we were able to go in, restore order, negotiate a truce among conflicting parties, hold reasonably honest elections which the right man won, withdraw our troops, and promote a very considerable amount of social and economic reform."[11]

To this list of ostensible accomplishments, the State Department has added three others (besides, of course, the prevention of a Communist takeover): the saving of American and foreign lives, the aversion of a bloody civil war, and the establishment of the first peacekeeping force in the hemisphere.[12]

There clearly is an element of truth in these assessments, but they are (to understate) quite incomplete and therefore misleading. Besides that, there was such a high element of luck in the Dominican drama that it would be disastrous for U.S. policy makers to see the intervention as a possible model and precedent for a similar operation elsewhere in Latin America. At this point, the reader may recall how the "successful" CIA-sponsored exile invasion of Guatemala in 1954 led to the totally unsuccessful Bay of Pigs operation against Castro in 1961. As I have argued elsewhere,[13] one of the unrecognized costs of the Guatemalan affair was that it firmly planted the notion that future Communist threats in Latin America could be met by similar techniques; until such threats developed, it was implicitly assumed, the political, social, and economic conditions that produced Communism in Guatemala could safely be forgotten. It would be tragic if the Dominican intervention should have the same results.

The outcome of the Dominican crisis was in good part a reflection of several very particular circumstances that are most unlikely to recur. As Abraham Lowenthal has remarked, "The Dominican Republic was a comparatively easy place for the United States to intervene and from which to withdraw."[14] For one thing, the smallness of the country facilitated military intervention and discouraged any armed resistance; the United States was able to concentrate an overwhelming military presence in Santo Domingo but yet move an impressive amount of troops and heavy equipment into the countryside in very short order.

An even more important factor in the relatively passive response to the intervention was the rudimentary sense of national consciousness and cohesion that existed in the Dominican Republic.[15] * The Trujillo era had fragmented and demoralized Dominican society, aborting the development of a sense of nationalism that could have provided the impetus for a national resistance movement. It is probably even true, as U.S. officials claim, that a great many Dominicans *supported* the intervention, preferring a U.S. occupation to a possible civil war or Communist takeover.† A U.S. intervention elsewhere in Latin America might very well be a quite different affair; indeed, today intervention might be quite different in the Dominican Republic itself, for one of the effects of the 1965 crisis was to stimulate a wave of anti-American nationalism, especially among the youth. And one need think only of Vietnam to understand the consequences of foreign military intervention in countries with strong nationalist movements.

Finally, it is most unlikely that the crisis would have been peacefully resolved, free elections held, and the U.S. troops withdrawn relatively quickly if Héctor García-Godoy had not emerged to play a key role. Certainly the United States could not again count on the fortuitous appearance of such an exceptionally able and far-sighted man to rescue it from the consequences of future interventions.

In any event, it is premature and remarkably short-sighted to consider the Dominican intervention a "success." For one thing, Communist, or, at least, radical and extremist strength in

* Draper recently has argued that the major reason the United States met no resistance was that "Bosch told his followers it was unthinkable to fight U.S. troops."[16] He does not tell us why he is confident it is the key factor.

† This should certainly not be overstated, though. Many moderate Dominicans to whom I spoke, even those who were very dubious about the constitutionalists, were angrily opposed to the intervention, preferring by far to run the risks of a continuation of the revolutionary process.

the Dominican Republic is far higher today than it was in April, 1965, in good part because of the intervention. More generally, as I have argued, the overall fabric of Dominican stability and democracy is still, to say the least, very fragile, with many of the traditional problems remaining essentially unchanged —the deep divisions in Dominican society, the proclivity for political violence, the widespread poverty and unemployment, the tenuous political subordination of the military, and the cynicism of many of the political leaders. If anything, the underlying or potential crisis might even be worse today, as the revolution and then the intervention even further fragmented and polarized the country, leaving it in what one writer has called a state of "political and social disintegration . . . [the effects of which are unlikely to] shortly or easily permit the development of a viable, functioning, pluralist system."[17]

Thus, the temporary "quiet" in the Dominican Republic should not be allowed to obscure the errors of U.S. policy. Moreover, even if the Dominican Republic does not again explode and the modest social and economic progress made under Balaguer continues and takes firmer root, the overall costs have been extremely high. For example, the OAS was seriously undermined and is currently in the political doldrums. All over Latin America the OAS has increasingly become an object of scorn, widely (if erroneously) seen, in Castro's words, as Washington's "Ministry of Colonies." As a result, in the last few years Latin American sentiment for new forms of hemispheric cooperation that would exclude the United States have arisen; and the OAS has had to shelve plans for institutional reforms that would have very modestly expanded its role in hemispheric political affairs, has been unable to establish a mediatory role in several South American border disputes that have recently flared up (occasionally even to the point of small-scale military skirmishes),* and, in general, has become increasingly irrelevant to the processes of Latin American economic, political, and social change.[18]

While the Alliance for Progress and the policy of the promotion of nonrevolutionary change in Latin America that underlies it were already in considerable difficulty by mid-1965, it is probable that they were further seriously weakened by the Dominican intervention. One of the major premises of the Alliance was that the privileged classes of Latin America and their allies in the military, the Church, and the established political parties could be brought to support, or at least bow before, the forces for democratic change as the only realistic alternative to much more radical and violent change. But the Dominican intervention opened the possibility of another alternative—the United States might, at the moment of truth, bail out the "oligarchies" rather than let them face the consequences of their own inadequacies and steadfast addiction to an outmoded and unjust status quo. Thus, it is at least plausible that the Dominican intervention diminished elitist incentives to accommodate to change, and it is probably not unrelated (although, of course, many other factors are at work as well) that in the last few years the political and social idealism has all but drained out of the Alliance, increasingly leaving it, to the extent that it has any life at all, as not much more than a traditional lending program.

Finally, the Dominican intervention contributed massively to the sharply increased alienation from the U.S. Government and even the political system as a whole that has become rampant among youths, intellectuals, and the non-Communist left in gen-

* However, in the most serious of the recent hemispheric conflicts, the El Salvadoran–Honduran clash in the summer of 1969, the OAS did act decisively to force an end to the fighting, the withdrawal of El Salvadoran troops from Honduran territory, and the initiation of negotiations for a political settlement.

eral in the late 1960's, as much or even more in the United States itself than in the rest of the world. Vietnam-and-the-Dominican-Republic, the-Dominican-Republic-and-Vietnam—the linkage is invariable (although, as I shall shortly argue, considerably oversimplified), the two traumatic crises of the mid-1960's seen as both the symbol and the inevitable outcome of the pathology of U.S. foreign policy. The costs to this country—to our national prestige, to our own self-respect, and perhaps even to our domestic stability—have been incalculable. Even if the Dominican "success" had not been deeply flawed in so many other ways, more such victories would be unmitigated disasters.

NO MORE DOMINICAN REPUBLICS?

WHATEVER THE OFFICIAL LINE, a number of U.S. officials privately agree that in the absence of more persuasive evidence of an imminent Communist takeover the Dominican intervention was a mistake, and it is clear that any future calls from U.S. embassies for the dispatch of U.S. troops would be received far more skeptically. Indeed, many of the U.S. errors in the Dominican Republic, especially in the first few weeks, were at least in part a reflection of the exceptionally fast-breaking nature of the crisis, which severely strained the machinery of government and left little time for reflection on alternatives, as well as a function of the underlying sets of assumptions and preconceptions that constituted established policy.

The poor performance of many U.S. officials in both the embassy and the State Department was virtually acknowledged by the speed with which they were replaced. Within a year of the intervention, Thomas Mann withdrew from overall supervision of Latin American affairs, Jack Hood Vaughn had been moved to the Peace Corps from his position as Assistant Secretary of State for Latin American Affairs, John Crimmins had replaced Bennett as Ambassador, C. Allan Stewart, a liberal career diplomat who had been Ambassador to Venezuela during Betancourt's Presidency, had replaced Kennedy Crockett as Chief of the Bureau of Caribbean Affairs, and there had been nearly a complete turnover in the political staff of the embassy.[19]

Moreover, the atmosphere in Washington today is quite different from that in 1965, largely, of course, because of the Vietnam tragedy. The hubris of the early 1960's is shattered, domestic concern over Cuba has almost completely disappeared, and the general foreign-policy emphasis is on finding ways of disengaging the United States from its overseas "responsibilities" rather than girding the country for further onslaughts at the gates. Nonetheless, the No Second Cuba doctrine, while muted, is far from dead, and it is probably still a lot safer for State Department officials to overestimate rather than underestimate potential Communist threats. It is even possible (although, I think, unlikely) that a manifestly unfavorable settlement of the Vietnam War could *increase* Washington's disposition to demonstrate its continued anti-Communist vigor in future Caribbean uprisings, much as Kennedy's defeats in Laos and the Bay of Pigs are said to have stiffened his disposition to turn to the military in Vietnam and the Cuban missile crisis. Alternatively, a U.S. disengagement in Asia and a deepening détente with the Soviet Union might be based on a *de facto* spheres-of-influence accord, in which the superpowers tacitly give each other carte blanche to arrange affairs in their backyards to their own taste.

In the near future, the most likely Caribbean trouble spot, aside from the Dominican Republic itself, is Haiti, which contains all the seeds of a major tragedy. It is widely feared in Washington that upon the passing of the incredible despotism of François Duvalier, whether through the death of the brutal dictator or an internal uprising, the thin fabric of Haitian society will completely dissolve into bloody chaos. As the Communist party presently seems to be one of the main opposition groups in Haiti,* the chances for a future U.S. or U.S.-OAS intervention are not remote. No one in Washington views such a prospect with anything but the grimmest foreboding, however, not only because in a country with no established political institutions, a vacuum of responsible and effective leadership, and the worst poverty in the hemisphere the outlook for an early withdrawal would be nil,[20] but also because U.S. intervention in a black country, even if humanitarian in its intentions and effects, would almost inevitably become entangled in America's racial crisis.

Surely there must be a way to break the thralldom in which the Cuban revolution has held U.S. policy. What is desperately necessary now is a new conception of the appropriate hemispheric role of the United States, one that provides a rationale for noninvolvement in any future Castroite uprisings without risk of unpleasant consequences both at home and abroad. Several steps are essential. Public opinion must be reeducated, but before that can be done American policy makers must reeducate themselves, opening up for reexamination a number of crucial premises that are now simply accepted as givens. Such a reexamination, I believe, would point to the need for two major actions: first, the United States in its public pronouncements and rhetoric must clearly de-couple genuine revolutions from "international aggression." Second, the Monroe Doctrine, which latterly has been interpreted to require the exclusion of hostile or antidemocratic political ideologies from the Western Hemisphere, must be jettisoned, or at least drastically modified.†

In 1965 the only even theoretically acceptable rationale for

* However, there are some indications that Duvalier may be encouraging the activities of the small group of Communists and deliberately magnifying their influence, in order to frighten the United States into supporting his regime.

† Not least, perhaps, because nondemocratic governments in Latin America are far more the norm than the exception.

the U.S. intervention in the Dominican Republic was not that the Dominican revolution objectively posed a threat to the security of the United States but that Washington had painted itself into a corner by unwise pronouncements that forced it to act in order to avert potentially very unpleasant domestic and international consequences. To break out of this vicious circle and avoid a repeat performance, it is crucial that U.S. political leaders act now, before another major crisis makes it far more difficult and dangerous, to make it clear that the Monroe Doctrine is obsolescent in the nuclear era and that indigenous change in Latin America, no matter how radical or violent, is no threat to the United States. To remain indefinitely prisoner to our historical clichés and Cold War propaganda, unable to change under pressure but seeing no need to do so in times of calm, would amount to an inexcusable abdication of statesmanship and intelligence.

There is good reason to be hopeful that public opinion, if properly led, would not be an insuperable obstacle to fundamental changes in U.S. policy. Not only has concern over the Castro "threat" already markedly diminished, but a great number of studies have firmly established that mass public opinion on foreign policy is usually amorphous, unstructured, and flexible, responsive, above all, to strong presidential leadership.* Indeed, on many foreign-policy issues there *is* no public opinion, properly speaking, until it is created by presidential action or rhetoric. Nonetheless, policy makers seem not to understand the broad latitude for innovation that a permissive public opinion grants them, or, alternatively, they find it convenient to ignore this latitude, for they habitually treat public opinion as

* One recent study concluded: "In the realm of foreign policy there has not been a single major issue on which Presidents, when they were serious and determined, have failed."[21] The Vietnam War would now have to be counted as a major exception, of course.

a given, as a set of rigid constraints which "won't allow" changes in existing policies. Explaining why the United States could not accept a Communist regime in the Dominican Republic, John Bartlow Martin gives us an almost classic formulation of the views so prevalent in official circles:

> I think we could not permit it on the simple ground that public opinion in the United States would not have tolerated a second Cuba in the Caribbean. It may be objected that this is making foreign policy on the basis of domestic politics. To my mind, in our open society, the makers of foreign policy must take into account domestic public opinion . . . and if the time comes when they do not, our society will no longer be an open one.[22]

Whether this sort of static, simplistic conception of the relationship of public opinion to policy is genuine, as in some cases, or a rationale for hard-line policies personally favored by officials, as in others, in either case it represents a breakdown of enlightened leadership that should no longer be tolerated.*

There are, indeed, a number of indicators that in recent years State Department sentiment for greater U.S. aloofness from Latin American and even Caribbean affairs has gained considerable strength.[23] But what should policy be toward the Dominican Republic, where the United States is engaged to an extent far greater than anywhere else in the hemisphere? In *that* country, it seems to me, it is too late for disentanglement, at least for some time to come, for since the intervention the United States has had an inescapable moral responsibility to do whatever it can to help the Dominican people move toward stable democracy, economic growth, and social justice. To be sure, the United States has so far had only modest success in con-

* Note that this argument is based on the assumption that effective presidential leadership has a great capacity to reeducate public opinion over time, whereas my earlier argument focused on the probable domestic costs of an *abrupt* break with traditional policies in the midst of a crisis, a quite different matter.

structively influencing Dominican public affairs. More generally, as many critics of American foreign policy have noted, the capacity of the United States to affect the internal politics and policies of other countries is not unlimited.

In the Dominican Republic, however, it has not been U.S. influence but wisdom and vision which have been in short supply. To alter slightly the classic lament for his country of a former Mexican President: "Poor Dominican Republic, so far from God and so close to the United States of America." The long history of U.S. interventionism in the country, the traditional Dominican receptiveness to U.S. advice, and the nearly total economic dependence on U.S. aid and trade (70–80 percent of Dominican trade is with the United States, and sugar alone accounts for half of all the foreign currency available to the Dominican Republic[24])—all provide enormous U.S. leverage. Obviously it is leverage which can be used for narrow and unenlightened ends as well as generous and constructive ones. And so, ultimately, the only real question concerning the Dominican Republic is not whether but how the United States is to exert its overwhelming and unavoidable influence.

THE MEANING OF THE DOMINICAN CRISIS

THE INTERVENTION of the United States in the Dominican revolution has widely been interpreted as symptomatic of a general pathology of American foreign policy under Lyndon Johnson,[25] if not, more sweepingly, of the entire range of the U.S. anti-Communist effort in the postwar period.[26] Under the less restrained of such interpretations, the United States is seen as a fundamentally militaristic, counterrevolutionary, or outright imperialistic power, whose actions in the Dominican Republic parallel Soviet behavior in Hungary and Czechoslovakia:

Where the great powers have staked out their sphere of influence, freedom of maneuver is possible only on the sufferance of the authorities in the seat of empire. . . . The parallel with Czechoslovakia is the Dominican Republic, where the United States launched an invasion to prevent a change of government, and justified it by saying it was on the invitation of certain Dominican leaders, and that unspecified agents of a foreign power threatened to take over the country.[27]

Despite my own criticisms of American policy in the Dominican crisis, these propositions seem to me to be quite dubious, or at least badly in need of substantial qualification. First, did the Dominican intervention reflect a broader "Johnson Doctrine," by which the United States asserted "a virtually unlimited claim of legitimacy for armed intervention in civil strife"?[28] While it is true that Johnson, in defending the Dominican intervention, argued that "the old distinction between civil war and international war has lost much of its meaning,"[29] the President was only making more explicit an assumption that he had inherited from the Kennedy Administration. More importantly, the rhetoric did not imply that the United States would in fact intervene in any and all civil wars involving a real or alleged Communist element, for the Dominican intervention was really an application of the much more limited and specific No Second Cuba policy in the Caribbean. And while no one can confidently say "what Kennedy would have done" in the concrete circumstances of April, 1965, it is an indisputable fact that the overall policy was much more a creation of the Kennedy Administration than of the Johnson Administration.

The evidence includes the following points. First, in early 1963 Kennedy's Assistant Secretary of State for Latin American Affairs told the House Committee on Foreign Affairs that the administration interpreted OAS resolutions as authorizing "the provision, upon request, of military forces to . . . help a government threatened by a Communist takeover."[30] Second, Martin writes that after the overthrow of Juan Bosch in 1963 the State Department informed him that the United States would not intervene "*unless a Communist takeover were threatened.*"[31] Third, in a 1969 interview W. W. Rostow noted that Kennedy had established a high-level government task force to study the legal basis for using U.S. military power in the Caribbean to prevent another Cuba.[32] Finally, Johnson's decision to intervene was based on the almost unanimous advice of the top policy makers in both the State Department and the U.S. Embassy in the Dominican Republic, most of whom were holdovers from the Kennedy Administration. As Geyelin has argued, to have chosen another course the President would have had "to invent his own alternatives and ignore the counsel of his principal advisers."[33] *

What of the broader implications of the Dominican intervention? The frequently-drawn parallel to the Vietnam War is, I think, questionable in a number of respects. Despite the similarities—a military intervention against a radical nationalist revolution—there were some very important differences as well. U.S. policy in Vietnam developed over a period of many years, whereas Dominican policy, while certainly reflecting a general cast of mind throughout the government, was also to a considerable degree a function of the unfortunate judgments of a few strategically placed individuals as well as the rapidity with which the crisis broke. Second, unlike in Vietnam, it is at least plausible that the U.S. intervention may have saved many lives, aborting what could have been a very bloody civil war. Third, after the initial intervention the United States opted for a negotiated political settlement rather than an imposed military

* Cf. also Senator Fulbright: "The principal reason for the failure of American policy in Santo Domingo was faulty advice given to the President by his representatives in the Dominican Republic . . . [on the basis of which he] could hardly have acted other than he did."[34]

"solution." Fourth, the United States established and supported a democratic regime instead of a military dictatorship: García-Godoy was no Marshall Ky or General Thieu, and the Dominican elections of 1966 bore no resemblance to the Vietnamese elections of 1967. Finally, although I am personally not persuaded that the political orientation of the Dominican Republic is of much significance to the United States, a far more plausible case linking the Dominican Republic to the U.S. national interest can be made than for Vietnam.

The parallel with the Soviet invasion of Czechoslovakia ultimately is even less convincing. Again there are some obvious similarities—a great power intervenes militarily against a revolutionary movement in a small country that is seen as an ideological threat to its sphere of influence. I am more persuaded, however, by the differences. The U.S. "sphere of influence" in the Caribbean is not to be compared with the tight and repressive Soviet political, military, and economic control of Eastern Europe. Nor is the action (however unjustifiable and unwise) of a democratic state in crushing a movement that had at least some potential for becoming totalitarian quite the same as a dictatorial state crushing an unmistakably democratic movement. Most importantly, it is not just the initial intervention that is of significance—in the Dominican Republic U.S. policy became increasingly liberal and oriented toward the restoration of constitutional democracy, whereas in Czechoslovakia Soviet policy has become increasingly repressive and oriented toward the restoration of reactionary dictatorship.

Finally, it is unlikely that the Dominican intervention can be seen as a reflection of a more general antiliberal or even counterrevolutionary policy. That U.S. hostility to Juan Bosch in 1965 was not part of a larger hostility to the democratic left in Latin America can be easily demonstrated by the considerable evidence that the United States has strongly supported the democratic left elsewhere in Latin America and in the Dominican Republic itself before and since 1965.[35] That the United States will not invariably intervene directly in Latin America every time there is a violent revolution that attracts Communist support is more difficult to show, as there have been no such revolutions in Latin America since the Dominican crisis.* Just the same, it is my belief that the Dominican intervention is more likely to have been a special case than the first step in a trend. The political climate today is quite different from that in 1965, and in any case few other countries in the Caribbean, and none elsewhere in Latin America, are at once so historically tied to the United States, so politically weak and vulnerable to armed uprisings, and so accessible to U.S. power.

Still, it is not difficult to conceive of circumstances in which U.S. intervention could recur, in Haiti, in the Dominican Republic itself, or elsewhere in the Caribbean. And so it will remain until the United States redefines the international situation and reaches a more rational understanding of its national interests.

* Although it is worth noting, in this connection, that the Nixon Administration has leaned over backward to avoid a crisis with the current Peruvian military government, probably the most radical nationalist regime to come to power in Latin America since Castro.

Notes

Preface

1. John Bartlow Martin, *Overtaken by Events.* (New York: Doubleday & Co., 1966); Tad Szulc, *Dominican Diary* (New York: Delacorte Press, 1965); Dan Kurzman, *Santo Domingo: Revolt of the Damned* (New York: G. P. Putnam's Sons, 1965); Theodore Draper, "The Dominican Crisis," *Commentary,* December, 1965; "U.S. Power and Responsibility—The New Dominican Crisis," *New Leader,* January 31, 1966; "A Case of Political Obscenity," *New Leader,* May 9, 1966; *The Dominican Revolt* (Commentary Report, 1968).

Chapter 1. Background to Revolution

1. Robert D. Crassweller, *Trujillo* (New York: Macmillan, 1966), p. 15.

2. For the best history of the pre-Trujillo era, see Sumner Welles's monumental classic, *Naboth's Vineyard* (New York: Paul P. Appel, 1966), 2 volumes.

3. On the Trujillo era, see Crassweller; Jesús de Galíndez, *La Era de Trujillo* (Santiago, Chile: Editorial de Pacifico, 1956); German Ornes, *Trujillo: Little Caesar of the Caribbean* (Thomas Nelson and Sons, 1958); Howard J. Wiarda, *The Dominican Republic* (New York: Praeger, 1969).

4. For a discussion of this period see Melvin M. Knight, *The Americans in Santo Domingo* (New York: Vanguard Press, 1928) and Dana G. Munro,

Intervention and Dollar Diplomacy in the Caribbean, 1900-1923 (Princeton: Princeton University Press, 1964).

5. Welles, p. 908.

6. Wiarda, p. 31, quoting a Dominican historian.

7. Much of the material in the next four pages is drawn from my book *The OAS and United States Foreign Policy* (Columbus: Ohio State University Press, 1967).

8. Crassweller, p. 213.

9. Arturo R. Espaillat, *Trujillo: The Last Caesar* (New York: Henry Regnery, 1963), pp. 75-81.

10. *New York Times*, December 21, 1963.

11. Crassweller, p. 213.

12. United States Congress, House Committee on Agriculture, *Extension of the Sugar Act of 1948*, Hearings (86th Congress, 2nd Session), 1960, Part II, especially p. 67.

13. Sixth Meeting of Consultation of Ministers of Foreign Affairs, *Actas*, Final Act, Resolution I.

14. Quoted by Arthur M. Schlesinger, Jr., *A Thousand Days* (New York: Fawcett, 1965), p. 769.

15. *Ibid.*, p. 770.

16. *Department of State Bulletin*, December 4, 1961 (Vol. 45, No. 1171), p. 931.

17. John Bartlow Martin, *Overtaken by Events* (New York: Doubleday & Co., 1966), p. 227.

18. Quoted in Munro, p. 291.

19. Juan Bosch, *The Unfinished Experiment* (Praeger, 1964), pp. 165-66.

20. Martin, p. 206.

21. *Ibid.*, pp. 179, 269.

22. *Ibid.*, p. 201.

23. See Martin's discussion of his efforts to get Bosch to modify the con-situation, pp. 326-30.

24. *Ibid.*, p. 512.

25. *Ibid.*, p. 347.

26. *Ibid.*, pp. 113, 465.

27. *Ibid.*, p. 129.

28. *Ibid.*, pp. 487, 509-10, 562.

29. Bosch, p. 141.

30. Martin, p. 451.

31. AID figures furnished to me in correspondence with the Department of State.

32. Martin, p. 551.

33. *Ibid.*, p. 570.

34. Personal interview.

35. Martin, p. 570.

36. *Ibid.*, p. 601.

37. *Ibid.*, p. 600.

38. *Ibid.*, p. 611.

39. Indeed, according to Martin the assassination of President Kennedy *delayed* recognition (p. 722). For the standard interpretation, see Theodore Draper, *The Dominican Revolt* (*Commentary* Report, 1968), p. 8. This is a slightly revised and expanded reprint of Draper's famous earlier article "The Dominican Crisis," *Commentary*, December, 1965 (Vol. 40, No. 6). See also Richard Barnet, *Intervention and Revolution* (New American Library, 1968) and my own earlier error in "Democracy vs. Stability: The Recent Latin American Policy of the United States," *Yale Review*, winter, 1966 (Vol. LV, No. 2).

40. Draper, pp. 15-16.

41. See footnote 31, *supra*.

42. Quoted in Selden Rodman, "A Close View of Santo Domingo," *The Reporter*, July 15, 1965, p. 24.

Chapter 2. The Revolution

1. Draper, *Dominican Revolt*, pp. 28-42.

2. Quoted by Rowland Evans and Robert Novak, *Lyndon B. Johnson: The Exercise of Power* (New York: New American Library, 1966), p. 513.

3. *Listin Diario* (Dominican Republic), September 18, 1968.

4. Quoted by Tad Szulc, *Dominican Diary* (New York: Delacorte Press, 1965), pp. 182-83.

5. Much of this information on the background of the constitutionalist leaders is drawn from the writing of two of the leading young scholars on Dominican politics, Abraham F. Lowenthal and José Moreno. See especially Moreno's Ph.D. dissertation, *Sociological Aspects of the Dominican Revolution* (Cornell University, 1967) and Lowenthal's "The Dominican Republic: The Politics of Chaos," in Arpad von Lazar and Robert R. Kaufman (eds.), *Reform and Revolution: Readings in Latin American Politics* (Allyn & Bacon, 1969).

6. On the ideology of the constitutionalists see especially Moreno, Szulc, and Dan Kurzman, *Santo Domingo: Revolt of the Damned* (New York: G. P. Putnam's Sons, 1965). Lowenthal tends to emphasize, in my view excessively, the opportunistic nature of the constitutionalist adherents, and comes very close to painting the struggle as involving nothing more than the "outs" vs. the "ins."

7. Wiarda, p. 4. Much of the discussion here of the Dominican socioeconomic structure is drawn from this source.

8. Lloyd Free, "Attitudes, Hopes and Fears of the Dominican People" (Princeton: Institute for International Social Research, mimeographed, 1962), p. 12. Also see the attitude study of Dominican youth by the psychiatrist Bryant Wedge, "The Case of Student Political Violence," *World Politics* (Vol. XXI, No. 2), January, 1969.

9. On the composition of the constitutionalist movement, see especially Moreno. Dr. Moreno, a Cuban by birth and formally a priest, was living in Santo Domingo gathering material for a Ph.D. dissertation in sociology when the revolution broke out. He then spent four months in the constitutionalist zone as both a participant in and a professional observer of the movement.

10. *Op. cit.*

11. *Listin Diario,* May 13, 1968.

12. Embassy cable quoted by Philip Geyelin, *Lyndon B. Johnson and the World* (Praeger, 1966), p. 246.

13. Juan Bosch, *Pentagonism, A Substitute for Imperialism* (Grove Press, 1968), p. 107.

14. See Connett's cable of April 25, quoted by Geyelin, p. 246.

15. Draper, *The Dominican Revolt,* p. 73.

16. U.S. Senate, Committee on the Judiciary, "Testimony of Brigadier

General Elías Wessin y Wessin," *Hearings* (89th Congress, First Session), October, 1965, p. 157.

17. Geyelin, p. 245.

18. Draper, "The Dominican Crisis," pp. 34-36. Draper, however, attributes the anti-Bosch policy to President Johnson and to Thomas Mann, while I have argued that there are clear signs that the policy stemmed from the Kennedy Administration.

19. Quoted by Marcel Niedergang, *La Révolution de St. Dominique* (France: Librairie Plon), p. 39.

20. Geyelin, p. 245.

21. See Szulc, Martin, Draper, Kurzman, Niedergang, and Bosch's own article, "The Dominican Revolution," *The New Republic,* July 24, 1965. According to Szulc, Bosch was prepared to return to the Dominican Republic early in the revolution but then changed his mind (pp. 38-39).

22. Martin, pp. 678-79.

23. Szulc, p. 28.

24. Although there is absolutely no doubt that Bennett refused U.S. mediation and made the accusations mentioned in the text, the former Ambassador has denied he told the constitutionalists to surrender. However, not only the constitutionalists but Martin (p. 653) maintain that he did so.

25. Martin, p. 654.

26. Much of the description here is drawn from the eyewitness account of an Argentine journalist, Gregorio Selser, *Aquí, Santo Domingo*! (Buenos Aires: Editorial Palestra, 1966).

27. *Ibid.,* p. 27.

28. Geyelin, p. 238.

29. The quote is from Niedergang, p. 76. The chaotic scene at San Isidro is mentioned by Geyelin and was described to me by several eyewitnesses.

30. Quoted by Geyelin, p. 250.

31. "American Foreign Policy and the Decision to Intervene," *Journal of International Affairs* (Vol. XXII, No. 2), 1968, p. 234.

32. "The Situation in the Dominican Republic," *Congressional Record,* September 15, 1965, p. 23859.

33. Martin, p. 661.

34. Seyom Brown, *The Faces of Power* (New York: Columbia University Press, 1968), p. 355 (emphasis in original).

35. Martin, p. 651.

36. *New York Times*, May 2, 1965. Cf. also Szulc: "From the few things we had seen since arriving in the Dominican capital . . . none of us had any doubts about the wisdom of his recommendation" (p. 79).

37. Moreno, p. 34.

38. Szulc, pp. 31-32.

39. Geyelin, quoting State Department cable, p. 250.

40. See Draper, *The Dominican Revolt.* As late as 1968 he was arguing that the evidence shows that the Dominican junta's request for U.S. troops was originally based on the Communist issue but was reworded at the direction of the embassy to refer only to the alleged threat to U.S. lives. His case is persuasive, but even so it would not in and of itself prove that the U.S. concern was simply a pretext.

41. Buchwald's column is reprinted in Selser.

42. See especially Kurzman, p. 21, for a discussion of the lists.

43. "The Dominican Crisis," p. 54.

44. Cf. José Figueres' essay in *Dominican Republic, A Study in the New Imperialism* (New York: Institute for International Labor Research, 1965). Although greatly concerned by the intervention, the former Costa Rican President and leading Latin American liberal found it impossible to dismiss the fact that a great many foreign observers feared that a new Cuba was in the making.

45. Charles Roberts, *LBJ's Inner Circle* (New York: Delacorte Press, 1965), p. 199.

46. *Intervention Against Communism* (Johns Hopkins Press, 1967), p. 47.

47. The administration's case is set forth in a monograph sponsored by the Center for Strategic Studies of Georgetown University, *Dominican Action—1965* (Washington, D.C., July, 1966) and in a speech by Senator Thomas Dodd in the *Congressional Record,* September 16, 1965, pp. 2329 ff., from all appearances inspired by the State Department and the CIA.

48. Moreno, p. 66.

49. *Ibid.*, p. 34.

50. *Op. cit.*

51. According to "J. B. Bender," identified only as a pseudonym for a U.S. "specialist in Latin American affairs involved in the crisis," it was the commando organization that most worried the Johnson Administration ("Dominican Intervention: The Facts," *National Review,* February 8, 1966).

52. Announcement of the Partido Comunista Dominicano, *El Nacional* (Dominican Republic), April 24, 1968.

53. "The Dominican Crisis: Correcting Some Misconceptions," *Department of State Bulletin,* November 8, 1965.

54. *Documents of the OAS Tenth Meeting of Foreign Ministers* (hereinafter cited as "*MFM Documents*"), *Document 47, First Report of the Special Committee,* May 7, 1965.

55. *MFM Document 42, Minutes of the Fourth Plenary Session,* May 7-8, 1965.

56. Personal interviews.

57. Martin, p. 675.

58. Draper, "The Dominican Crisis," p. 60; Mann, interview with Max Frankel, *New York Times,* May 9, 1965; Mann, "The Dominican Crisis: Correcting Some Misconceptions," *op. cit.,* especially p. 731; Szulc, quoting Mann, p. 303-304.

59. Free.

60. *Excelsior* (Mexico), April 28, 1965.

61. U.S. House Committee on Foreign Affairs, Subcommittee on Inter-American Affairs, *Communism in Latin America,* Hearings (89th Congress, 1st Session), 1965; and the committee's *Report No. 237,* April 14, 1965.

62. See Draper, *The Dominican Revolt,* and the Communist party's own assessment, reprinted in Martin, pp. 770-790.

63. Martin, p. 664.

64. For a similar analysis, see Kurzman, p. 160.

Chapter 3. The Objectives of the Intervention

1. Senator William Fulbright, "The Situation in the Dominican Republic," Speech in the U.S. Senate, *Congressional Record,* September 15, 1965, p. 23859.

2. In Richard M. Pfeffer, *No More Vietnams?* (Harper & Row, 1968), p. 153. Cf. also Kurzman: "The United States tried to stop not just the Com-

munists but the revolution itself" (p. 11); Michael Harrington: "Lyndon Johnson celebrated the return to the *status quo ante* in the Dominican Republic." ("Where and When to Intervene," *The New Republic*, November 30, 1968, p. 26); James Petras: "a series of violent internal struggles (Cuba, Dominican Republic) . . . [reveals] the profound stake that the U.S. has in stabilizing the status quo within each country" ("The United States and the New Equilibrium in Latin America," *Public Policy*, fall, 1969, pp. 129-30).

3. The two major works in this vein are Fred Goff and Michael Locker, "The Violence of Domination: U.S. Power and the Dominican Republic," in Irving L. Horowitz *et al.* (eds.), *Latin American Radicalism* (New York: Random House, 1969), and Richard J. Barnet, *Intervention and Revolution* (Cleveland: World Publishing Co., 1968), chap. 8. While Barnet does not accept the New Left position in its entirety, his treatment of U.S. policy in the Dominican Republic since 1960 emphasizes its alleged economic roots, and he flatly asserts that the Dominican intervention of 1965 was a "plausible case" in which "the protection or recovery of economic interests was a paramount consideration" (p. 17).

4. Goff and Locker, p. 280.

5. *Ibid.*, pp. 280-83.

6. Quoted by Draper, *The Dominican Revolt*, p. 172.

7. *Ibid.*

8. *Ibid.*, *passim*, especially p. 120.

9. *Ibid.*, p. 141.

10. *Ibid.*, p. 57, emphasis added.

11. *Op. cit.*

12. Draper, *The Dominican Revolt*, p. 206.

13. *Op. cit.*, p. 361.

14. For details on the economic-assistance program see *MFM Document 405, Report of the OAS Secretary General Regarding the Dominican Situation*, November 1, 1965.

15. In Pfeffer, p. 30.

16. See especially the *New York Times*, May 20, 21, 1965; Szulc, pp. 202-203, 209-10, 241, 256; and Rodman.

17. According to Szulc, in private Bennett was given to referring to the constitutionalists as "Communist scum" (p. 103).

18. Draper goes even further: "Martin was the living symbol of U.S. faith in democracy and social justice" (*The Dominican Revolt,* p. 148).

19. Sadly enough, in Bosch's own book, *The Unfinished Experiment,* which appeared shortly before the revolution, he has nothing but the highest praise for Martin.

20. Martin, p. 15.

21. *Ibid.*, p. 197.

22. *Ibid.*, p. 320.

23. *Ibid.*, p. 202.

24. *Ibid.*, p. 213.

25. *Ibid.*, p. 180.

26. *Ibid.*, p. 205.

27. *Ibid.*, p. 369.

28. *Ibid.*, *passim, especially* pp. 128-29.

29. *Ibid.*, p. 128.

30. *Ibid.*, p. 486.

31. *Ibid.*, p. 127.

32. *Ibid.*, pp. 203-205, 213, 256-57, 273.

33. *Ibid.*, especially pp. 272-74.

34. *Ibid.*, p. 313.

35. *Ibid.*, p. 203.

36. *Ibid.*, p. 205.

37. *Ibid.*, pp. 565-66.

38. This is attested to by several U.S. and Dominican officials who were either at Martin's meeting with Imbert or were later told the details by Martin himself.

39. Martin, p. 681.

40. *Ibid.*, pp. 54-55, 205.

41. *Ibid.*, p. 205.

42. "The Dominican Crisis: An Inter-American Dilemma," *The Canadian Yearbook of International* Law (Vancouver: University of British Columbia, 1966), IV, 1966, p. 181.

43. Draper, *The Dominican Revolt,* pp. 78-79.

44. See chap. 2.

45. Draper, *The Dominican Revolt,* p. 16.

46. The following paragraphs are based on Rómulo Betancourt, *Golpes de Estado y Gobiernos de Fuerza en America Latina* (Caracas: Prensas Venezolanas de Editorial Arte, 1966) ; José Figueres, "Revolution and Counter-Revolution in Santo Domingo," in Institute for International Labor Research, *Dominican Republic, A Study in the New Imperialism, 1965;* and personal interviews with one of the three men directly involved, as well as with a number of Latin American delegates to the OAS.

47. See their letter in *Life Magazine,* June, 18, 1965.

Chapter 4. The Initial Negotiations

1. Martin, p. 658.

2. *MFM Document 405, Report of the Secretary General on the Dominican Situation,* November 1, 1965.

3. *Ibid.,* p. 3.

4. Martin, pp. 661-62, 672.

5. *Ibid.,* p. 662.

6. *Op. cit.*

7. *Op. cit.,* p. 125.

8. *Congressional Record,* September 16, 1965, pp. 23311-14; cited by Draper, *The Dominican Revolt,* pp. 167-68.

9. For a full discussion of the OAS, see my book *The OAS and United States Foreign Policy.*

10. Geyelin, p. 239.

11. Senate speech, *op. cit.*

12. Geyelin, p. 254.

13. Rowland Evans and Robert Novak, *Lyndon B. Johnson: The Exercise of Power* (New York: New American Library, 1966), p. 517.

14. *MFM Document 24, Minutes of the Second Session of the General Committee,* May 1, 1965.

15. E.g., President Leoni of Venezuela sent the following message to President Johnson: "I was deeply disturbed at the news that . . . the armed forces

of your country had landed on the territory of a sister Republic, in inexplicable disregard of the principles of the inter-American system" (OAS Document OEA-00303, April 29, 1965).

16. *MFM Document 32, Minutes of the Fourth Session of the General Committee,* May 3, 1965.

17. *Ibid.*

18. Colombian representative, *MFM Document 14, Minutes of the Opening Plenary Session,* May 1, 1965.

19. *MFM Document 32, Minutes of the Fourth Session of the General Committee,* May 1, 1965. Others taking roughly similar positions included the delegates of Colombia, Venezuela, and Peru.

20. Szulc, pp. 96, 145.

21. *MFM Document 47, First Report of the Special Committee,* May 7, 1965.

22. *New York Times,* May 16, 1965.

23. Moreno, p. 41.

24. *MFM Document 81, Second Report of the Special Committee,* May 19, 1965, and *MFM Document 86, Minutes of the 10th Plenary Session,* May 20, 1965.

25. *MFM Document 81, Second Report of the Special Committee,* May 19, 1965.

26. For a similar analysis see Szulc, p. 166; Abraham F. Lowenthal, "The Dominican Intervention in Retrospect," *Public Policy* (Vol. XVIII, No. 1), fall, 1969, pp. 133-34.

27. *National Review,* August 23, 1966.

28. Szulc, pp. 255, 262-64.

29. See my article "Democracy vs. Stability: The Recent Latin American Policy of the United States," *Yale Review,* winter, 1966.

30. Szulc, p. 290. See also Draper, *The Dominican Revolt,* pp. 181-84.

31. See p. 31.

32. Szulc, pp. 286-90; Draper, *The Dominican Revolt,* pp. 181-84.

33. Draper, *The Dominican Revolt,* p. 182.

34. *Ibid.,* p. 184.

Chapter 5. The Negotiations for the Provisional Government

1. *MFM Document 131, Minutes of the Tenth Session of the General Committee,* June 2, 1965.

2. *MFM Document 341, Telegram of Ad Hoc Committee,* August 30, 1965.

3. *MFM Document 109, Telegram of Constitutionalist Foreign Minister,* May 30, 1965.

4. *MFM Document 50, Minutes of the Fifth Plenary Session,* May 8, 1965.

5. See especially the statement of the Costa Rican representative, *MFM Document 74, Minutes of the Seventh Plenary Session,* May 14, 1965.

6. See below, *passim.*

7. For a similar interpretation, see the excellent article by Dona Baron, "The Dominican Republic Crisis of 1965," in Andrew W. Cordier (ed.), *Columbia Essays in International Affairs, Volume III, 1967* (New York: Columbia University Press, 1968).

8. *UN Security Council Document S/6369, Report of the Secretary General on the Situation in the Dominican Republic,* May 19, 1965.

9. For a fuller discussion of the two constitutions, see Howard Wiarda, "Contemporary Constitutions and Constitutionalism in the Dominican Republic," *Law and Society Review,* June, 1968.

10. See Szulc, and the various reports of the Human Rights Commission to the Tenth Meeting of Consultation.

11. *MFM Document 134, Telegram of the Constitutionalist Foreign Minister,* June 2, 1965.

12. *MFM Document 251, First General Report of the Ad Hoc Committee,* July 17, 1965.

13. See the texts of some of these announcements in *MFM Document 374, Second General Report of the Ad Hoc Committee,* Appendix 4, November 1, 1966.

14. *UN Security Council Document S/6447, Report of the Secretary General on the Situation in the Dominican Republic,* June 16, 1965.

15. Juan Bosch, *Pentagonism: A Substitute for Imperialism,* p. 117. See also the paper released by the constitutionalists at the Second Special Inter-American Conference, in which it is charged that Bunker imposed the settlement after severe armed incursions by the IAPF.

16. Moreno, p. 177.

17. The constitutionalist reply is in the *First General Report of the Ad Hoc Committee,* pp. 12-18.

18. *MFM Document 192, Ad Hoc Committee Message to Tenth Meeting of Consultation,* June 22, 1965.

19. Crassweller, p. 83.

20. For discussions of the Dominican oligarchy, see Crassweller, *passim;* Martin, especially p. 134; and Wiarda, *The Dominican Republic,* pp. 101-103.

21. Martin, p. 453.

22. Crassweller, p. 113.

23. In Franklin J. Franco, *Republica Dominicana: Clases, Crises, y Comandos* (Cuba: Casas de las Americas, 1966).

24. In Martin, especially p. 788.

25. Statement of President Johnson, transcript of presidential news conference, *New York Times,* August 30, 1965.

26. Article 8 of the Act of Dominican Reconciliation, text in Appendix 10 of the *Second General Report of the Ad Hoc Committee.*

27. See the various reports of the commission to the Tenth Meeting of Consultation and the analysis of its work in Anna P. Schreiber and Phillipe E. Schreiber, "The Inter-American Commission on Human Rights in the Dominican Crisis," *International Organization,* Volume XXII, No. 2 (spring, 1968).

28. Formally, the Ad Hoc Committee agreed that the Institutional Act should specify that "the Provisional Government shall initiate or continue necessary, urgent programs for the economic recovery and development of the nation and the social betterment of the population. To that end, it may request of the agencies of the inter-American system and other international organizations whatever technical and financial assistance is required" (Article 12, in *Second General Report of the Ad Hoc Committee,* p. 31).

29. Richard M. Pfeffer (ed.), *No More Vietnams?* (New York: Harper & Row, 1968), p. 120 (emphasis added).

30. *New York Times,* June 7, 1965.

Chapter 6. The Provisional Government

1. *New York Times,* September 6, 1965.

2. Senate Committee on the Judiciary, *Testimony of Wessin y Wessin,* pp. 165-66.

3. Quoted by the *New York Times,* September 15, 1965.

4. *UN Security Council Document S/6975, Report of the Secretary General on the Situation in the Dominican Republic,* November 25, 1965.

5. *Listin Diario,* January 4, 1966.

6. *Listin Diario,* January 8, 1966.

7. *New York Times* January 9, 1966.

8. *Department of State Bulletin,* June 21, 1965, p. 1017.

9. *MFM Document 182, Minutes of the 16th Plenary Session,* June 18, 1965.

10. *New York Times,* September 5, 1965.

11. *Op. cit.*

12. Text of the letter in *MFM Document 430, Ad Hoc Committee Telegram 1011 to 10th Meeting of Consultation,* February 23, 1966.

13. This story was told to me by several participants in the Dominican crisis; it also appeared in a column by Otto Zausmer, *Boston Globe,* April 7, 1968.

14. *MFM Document 432, Minutes of the 23rd Plenary Session,* February 18, 1966.

15. See *New York Times,* June 13, 1967.

Chapter 7. The Elections and After

1. See, for example, Ruth Shereff, "Liberals in Wonderland," *Commonweal,* May 5, 1967.

2. Evans and Novak, p. 525.

3. *Ahora,* April 11, 1966.

4. Bosch describes some of these meetings in his "Trujijohnson, Pérez, y Balaguer," *Ahora,* March 31, 1969.

5. Bosch, unsurprisingly, is not. At first, he writes, he thought the U.S. attitude "seemed logical," since only through free elections could the United States "save face." Later, though, he realized he couldn't win, because "Trujijohnson" didn't want him to win. Shortly before the elections, Bosch claims, a high Venezuelan official told him that Johnson had told President Leoni of Venezuela that he, Johnson, would not allow Bosch to be elected President (*ibid.*). This story seems highly implausible for a variety of reasons, not least because much of the embittered Bosch's recent recollections of the Dominican crisis have not been notable for their accuracy.

6. *New York Review,* February 23, 1967.

7. *MFM Document 449,* May 27, 1966.

8. *MFM Document 439, First and Second Reports of the Technical Assistance Mission to the Dominican Republic on Electoral Matters,* April 25, 1966.

9. *UN Security Council Document S/7342, Report of the Observers of the Dominican Elections,* June 7, 1966.

10. Barnet, p. 178.

11. Shereff, *op. cit;* Norman Gall, "The Strange Dominican Election," *New Leader,* June 20, 1966.

12. Barnet, p. 178.

13. *MFM Document 439, op. cit.*

14. *New York Times,* March 26, 1966.

15. On this aspect of the campaign see Henry Wells, "The Dominican Search for Stability," *Current History,* December, 1966.

16. See Donald Grant, "The Dominican Tragedy," *The Progressive,* September, 1966.

17. See especially the *New York Times,* April 25, 1968, and *Listin Diario, passim.*

18. The figures come from the *New York Times,* June 14, 1967, and a speech by Ambassador Crimmins, *Listin Diario,* November 22, 1968.

19. *Listin Diario,* September 18, 1968.

20. *New York Times,* April 6, 1969.

21. For discussions of unemployment and growth rates, see T. D. Roberts *et al., Area Handbook for the Dominican Republic* (Washington, D.C.: Government Printing Office, 1966), esp. chap. 1, pp. 56-58; also, the *New York Times,* April 25, 1968; *Listin Diario,* February 5, 1969.

Chapter 8. Conclusions

1. Fulbright, *op. cit.,* p. 23859.

2. "The Dominican Crisis: Correcting Some Misperceptions," *Department of State Bulletin,* November 8, 1965.

3. This has been implied by several critics; see, especially, the discussion by Eqbal Ahmad in Pfeffer, p. 14.

4. "The Ethics of Intervention," *Review of Politics,* July, 1965, p. 302.

5. See especially Pfeffer, *passim.*

6. *Roberts,* p. 205.

7. *Evans and Novak,* p. 510.

8. See the moving descriptions in Szulc, especially p. 240.

9. *Area Handbook for the Dominican Republic,* p. 394.

10. For an excellent study, see Willard F. Barber and C. Neale Ronning, *Internal Security and Military Power* (Ohio State University Press, 1966).

11. In *Pfeffer,* pp. 2-3.

12. *New York Times,* May 28, 1965.

13. *The OAS and United States Foreign Policy,* pp. 128-29.

14. "The Dominican Intervention in Retrospect," *Public Policy* (Vol. XVIII, No. 1), fall, 1969, p. 144. A number of the comments that follow parallel Lowenthal's discussion, in good part because some of the ideas in Lowenthal's essay and this book grew out of a series of meetings on the Dominican crisis sponsored by the Center for International Affairs at Harvard University, in which both Lowenthal and this author participated.

15. Dinerstein, pp. 48-49.

16. In Pfeffer, p. 35.

17. Howard J. Wiarda, "From Fragmentation to Disintegration: The Social and Political Effects of the Dominican Revolution," unpublished paper delivered at the Southern Political Science Association Convention, Gatlinburg, Tennessee, November 10-12, 1966.

18. For further discussion of these points, see my article "The Decline of the OAS," *International Journal,* summer, 1969.

19. For inside stories on the Johnson Administration's reevaluation of the crisis, see the *New York Times,* April 24, 1966, and June 19, 1966.

20. Cf. Lowenthal, *Public Policy,* p. 147.

21. Aaron Wildavsky, "The Two Presidencies," *Trans-Action,* (Vol. 4, No. 2), December, 1966, p. 7.

22. *Op. cit.,* p. 739.

23. See, for example, the eloquent critique of Martin's deep involvement in day-to-day Dominican politics by the influential former career ambassador Philip Bonsal, "Open Letter to an Author," *Foreign Service Journal,* February, 1967.

24. Wiarda, *The Dominican Republic,* p. 146; Martin, p. 162.

25. This is Draper's position. See especially his *Dominican Revolt,* p. 2 ("the Dominican events were symptomatic of an American crisis, or more exactly, a crisis in the conduct of foreign affairs . . .") and *Abuse of Power* (New York: Viking Press, 1966), especially pp. 3-4.

26. See especially Barnet and the recent writings of others in the "revisionist" school.

27. Ronald Steel, "Up Against the Wall in Prague," *New York Review of Books,* September 26, 1968.

28. Barnet, p. 174.

29. *Ibid.,* p. 11.

30. Subcommittee on Inter-American Affairs, *Castro-Communist Subversion in the Western Hemisphere,* Hearings, 88th Congress, 1st Session, 1963, p. 48.

31. *Op. cit.,* p. 570, emphasis added.

32. *New York Times,* April 21, 1969.

33. *Op. cit.,* p. 245.

34. *Op. cit.,* p. 27859.

35. See Chapter 3.

Selected Bibliography

Background Material on the Dominican Republic and on U.S.–Dominican Relations Prior to 1965

1. Juan Bosch, *The Unfinished Experiment* (Praeger, 1969).
2. Robert D. Crassweller, *Trujillo* (Macmillan, 1966).
3. Arturo Espaillat, *Trujillo: The Last Caesar* (Henry Regnery, 1963).
4. Jesús de Galíndez, *La Era de Trujillo* (Santiago, Chile: Editorial de Pacifico, 1956).
5. Albert C. Hicks, *Blood in the Streets* (Creative Age Press, 1946).
6. Melvin M. Knight, *The Americans in Santo Domingo* (Vanguard Press, 1928).
7. Abraham F. Lowenthal, "Foreign Aid as a Political Instrument: The Case of the Dominican Republic," *Public Policy,* Volume XIV.
8. Dana G. Munro, *Intervention and Dollar Diplomacy in the Caribbean, 1900-1923* (Princeton University Press, 1964).
9. German Ornes, *Trujillo: Little Caesar of the Caribbean* (Thomas Nelson & Sons, 1958).
10. Jerome Slater, "The United States, the Organization of American States, and the Dominican Republic, 1961-63," *International Organization* (Vol. XVIII, No. 2), 1964.
11. Sumner Welles, *Naboth's Vineyard* (Paul P. Appel, 1966).
12. Howard J. Wiarda, *Dictatorship and Development: Methods of Control in Trujillo's Dominican Republic* (University of Florida Press, 1968).
13. ——, *The Dominican Republic* (Praeger, 1969).

The United States and the Dominican Revolution

A. BOOKS AND MONOGRAPHS

1. Victor Alba, *Les Sumergidos* (Mexico: B. Costa-Amic, 1965).
2. Richard J. Barnet, *Intervention and Revolution* (New American Library, 1968), Chapter 8.
3. Juan Bosch, *Pentagonism: A Substitute for Imperialism* (Grove Press, 1968).
4. Seyom Brown, *The Faces of Power* (Columbia University Press, 1968), Chapter 19.
5. Danilo Brugal Alfau, *Tragedia en Santo Domingo* (Santo Domingo, 1966).
6. Theodore Draper, *The Dominican Revolt* (*Commentary* Report, 1968).
7. Julio C. Estrella, *La Revolucion Dominicana y La Crises de la OEA* (Santo Domingo: Revista Ahora, 1965).
8. Rowland Evans and Robert Novak, *Lyndon B. Johnson: The Exercise of Power* (New American Library, 1966), Chapter XXIII.
9. Ramon A. Ferreras, *Guerra Patria* (Santo Domingo, 1966).
10. Franklin J. Franco, *Republica Dominicana: Clases, Crises, y Comandos* (Havana: Casas de las Americas, 1966).
11. Georgetown University Center for Strategic Studies, *Dominican Action—1965* (Georgetown University, 1966).
12. James A. Clark, *The Church and the Crisis in the Dominican Republic* (Newman Press, 1967)
13. Philip Geyelin, *Lyndon B. Johnson and the World* (Praeger, 1966), Chapter 10.
14. Institute for International Labor Research (Norman Thomas, ed.), *Dominican Republic, A Study in the New Imperialism,* 1965.
15. Dan Kurzman, *Santo Domingo: Revolt of the Damned* (G. P. Putnam's Sons, 1965).
16. Jay Mallin, *Caribbean Crisis* (Doubleday, 1965).
17. John Bartlow Martin, *Overtaken by Events* (Doubleday, 1966).
18. Marcel Niedergang, *La Revolution de St. Domingue* (France: Librairie Plon, 1966).
19. Charles Roberts, *LBJ's Inner Circle* (Delacorte Press, 1965), Chapter XIII.
20. Gregorio Selser, *Aquí, Santo Domingo!* (Buenos Aires: Editorial Palestra, 1966).
21. Tad Szulc, *Dominican Diary* (Delacorte Press, 1965).

22. A. J. and Ann van Wynen Thomas, *The Dominican Republic Crisis, 1965* (The Hammarskjöld Forum, Association of the Bar of the City of New York, 1966).

B. ARTICLES

1. Dona Baron, "The Dominican Republic Crisis of 1965," in Andrew W. Cordier (ed.) *Columbia Essays in International Affairs, Volume III, 1967* (Columbia University Press, 1968).
2. "J. B. Bender" (pseudonym), "Dominican Intervention: The Facts," *National Review,* February 8, 1966.
3. Paul Bethel, "The Dominican Intervention: The Myth," *National Review,* February 8, 1966.
4. ——, "The Dominican Republic Goes to the Polls," *Reporter,* June 2, 1966.
5. Juan Bosch, "The Dominican Revolution," *The New Republic,* July 24, 1965.
6. ——, "Communism and Democracy in the Dominican Republic," *Saturday Review,* August 7, 1965.
7. ——, "Trujijohnson, Pérez, y Balaguer," *Ahora,* March 31, 1969.
8. Max Clos, "Santo Domingo's Activist Adventurers," *Reporter,* June 17, 1965.
9. Theodore Draper, "The Roots of the Dominican Crisis," *The New Leader,* May 24, 1965.
10. ——, "The Dominican Crisis," *Commentary,* December, 1965.
11. ——, "U.S. Power and Responsibility—The New Dominican Crisis," *The New Leader,* January 31, 1966.
12. ——, "A Case of Political Obscenity," *The New Leader,* May 9, 1966.
13. Norman Gall, "The Strange Dominican Election," *The New Leader,* June 20, 1966.
14. Fred Goff and Michael Locker, "The Violence of Domination: U.S. Power and the Dominican Republic," in Irving Louis Horowitz *et al* (eds.), *Latin American Radicalism* (Vintage, 1969).
15. James Nelson Goodsell, "Dominican Dilemma," *The New Republic,* February 5, 1966.
16. Donald Grant, "The Dominican Tragedy," *The Progressive,* September, 1966.
17. Sam Halper, "A Second Chance," *The New Leader,* June 20, 1966.
18. Abraham F. Lowenthal, "The Dominican Intervention in Retrospect," *Public Policy* (Vol. XVIII, No. 1), fall, 1969.
19. ——, "The Dominican Republic: The Politics of Chaos," in Arpad von Lazar and Robert R. Kaufman (eds.), *Reform and Revolution: Readings in Latin American Politics* (Allyn & Bacon, 1969).
20. John P. S. McLaren, "The Dominican Crisis: An Inter-American

Dilemma," in *The Canadian Yearbook of International Law,* Volume IV, 1966 (University of British Columbia, 1966).
21. J. C. M. Ogelsby, "The Prospects for Democracy in the Dominican Republic," *International Journal,* spring, 1966.
22. F. Parkinson, "Santo Domingo and After," in *The Yearbook of World Affairs, 1966* (Praeger, 1966).
23. James Petras, "Dominican Republic: Revolution and Restoration," *Liberation,* September, 1966.
24. Selden Rodman, "A Close View of Santo Domingo," *The Reporter,* July 15, 1965.
25. ——, "Why Balaguer Won," *New Republic,* June 18, 1966.
26. ——, "Balaguer: The First Nine Months," *New Republic,* March 25, 1967.
27. Anna P. and Philippe E. Schreiber, "The Inter-American Commission on Human Rights in the Dominican Crisis," *International Organization,* spring, 1968.
28. Ruth Shereff, "Liberals in Wonderland," *Commonweal,* May 5, 1967.
29. Jerome Slater, "The Limits of Legitimization in International Organizations: The Organization of American States and the Dominican Crisis," *International Organization* (Volume XXIII, No. 1), 1969.
30. Tad Szulc, "When the Marines Stormed Ashore in Santo Domingo," *Saturday Evening Post,* July 31, 1965.
31. Bryant Wedge, "The Case Study of Student Political Violence," *World Politics* (Vol. XXI, No. 2), January, 1969.
32. Henry Wells, "The Dominican Search for Stability," *Current History,* December, 1966.
33. Howard J. Wiarda, "From Fragmentation to Disintegration: the Social and Political Effects of the Dominican Revolution," *América Latina* (Rio de Janeiro), April-June, 1967.
34. ——, "Contemporary Constitutions and Constitutionalism in the Dominican Republic," *Law and Society Review,* June, 1968.
35. ——, "The Dominican Revolution in Perspective," *Polity* (Vol. I, No. 1), fall, 1968.

C. DOCUMENTS OF THE U.S. GOVERNMENT, THE ORGANIZATION OF AMERICAN STATES, AND THE UNITED NATIONS

1. Documents of the OAS Tenth Meeting of Consultation of Ministers of Foreign Affairs.
2. Senator William F. Fulbright, "The Situation in the Dominican Republic," *Congressional Record,* September 15, 1965, pp. 23855-23865.
3. United Nations Security Council Documents, 1965-66.
4. U.S. Congress, House, Committee on Foreign Affairs, Subcommittee on Inter-American Affairs, *Communism in Latin America,* Hearings (89th

Congress, First Session), 1965, and *Committee Report No. 237*, April 14, 1965.
5. U.S. Congress, Senate, Committee on Foreign Relations, *Background Information Relating to the Dominican Republic*, Committee Print (89th Congress, First Session), 1965.
6. U.S. Congress, Senate, Committee on the Judiciary, *Testimony of Brigadier General Elías Wessin y Wessin*, Hearings (89th Congress, First Session), October, 1965.

D. NEWSPAPERS AND MAGAZINES OF THE DOMINICAN REPUBLIC

1. *Ahora!* (weekly newsmagazine), 1965-69.
2. *El Caribe*, 1965-69.
3. *Listin Diario*, 1965-69.

E. UNPUBLISHED WORKS

1. José A. Moreno, *Sociological Aspects of the Dominican Revolution* (Ph.D. Thesis, Cornell University, 1967).
2. Howard J. Wiarda, "The Context of U.S. Policy Toward the Dominican Republic," 1966.
3. Larman Wilson, "The United States and the Dominican Republic: A Post-Election Assessment," 1967.

Index

C

D

E

F

G

H

I

J

K

S

T

U

V

W

Y

70 71 72 73 10 9 8 7 6 5 4 3 2 1